Attachment and
Adult Psychotherapy

Attachment and Adult Psychotherapy

Pat Sable, Ph.D.

JASON ARONSON INC.
Northvale, New Jersey
London

This book was set in 12 pt. New Aster by Alpha Graphics of Pittsfield, NH, and printed and bound by Book-mart Press, Inc. of North Bergen, NJ.

Library of Congress Cataloging-in-Publication Data

Sable, Pat.
    Attachment and adult psychotherapy / Pat Sable.
        p. : cm.
    Includes bibliographical references and index.
    ISBN 0-7657-0284-3
    1. Attachment behavior. 2. Psychotherapy. 3. Adulthood—Psychological aspects. I. Title.
    [DNLM: 1. Object Attachment. 2. Psychotherapy. 3. Emotions.
WM 460.5.O2 S117a2000]
RC455.4.A84 S23 2000
616.89'14—dc21   00-035537

Printed in the United States of America on acid-free paper. For information and catalog write to Jason Aronson Inc., 230 Livingston Street, Northvale, NJ 07647-1726, or visit our website: www.aronson.com

For my grandchildren

Megan

Brandon

Garrett

Bronte

Monet

Emerson

Contents

Acknowledgments

This book grew out of the inspiration of John Bowlby's ideas and his conviction that attachment was significant in our emotional lives throughout the life cycle. I feel fortunate to have known Dr. Bowlby early in the evolution of attachment theory and appreciate the support and encouragement he gave to my interest in applying its concepts to clinical practice with adults. I also feel fortunate to have had the help of so many friends and colleagues during my years of study and teaching and finally writing this book. Beginning with Maurice Hamovitch, my professors and, later, colleagues at the University of Southern California School of Social work were enthusiastic and supportive, allowing me the freedom to pursue the exciting potential I saw in attachment.

Peter Marris has been a longstanding, invaluable source of support and guidance, furthering my understanding of the meaning that is found in our closest relationships.

Judith Schore and Allan Schore have given generously of their time, read and commented on portions of the book, and helped me to better understand the principle of affect regulation.

Among the many attachment researchers, theorists, and therapists who have contributed to my thinking, I am particularly indebted to Jeremy Holmes, Robert Weiss, Morris Eagle, and Arietta Slade for their helpful discussions and clarifications of a clinical attachment.

The other group of people who deserve acknowledgment are my patients, who gave me the privilege of sharing their personal stories, all of which are disguised for the sake of confidentiality.

I am grateful to Andréa Vaucher for her expertise in editing the final manuscript.

Most of all, I thank my attachment figures—my parents, Ernie, sons Jim and John, grandchildren, and dogs—for showing me the real meaning of attachment.

Introduction

In the summer of 1982, our Los Angeles attachment study group traveled to London to spend a week with John Bowlby, his family, and several of his British colleagues in the attachment field. We wanted to renew and strengthen the connections of a small attachment community that had developed during Bowlby's final visit to Los Angeles in 1980 and looked forward to continuing our exchange of ideas. At the Tavistock Clinic, where Bowlby had directed a children's department throughout most of his long and distinguished career, we took part in informal discussions and made case presentations that Bowlby commented upon. At the time, only limited attachment-based research or literature was available; Bowlby's most thorough discussion of clinical treatment, in *Loss*, the last volume of his trilogy, *Attachment and Loss*, had only recently been published. There was still only very minor exposure to Bowlby's thoughts about therapy, especially with adults, and at Tavistock, as I described my work with a young adult woman whose cluster of symptoms fit the criteria for agoraphobia, I eagerly awaited Bowlby's recommendations. I anticipated that Bowlby would offer insightful interpretations and behavioral techniques; instead he simply stated that the methods of practice were less consequential than understanding the pattern of family relationships and events in my patient's life that had initiated her agoraphobic condition. The importance of these remarks resonated clearly when I recalled an earlier exchange with Bowlby during his Los Angeles visit. After reading a draft of one of my manuscripts (Sable 1983), Bowlby had stressed the significance of my client, Kelly, asking me if I was trying to tell her that her problems came from incidents that had happened to her in her family. The explicit realization of this, she declared, made her feel less hopeless and helpless because now, as an adult, she could do something about herself and therefore get better. That session with Kelly had proven to be a turning point in our four years of work together.

My exchanges with Bowlby underlined his novel approach of singling out real-life experiences, and our conversations about clinical issues illustrated his originality, his clear and direct style of expression, and his basic philosophy concerning the effects of the environment on psychological development. Today, now that the role of real experiences is no longer a charged subject (Holmes 1993a), this message is not unfamiliar. But in the early 1980s Bowlby was formulating a new perspective on human social behavior, which, though based on scientific research, touched our most profound feelings—those related to our inherent need for secure connection to others and to our anguish and yearning when these bonds are threatened or disrupted by separation and loss. Psychological health is directly related to the power of these basic attachment and loss experiences, both present and past, and to the personal meaning that is attributed to them.

This past decade has spawned extensive attachment-based research and there is now substantial empirical support for Bowlby's conviction that early family experience is related to later personality functioning (Amini et al. 1996). Attachment theory has come to be regarded as a discipline in its own right, and Bowlby's ideas, once considered bold and speculative, have moved into the mainstream and are an accepted aspect of psychodynamic thinking (Holmes 1993a, Insel 1997, Karen 1994). There is also mounting interest in adult attachment and in the way affectional experiences relate to emotional wellbeing or psychological distress throughout the life cycle (Bretherton 1995, Feeney 1999).

In spite of this growing acceptance of attachment and its compatibility with the current evolution of psychoanalysis into an interpersonal approach (Bretherton 1995, Lyons and Sperling 1997, Patrick et al. 1994, Slade 1999), attachment theory has not significantly influenced clinical practice (Holmes 1996, Lieberman and Zeanah 1999, Slade 1999). Though Bowlby (1982, 1988a) was himself a clinician and stated in his writings that he formulated the theory to be used in the diagnosis and treatment of emotionally distressed persons, it has more often prompted adjunct research in developmental psychology. Noting that he welcomed research findings, Bowlby nonetheless expressed disappointment that the theory had not had greater impact on practicing clinicians.

In trying to explain this enigma, Holmes (1995) states that traditional psychotherapists resist the theory because it is more focused on security and deficiency than on sexuality and conflict, which makes it too different from prevailing psychoanalytic thought. Lieberman and Zeanah (1999) suggest that its focus on security and protection make attachment theory seem incomplete and constricting, and that therapists do not know how to apply the concepts in their everyday practices. Furthermore, the language of attachment is descriptive and external, rather than experiential and internal, making it appear off limits to most therapists (Holmes 1996). Others have wondered whether Bowlby's call for a theory based on research made it seem too mechanistic, behavioral, and bland (Berman and Sperling 1994, Bowlby 1979, 1988a, Hamilton 1987). Another speculation is that the ideas are so basic to human nature that they are almost unnoticeable and thus not notable. Moreover, using Bowlby's theory in practice forces clinicians to confront intense emotions, including the pain of separation anxiety, grief, and mourning, which can elicit defensive processes, called up as clinicians exclude their own responses to unhappy experiences (Hamilton 1985, 1987). Finally, although he described attachment as a life-span phenomenon, Bowlby focused more on childhood and the nature and function of the mother–child bond. He also gave more attention to theory and research and did not write as much about clinical applications (Hamilton 1987, West and Sheldon-Keller 1994). The majority of publications written on the subject by other therapists have been concerned with theory and developmental research (Lieberman and Zeanah 1999) rather than with the systematic application of attachment theory to practice issues.

The focus of this book is to give an attachment perspective of psychopathology and an application of the theory to therapy with adults. One goal is to illustrate that Bowlby has built a bridge between research and theory that advances our understanding of personality development, both healthy and pathological, and that provides guidelines for effective treatment. Despite the difficulty of measuring and specifying pathology, or of relating childhood experiences to adult dysfunction, attachment now has an empirical foundation that changes the way we conceptualize our clients' experiences and thus the context of clinical practice. Research has shown that the quality of one's attachment relationships is at the very core of adaptive functioning, and affects emotional and mental coherence as well as behavioral dispositions (Atkinson 1997, Grossman 1995). This shift in perspective on development and pathology has a significant impact on assessment and treatment. Psychological symptoms are seen as evolving out of individuals' interpersonal experiences and these are manifest in a variety of clinical symptoms, such as agoraphobia, disordered mourning, or borderline personality disorder. Treatment provides an opportunity to explore attachment experiences, both current and past, in a protective setting with a safe person in order to understand and change certain attitudes, feelings, and behaviors that may no longer be relevant to the present and to what is learned in the therapeutic process (Bowlby 1991). The personal relationship and emotional contact with the therapist furnish an opportunity to experience secure attachment, counteracting and healing painful wounds from earlier relationships.

When I began teaching attachment theory in the School of Social Work at the University of Southern California and lecturing in the community, nearly two decades ago, there was no precedent for presenting these ideas within a framework. My first task was to decide how and where to integrate the material. This involved comparing basic concepts to other personality theories. In Chapter 1, I place attachment theory in its historical context, and present an overview of the evolution of its main ideas.

In applying attachment theory to clinical work with adults, I needed to define adult attachment and justify the perception of adult psychological disturbance in terms of affectional bonds. Chapter 2, therefore, defines and discusses concepts of attachment in adults, and how adult affectional relationships relate to and differ from those of infants and children. Chapter 3 deals with an overall concept of adult attachment disorder, including the patterns of personality development that render individuals vulnerable to symptom formation at times of stress. Derived both from Bowlby's conceptualizations of attachment behavior patterns and Ainsworth's (Ainsworth et al. 1978) research, these attachment styles have had wide exposure in the attachment literature and constitute one of the more accessible concepts for clinicians trying to assimilate attachment theory into their theoretical thinking. As West and Sheldon-Keller (1994) point out, attachment theory must be useful to clinical practice if we expect therapists to modify their treatment techniques to admit attachment ideas. This chapter also introduces Bowlby's basic approach to psychotherapy.

With Chapter 4 the discussion begins to address the application of attachment theory to understanding and treating different forms of emotional disturbance. This chapter considers Bowlby's major concepts of separation anxiety and anxious attachment, while Chapters 5 and 6 illustrate how these concepts are manifest in the syndromes of agoraphobia and post-traumatic stress disorder. Chapter 7 considers Bowlby's other major concept, encompassing loss, grief, and mourning, as well as the clinical manifestations of this concept in disordered grief or depression. Chapter 8 explores defensive processes and emotional detachment. This condition, also referred to as unresolved attachment, reflects a greater degree of exclusion, or repression, of attachment behavior and may not be diagnostically very different from the dynamics of borderline personality described in Chapter 9.

The discussion of emotional abuse in Chapter 10 illustrates the theory's application and flexibility with regard to a more recently recognized psychological condition. As in the previous chapters, it is emphasized here that the foundation for any therapeutic change is the therapist's ability to provide the experience of an attachment relationship, and to assist patients in understanding the relevance of their affectional history on current distress. Although clinical examples are generally of individual adults, the approach is also applicable to child, family, or group treatment. Chapter 11 shifts gears somewhat and explores the devotion, affection, and attachment feelings we have for our family pets, especially dogs and cats. This chapter may offer new insight into the prominent use of pets in the media and in advertising, and suggests ramifications for therapeutic understanding. The final chapter of the book summarizes the basic concepts related to applying attachment theory in treatment, and explores Bowlby's legacy, including implications for prevention and social policy.

Holmes (1996) sees attachment theory as being on the cutting edge in the search for common ground among various psychotherapies. Because of the theory's emphasis on relationships, he foresees it offering a unified framework capable of synthesizing ideas from psychodynamic thinking, cognitive science, and neurobiology. At the beginning of this new millennium, however, concepts of adult attachment, as well as their clinical application, are still in an early stage of development (Holmes 1996, Kobak 1999, Lieberman and Zeanah 1999, Weiss 1994a). Because Bowlby achieved prominence for his pioneering work on the mother–child bond, initial attention to his concepts tended to revolve around their relevance to child development. However, Bowlby believed that components of attachment extended into adulthood, influencing feelings of security and the meaning given to experiences and relationships. The wide range of emotions we feel, and the ways in which we live our lives, reflect in large measure the condition of our attachment relationships. Adult pathology is related to these affectional experiences, both in the present and past, and only by understanding these experiences can we fully appreciate why people think, feel, and act the way they do.

When individuals seek psychotherapy, they are usually upset about some aspect of an attachment relationship (Sable 1979, Weiss 1994b). A framework of attachment gives us a new perspective for appraising and dealing with these difficulties. Having this framework allows acceptance and affirmation of the attachment experiences that clients report have caused them pain and suffering and offers guidelines for treatment. Hopefully, mental-health professionals will find that exposure to these attachment concepts adds to their knowledge base and will be useful when they begin thinking about clients' lives. Bowlby attempted to revise our thinking about mental health and mental disturbance. I remember his forthright manner and the simple, everyday language he used to describe his theory and ideas about treatment. In Los Angeles, while I was walking across campus with him on the way to a lecture he was about to give, he said that the true test of theory is its applicability to alleviating the distress of our clients. It is that effort to which this book is addressed.

1

The Roots of
Attachment Theory

John Bowlby (1977, 1980) described his attachment framework as a way to account for the propensity of persons to form lasting affectional bonds to particular others, and to explain psychological disturbances, including anxiety, anger, depression, and emotional detachment, that could result from disruptions such as separation or loss or threat of separation. Attachment theory explains how certain early experiences are carried into adult relationships, affecting the way we behave and get along with others. It is concerned with the processes and feelings involved in the making and breaking of close personal ties of affection, and how these relate to mental health or emotional disturbance. Drawing on an ethological perspective and integrating psychoanalytic object relations theory with concepts from evolutionary biology, systems theory, and cognitive psychology, Bowlby developed a paradigm that updated Freud's theory of motivation and emphasized the significance of affectional bonds on personality development, whether healthy or pathological. In introducing the concept of attachment into psychological literature, Bowlby (1958) began an exploration of a point of view that has come to be accepted as a distinct theory of personality with its own unique ideas about the nature of interpersonal relationships and experiences.

Born in 1907, John Bowlby was the son of a prominent British surgeon, and the fourth child in a family of three girls and three boys. His training in psychoanalysis and child psychiatry coincided with the early development of object relations theory in Britain, where he was analyzed by Joan Riviere, supervised by Melanie Klein, and professionally associated with Anna Freud and Donald Winnicott. While working in a school for troubled children at the outset of his career, Bowlby first discovered the phenomenon of separation when he observed the distress of family members forced to be apart from each other. Later, while in analytic training, he worked in a child guidance clinic where he was struck by the activities of social workers who treated entire families because they thought that unresolved conflicts from the parents' childhood could be related to current difficulties with their children. Bowlby felt that traditional theory underestimated the impact of these environmental factors and parental attitudes and behavior in the inception of psychopathology and became determined to learn more about real experiences. Unfortunately, this conviction quickly led to rebuke and sometimes outright hostility from his colleagues; Bowlby's developing theory was essentially airbrushed out of psychodynamic thought and practice for two decades (Holmes 1995).

With the outbreak of World War II, Bowlby spent five years as an Army psychiatrist. When he left the service, he became director of a children's department at the Tavistock Clinic in London. He renamed the division the Department for Children and Parents, and, until his death in 1990 at the age of 83, he maintained an office and title there. Bowlby lived to see his work substantiated by research findings and his major concepts—attachment, separation, and loss—filter into popular attitudes and be applied to clinical thinking, changing how we understand early psychological development and the affectional needs of small children. His publications, such as the famous report for the World Health Organization (Bowlby 1951) on homeless children and maternal deprivation, led to worldwide changes in hospital practices and social policies and stimulated an interest in prevention (Karen 1994, Solnit 1990). A paper on family therapy (Bowlby 1949) is credited as one of the first published on the topic. The later trilogy, *Attachment and Loss* (Bowlby 1969a, 1973, 1980), completed toward the end of his career, is an eloquent, comprehensive presentation of his theory and the findings on which it is based. Its topics remain timely, even urgent today, with the high incidence of divorce and family violence, with more mothers working, and in light of the ongoing debate about children's emotional needs and the value and quality of day care (Karen 1994).

Bowlby's final major publication was a biography of Charles Darwin (1991). Though writing about Darwin, Bowlby could easily have been describing his own spirit when he stated, "What is striking is the courage with which he questioned the accepted doctrines and his determination to think things out for himself" (p. 212). Like Darwin, Bowlby embarked on a journey of observation and discovery. Self-confident and steadfast in his determination to chart his own course, Bowlby combined his outstanding intelligence and attention to detail with a capacity to clarify thought so precisely that people might walk away mistakenly thinking "everyone knows that."

Well, we know it now. We can now articulate that children need loving attachments with consistent caregivers, and that separation and loss can be traumatic, painful, and deeply damaging. But it was Bowlby who gave us this basic view of human nature and a reference point from which to evaluate the meaning of our relationships. Though unassuming and somewhat reserved and formal, Bowlby had a depth of understanding and a command of language that enabled him to put practical and seemingly plain common-sense words to our most basic emotions. He was sensitive to the vulnerability of children and aware that adults, too, needed people they could rely on if they were to maintain a sense of well-being. In many ways, Bowlby was the embodiment of the concept of the secure base that he promoted. Married for many years to Ursula Longstaff, and the father of four children, Bowlby spent holidays with his family on the Isle of Skye in Scotland, the place where he died and is buried. To colleagues, he listened attentively and respectfully; he was supportive and encouraging even in the early years when those in agreement with his ideas were more often admonished than acknowledged. At a small gathering at a conference at Lake Couchiching in Canada in the summer of 1978, sponsored by the Clarke Institute of Psychiatry of Toronto, where I first met him, I saw his eyes dart to a man who was discussing his theory and who kept using the term "introject." Bowlby made a few brief comments, never letting on that he disapproved of the term. Nor did he ever complain about the muggy weather and bug infestation like the rest of us did! In fact, and consistent with his known fondness for the country, he took early morning walks with Henry Hansburg, a colleague who developed one of the first research measures of attachment and separation (the Separation Anxiety Text, Hansburg 1972). Similarly, while in Los Angeles, he chose to spend an unscheduled day leisurely exploring the canyon area where I live.

FREUD, OBJECT RELATIONS AND ATTACHMENT

Historically, attachment theory grew out of the object relations tradition in psychoanalysis (Bowlby 1988a, Greenberg and Mitchell 1983) that began with Melanie Klein (1948) and was extended and further refined by the British school of object relations theorists (Winnicott 1965, Fairbairn 1963, and Balint 1965. The object relations emphasis on the internalization and representations of interpersonal experiences, beginning with the mother–child bond, made it a school of thought distinct from Freud's classical theory.[1] Bowlby broadened the object relations view, which held that an infant is naturally inclined to seek its mother, by using an ethological orientation, instead of psychic energy and drive theory, to explain why the mother is indispensable to the child. Bowlby (1969a) pointed out that even when theorists such as Fairbairn eliminated drive theory, they proposed no clear-cut substitution for it. An ethological perspective is unique to attachment; it conceptualizes an instinctive pattern of behavior that disposes the infant to seek proximity and to form an affectional bond—or attachment—to its caregiver, not primarily for oral needs or alimentary rewards, but for the biological function of safety and protection.

Attachment actually guarantees the infant's survival. As was the case in the beginning of human evolution when protection from predators was vital to survival of the species, infants and small children in our society today need

---

1. Throughout this book, the term "mother" refers to the individual who cares for an infant and to whom it becomes attached.

to be close to their caregivers and can be at greater risk of injury or assault if left alone and unprotected. There are studies, for example, that indicate that children are more likely to be hurt in traffic accidents when they are unaccompanied by an adult or are with their peers. Natural disasters or perils are also potentially threatening. In Los Angeles, for example, there are earthquakes, fires, and floods; in canyons, coyotes and rattlesnakes are particularly hazardous to both young children and family pets. The human infant, like the puppy, kitten, and nonhuman primate, is preprogrammed with behavioral equipment with which to respond to environmental threat, to signal distress or danger, and to turn to a familiar figure for safety from predation (Bowlby 1973, Holmes 1993a).

SEPARATION AND LOSS

When Bowlby read the work of the ethologists Lorenz (1952) and Tinbergen (1951) in the 1950s, he saw how their investigative concepts and techniques might potentially explain aspects of human behavior such as the distress exhibited by young children when separated from their parents. About the same time, Bowlby had hired James Robertson, a social worker who had worked with Anna Freud at the Hampstead nurseries during World War II. Roberston worked as his research assistant, making observations of hospitalized and institutionalized children who were removed from parents to whom they were attached, and then cared for by unfamiliar persons in strange surroundings (Bowlby 1973, Heinicke and Westheimer 1966, Robertson and Bowlby 1952). As Robertson discussed his observations with other professionals in the community, he became exasperated at his colleagues' refusal to believe his depiction of the extent of the children's misery. With Bowlby's support, Robertson made a series of films (Bowlby et al. 1952), beginning with *A Two-Year Old Goes to Hospital* (1952), to demonstrate the impact of separation (Grosskurth 1986). Bowlby, meanwhile, tried to interpret the responses that Robertson had identified and relate them to his evolving theoretical ideas (Karen 1994).

It was found that at the onset of separation there begins a sequence of behaviors designated as protest, despair, and detachment. All part of a single separation process, these responses occur along a continuum, with feelings fluctuating back and forth. During the stage of protest, fear and separation anxiety are prominent, indicating an urgent attempt to search out and recover a missing person. The phase of despair is more subdued and, though there is still preoccupation with reunion, hope fades and the child becomes withdrawn and less active, as though in a state of mourning. Whereas in the protest stage the heart rate accelerates, in the despair phase it now decreases. From an evolutionary perspective, this restraint conserves energy, whether for the young child who is in danger of becoming exhausted or the animal in the wild who must remain unobtrusive and hide from predators until its mother returns (Hofer 1995). Finally, if separation is prolonged, or if conditions during the separation are severe, defensive processes may close off attachment feelings, leading to an emotional detachment. This is especially evident in reunion behavior following detachment, where the child seems to have lost interest in mother, and refuses to acknowledge her presence or accept her comfort. If the separation has not been too lengthy or exacerbated by difficult circumstances such as inadequate substitute care, detachment does not persist and attachment is renewed. If the interruption is prolonged or repeated, however, detachment can persist indefinitely, even into adulthood (Bowlby 1973).

In identifying these universal responses to separation, Bowlby saw similarities to descriptions of adult bereavement (see Marris [1958], Parkes [1972]), and later revised the stages to describe grief and mourning. In the revision, he added an initial phase of numbing, referring to a brief time during which a person becomes dazed and distant in order to enable the shock of permanent loss to be absorbed a little at a time (Bowlby 1980, Parkes 1972). Subsequent stages of grief and mourning—yearning and searching, disorganization and despair, and then eventual acceptance—resemble the separation process, part of our biologically programmed effort to retrieve absent figures, which is only gradually relinquished with time and the realization that the loss is irreversible. With either separation or loss, this portrayal of responses as lying along a continuum, and including the possibility of anger at any phase, makes it possible to explain a fluctuating variety of emotions, whether in young children or adult clients. Moreover, Bowlby's (1973) position that childhood reactions such as emotional detachment could persist and have long-term detrimental effects on personality formation made it possible to begin to connect childhood separation and bereavement to later psychological disturbances.

ATTACHMENT

According to Bowlby (1973), once he discovered the significance of separation and loss, he had to understand the origin and nature of the bond whose disruption caused such distress at every age. Using an evolutionary and ethological perspective, he hypothesized an attachment behavior system designed to regulate and ensure proximity to one or a few specific individuals who provide protection and psychological security. Other systems that are interconnected with attachment to ensure survival and procreation include sexual mating, caregiving, and exploration. Bowlby used the term "attachment" to describe a relatively enduring bond that forms between two individuals over time in response to exposure, interaction, and familiarity. The tendency to form an attachment to someone perceived to be stronger and/or wiser is a basic component of our instinctive equipment that assures an infant will be protected and feel secure. As such, this attachment is the foundation of future emotional stability. Winnicott (1965) calls it having a "good-enough mother" and Erikson (1950) talks about the infant developing basic trust.

By stating that attachment provides the biological function of protection and safety, Bowlby gave the bond a scientific grounding that shifted theory away from concepts based on feeding, orality, or dependency. He had become enthusiastic about Lorenz's (1952) findings on the following responses of ducklings and goslings, and Harlow's (1958) experiments with infant monkeys who showed a clear preference for soft, furry surrogate mothers over the wire mothers who fed them. He saw a possible alternative model to psychoanalytic primary drive or dependency theory, which holds that children develop ties to the mother because she gratifies physiological and sensual needs. Instead, Bowlby posited an innate potential in human infants, similar to what is seen in infant monkeys: to attach to preferred and discriminated figures for proximity and comfort, not for food. Furthermore, this predilection is so strong that attachment will form even if caregiving is inadequate or abusing and, once created, will persist and resist redirection to other figures. This explains why abused and neglected children are attached to their parents and why battered spouses have difficulty withdrawing from destructive relationships. We intuitively expect our bonds of attachment to protect us from physical or psychological harm and find it almost unnatural to acknowledge that they could be disappointing or even dangerous.

It is because the theory emphasizes the physical proximity of familiar persons and places, as well as emotional availability, that Holmes (1993a) contends it is both relational and spatial. Schore (2000) points out that it is also a theory of affect regulation because it is concerned with how individuals regulate both positive and negative feelings. By stating that attachment provides the evolutionary function of survival, Bowlby explains how a mother allays anxiety and increases security and also how attachment behaviors such as crying, clinging, and pleading promote contact by attracting caregivers when they are needed. Distinguished from the term attachment, "attachment behaviors" are defined as a repertoire of social behaviors, equal in status to feeding, mating, and parental behavior, that are used to attain and retain a certain degree of proximity to attachment figures throughout life (Bowlby 1969a, 1980). The baby is born equipped with a number of instinctive behaviors that gradually become organized into increasingly complex behavioral systems as it interacts with the environment and develops models of itself and others. At first the infant cries at mother's departure, or is frightened, but later it can smile, crawl, and begin to use words. This set of actions is directed toward achieving a goal or "set-goal" of safety and well-being by remaining within the protective range of the attachment figure (Bowlby 1969a, 1979).

Bowlby used ethological and evolutionary ideas to explain that behavioral systems of attachment arose in the "environment of evolutionary adaptedness" and were a necessity for survival of the species. Thus, attachment has its own motivation—protection from danger—that is not derived from feeding or mating. The concept of cybernetically controlled behavioral systems is based on twentieth-century science, and replaces Freud's psychic energy model of drive and instinct. Behaviors regulated by such systems are referred to as "goal-corrected"; there is an ability to assimilate feedback and adjust behavior as circumstances change. The set-goal concept implies that there is an underlying readiness to be activated, and also that there are differences between the causes that activate a behavioral system and its functions or purposes for being activated. "Whereas an attachment bond endures," Bowlby (1980) explains,

> the various forms of attachment behaviour that contribute to it are active only when required. Thus the systems mediating attachment behaviour are activated only by certain conditions, for example strangeness, fatigue, anything frightening, and unavailability or unresponsiveness of attachment figure, and are terminated only by certain other conditions, for example, a familiar environment and the ready availability and responsiveness of an attachment figure. When attachment behaviour is strongly aroused, however, termination may require touching, or clinging, or the actively reassuring behaviour of the attachment figure. [p. 40]

To understand adult disorders, it is important to realize that attachment behavior, while more urgent and obvious in the young, is not confined to childhood. Because the function of attachment is to assure safety and security, the systems are liable to be activated and overtures for closeness and comfort from affectional figures made whenever there is internal pressure or external threat. Whereas certain behavior in adults, such as fear of being alone following a frightening event, might traditionally be seen as childish and overdependent, attachment theory perceives distress upon separation or threat of disruption as adaptive and essential for forming and maintaining affectional bonds for protection, especially in the face of danger.

A SECURE BASE

Ethology gave Bowlby a biological basis for his belief that children require a stable caregiver and become seriously distressed if the attachment to that caregiver is disrupted. A "good-enough mother" (Winnicott 1965) is affectively attuned to her infant, shielding it against overwhelming stimulation and discomfort, as well as initiating social interaction. Her sensitive and responsive availability regulates autonomic and behavioral functions and gives meaning to her baby's signals, facilitating its eventual ability to identify its own feelings as well as the situations that elicit them (Bowlby 1973, 1991, Karen 1994, McDougall 1989, Schore 1994, Spezzano 1993, Stern 1985). Schore's (1994) definition of attachment as a process of "psychobiological attunement" conveys that the maternal holding environment described by Winnicott includes both physiological and psychological provisions. In other words, the overall quality of parental handling—particularly with regard to protection, reliability, and responsiveness to the child's affective states—provides the foundation for healthy development, a secure base from which the child may venture forth and explore the universe and to which he or she may return when seeking refuge (Holmes 1995).

Bowlby sees attachment as complementary to exploration. From a springboard of secure attachment, children spend more time away, tolerating separation with less distress (Ainsworth 1989). When caregivers are available and responsive to their children's attachment behaviors, children develop feelings and expectations that others are reliable and that they themselves are worthy of receiving care and attention. It is the confidence that one can turn to others, knowing someone will be there if called upon, that frees one to rove, initiating new activities and options.

Attachment, however, takes precedence over exploration. If one is sick or hungry, feels threatened with danger in the environment, or is concerned about the reliability of a bond, attachment behaviors are activated in order to connect with an attachment figure and preserve or regain feelings of security (Ainsworth 1989, Bartholomew 1990, Bowlby 1980). Bowlby compares attachment behavior to an elastic band that allows movement and exploration away from a secure base when conditions are calm and attachment figures willing and readily available should they be needed. Lacking a secure base, curiosity and willingness to risk are inhibited, and the ability to tolerate separation is diminished (Ainsworth 1989, Bowlby 1969a, 1973, Karen 1990).

The concept of a secure base comes from the work of Mary Ainsworth, a developmental psychologist whose research interests and techniques broadened attachment theory. Ainsworth's path first crossed Bowlby's in the early 1950s when she answered an advertisement for a position in a research unit at Tavistock Clinic. After a brief period in London, followed by naturalistic studies of mothers and infants in Africa, she returned to a university position in Baltimore. In the late 1960s, Ainsworth (Ainsworth et al. 1978) devised the "Strange Situation" procedure, a standardized assessment of mother–child interaction that used direct observations and methodical rating to measure the emotional impact of parents on their children.

Although Bowlby had advocated that theory be based on direct observational studies as well as on retrospective reports of therapy, no one had previously found a way to assess and classify relatedness, or to determine how experiences became organized into internal representations. Ainsworth furnished empirical support for Bowlby's evolving theory by showing that the quality of attachment relationships could be measured, and also that everyday details of parenting had lasting effects on personality. The Strange Situation procedure is a twenty-minute structured laboratory observation of separation and reunion behaviors in 1-year-olds, which also compares the laboratory behavior with home observations made earlier. Ainsworth demonstrated that children's attachment and exploratory behaviors during the test were related to their caregiving experiences and, in particular, that secure children were more easily comforted and able to resume exploration (following two brief separations) than those classified as insecure. Her demonstration of the continuity of attachment behavior, which has been replicated with children of various ages and cultures and modified and applied to adults, was important for relating early experience to later distress. The many students and researchers Ainsworth inspired have used the protocol extensively, contributing much of the current data on attachment.

Ainsworth is also known for prescribing the kinds of maternal behavior that help in the formation of a secure base. Her research findings (e.g., that an infant who is promptly picked up when it cries, cries less at 1 year of age) were included in Bowlby's concept of attachment. However, it must also be noted that Ainsworth was influenced by Bowlby as well. By the 1970s, she was espousing research that recognized his thinking, such as the distinction between attachment and dependency.

ATTACHMENT VERSUS DEPENDENCY

In an interview (Hunter 1991) shortly before his death in 1990, Bowlby said that there were two main points in his work to which therapists had not paid much attention: one was that a person's desire for reassurance, comfort, and protection, especially when unhappy or distressed, should not be misconstrued as pathological or a regression to immature behavior, but recognized as a natural state when one is upset. The other was the significance of real experiences (Hunter 1991). According to the first point, it would not be weak or childish to exhibit attachment behavior under conditions of danger or stress such as frequently occur when someone seeks treatment. In fact, an affectional figure who responds to another's attachment behavior with sympathy and support alleviates distress and furthers the development of self-reliance and autonomy (Bretherton 1997).

Although there is minimal discussion of dependency in current writing on attachment, clinicians often use the concept to explain adult pathology (West and Sheldon-Keller 1994). But Bowlby (1982) opposed the object relations perspective of dependency or dependency need, distinguishing those terms from the concept of attachment. He stated that dependency is not only a confusing and pejorative term, but it also implies observable behavior markedly different from that characterizing attachment. Human infants are dependent on the care of others for survival, but are not yet attached. Attachment is an emotional bond that forms over time with caregiving, familiarity, and continuity, whereas dependency may diminish as the child grows older. Because attachment is characterized by connection to a specific person, it is not easily relinquished or replaced. Dependency, on the other hand, alludes to specific tasks, such as feeding in the young, or furnishing a range of goods and services, and at later ages certain nurturant social roles. Besides the fact that those tasks can be filled by any number of people, what may be called overly dependent behavior, such as wanting others when distressed, is often judged as something that eventually ought to be outgrown.

To be dependent on someone is not the same as being attached. One may be attached to someone but not dependent on him or her, as in the case of attachment to an elderly parent. Conversely, it is possible to be dependent on another without being attached. A sudden urban blackout quickly demonstrates one's dependency on a complex of others to whom one is not attached. Furthermore, as Parkes (1991) writes, perceiving adult relationships in terms of dependency is simplistic and does not reflect the complexity of interactions that occur between two people. From a bereavement study of spouses who sought psychotherapy, Parkes concluded that spouses who cited dependency on their mates or of their mates on them were actually describing a variety of underlying insecure aspects of the attachment relationship.

In addition to their different features, opposite values are implied and conveyed with the terms dependency and attachment (Bowlby 1969a). An adult labeled dependent is envisioned as one with a need to mature and become independent. On the other hand, it is desirable for an adult to be attached to another, or for family members to be attached to one another; no immaturity or helplessness is assumed. In fact, it is the absence of attachment, or detachment, that connotes pathology.

These value judgments are built into the concept of dependency. They are reflected in clients' self-appraisals, which are reinforced by a culture that equates independence with maturity. How many times have therapists heard clients admit, with shame and embarrassment, their dependency, and how often have therapists agreed with the assessment and made resolution of dependency needs a goal of treatment? If they are worried about a client's dependency needs, therapists may resist providing a secure base for that client for fear he will become overdependent. The client may react to the therapist's fostering independence as he did to the critical parent who made the client feel childish when seeking comfort; the client may then become afraid to express the very feelings he needs to express. Dependency becomes a blanket label that can be misleading, preventing the patient from realizing and dealing with some pressing attachment problems, such as a lack of intimacy or commitment in a relationship. In accusing oneself or one's partner of being overdependent, the importance of secure attachment to an adult may be overlooked, de-emphasized, or even denied.

This bias is illustrated by a couple who sought treatment because they found themselves arguing over money, their sexual relationship, and conflicting work schedules. Jason claimed that his wife was too dependent on him for financial support and company, and Wendy complained that Jason was cold, distant, and nonsupportive, both emotionally and financially. By rethinking and restating their situation in attachment terms, Jason saw that a crucial factor in their conflict was his perception of Wendy's attachment behavior as a sign of overdependence and immaturity. Once this realization surfaced, treatment could focus on helping the couple understand the way these misattributions and misconceptions about attachment needs were affecting their marriage.

REAL-LIFE EXPERIENCES

The other area of his work to which Bowlby wanted to draw attention regarded the significance of real-life events, such as separation or loss, on personality development (Hunter 1991). Although familial situations such as child abuse and neglect, and outside traumatic events such as urban violence and natural disasters are now receiving attention, specific personality theory concerning the effects of these conditions and events, as well as guidelines for their treatment, has been less well defined (Bowlby 1988a, Greenberg and Mitchell 1983, Hinde and Stevenson-Hinde 1991, Sanville 1991, van der Kolk 1987, Westen 1991). According to Bowlby (1988a), this gap in theory, and thus in clinical application, goes back to Freud and to the tendency of psychoanalytic theory to emphasize fantasy and to regard real-life events as significantly less important. Initially, Freud acknowledged that traumas, such as sexual abuse, had a role in the causation of hysteria, but he later reversed his opinion and claimed that these incidents had not really occurred—that they were conjured from the patient's imagination, wishful thinking, or through a misinterpretation of events. This shift away from external trauma and events led to an emphasis on the patient's internal world—or fantasy—and the unconscious defenses that kept feelings and thoughts out of awareness. Personal reality was relegated to a background position in developmental theory. Bowlby himself (Hunter 1991) stated that though he was confronted with instances of child abuse and neglect early in his career while working in a child guidance clinic, he was slow to grasp their consequence.

Freud's assertion that the role of fantasy was as important as actual events is alienating to most clinicians today (Lowenstein 1985, van der Kolk 1987). Object relations theories, direct observational studies of young children and animals, and clinical practice experience have given us evidence that the environment in which a child grows up is crucial in the determination of future mental health (Bowlby 1988a, Sanville 1991, Stern 1985, Trowell and Miles 1991). Additionally, we recognize that individuals are shaped by a wide range of sociocultural factors, including race, gender, and sexual orientation, and must be understood in terms of this total context.

WORKING MODELS OF ATTACHMENT

Attachment theory, like psychoanalytic and object relations theories, presupposes that early experiences are organized internally, and become the foundation of later adult personality (Berman and Sperling 1994, Greenberg and Mitchell 1983, Weinfield et al. 1999). In alleging the continuity and persistence of attachment behavior beyond infancy and childhood, Bowlby (1969a) introduced the concept of inner "working models" to describe a network of cognitive and emotional representations, as well as behavioral dispositions. Individuals use this network to reflect on relationships and conditions of the moment, to forecast the future, and to determine plans of action. Working models are seen as a dynamic internal process through which individuals select, organize, and store images and ideas about themselves and their interactions with others. These mental mechanisms start to form during infancy and are an assemblage of both conscious and unconscious memories, thoughts, feelings, and strategies for affect regulation (Bowlby 1969a, Bretherton 1985, Kobak and Sceery 1988, Schore 1994). Although not unlike object relations theories of internalization, which perceive that an individual lives in an external and an internal world simultaneously, representative models of attachment have a biological-ethological base (Nelson 1999) and are primarily constructed from attachment-related experiences, rather than fantasy, drives, or defenses. Children absorb impressions and messages from the people around them, and are affected not only by how they are treated, but by what they see and are told. Initially, their representations are quite rudimentary, but gradually become more elaborate and abstract with development and an expanding world of grandparents, other relatives, and friends with whom they share experiences. Once constructed, these inner models tend to be so taken for granted that they operate almost automatically and unconsciously, enabling individuals to function more efficiently by interpreting and generalizing thoughts from the available data of previous experience (Bowlby 1973, 1988b). By the time one reaches adulthood, these reproductions are a fairly accurate record of actual environmental events and interactions and are the set of rules and expectations used to interpret and anticipate the emotions and behavior of others. The representations vary from simple maps of the environment to more complicated internal beliefs and attitudes about oneself and one's capabilities and what can be expected from others.

When, over the years, caregivers and later affectional figures have been readily available and lovingly responsive to attachment behaviors while also encouraging exploration of the world, people will erect models in which they portray themselves as self-reliant and worthy of comfort and care, and will see others as loving and reliable. As Bowlby (1973) notes, cognitive structures usually develop in complementary fashion and are mutually confirming. Children who feel loved and wanted by their caregivers and other significant attachments are more apt to feel confident that others will find them lovable too; as adults they will feel lovable and capable of establishing satisfactory relationships. Feelings of self-reliance and self-confidence are "woven into the fabric of the working models" (Bowlby 1973, p. 205), resulting in representations that are compatible, consistent, and flexible enough to handle changes in the environment with a minimum of tension and difficulty. A person with such representations, or working models, is capable of both accepting assistance when it is needed and offering support to others. This person would also be able to communicate deeply and express interest in understanding another's feelings and points of view (Bowlby 1973, 1988a).

On the other hand, if the desire for comfort or exploration has been thwarted, these working models will reflect feelings of incompetence or unworthiness. Furthermore, when the information that reaches cognitive structures is inconsistent, contradictory, or painful, certain attachment thoughts and feelings may be defensively excluded from awareness. This leads to the creation of rigid and contradictory models that are difficult to update or modify and that may restrict adaptive functioning (Bowlby 1973, 1988a, Bretherton 1988), as it becomes increasingly difficult to process new information. This tendency is exacerbated by the fact that mental structures tend to be stable and to persist. The distortions caused by multiple conflicting models and the defensive resistance to change can affect reactions to subsequent situations, rendering such individuals more vulnerable to psychological disturbance when confronted with stressful events such as separation or loss (Bowlby 1973, 1988a).

> The construction of conflicting representations of attachment relationships is illustrated by the experiences of Kelly, a young, adult, single woman who will be discussed in greater detail in later chapters. Kelly sought therapy for her fears of getting close to others, feeling anxiety in unfamiliar conditions, and inability to improve her career or social life (Sable 1983, 1992). She had grown up in a chaotic and disorganized family where both parents were alcoholic, argumentative, and physically abusive to each other. Although Kelly saw her father as a volatile and frightening man, her mother told her how "lucky" she was to have such a "good" father. Her mother, hospitalized off and on during Kelly's childhood for psychiatric distress, which included suicide attempts, often threatened her daughter with abandonment or severely punished her for minor misdeeds. Kelly was discouraged from crying with impatient remarks such as "stop acting like a baby."
>
> Baffled by a disturbed family environment where she could not reconcile her impressions with what she was told, Kelly shut out most of her childhood memo-

ries from consciousness. Explaining that people were too confusing and difficult to figure out, she gave up trying to relate, preferring to be "invisible," to "slip by like a shadow," or freezing in fear and alarm if someone tried to get close to her. Overt conflicting communication, compounded by prohibitions against expressing or clarifying feelings, led to such confusion that Kelly began deactivating her attachment behavior and feelings early on in her life, determined to be independent and rely only on herself. That no one could make her feel safe at this early age strongly suggests that her childhood experiences were traumatic, setting the stage for her adult feelings and behavior. As an adult, Kelly was emotionally detached, both from her feelings and in her relationships with others.

Memories can be registered and stored in ways that further hamper making sense of one's experience. Information can be stored "semantically" in generalized propositions based on personal experiences, such as Kelly's perception of her father as volatile and frightening. Experience can be also stored "episodically," based on specific episodes or events, as when Kelly's mother told her daughter she was lucky to have such a "good" father. When the sense of an experience is discordant with what one is told or how one imagines a situation, conflict and defenses are more likely to arise. This is why clients are encouraged to recall the actual events of their lives, to reappraise situations and occasions with their parents, and to correct images in semantic storage that are not conscious or in line with current or historical evidence (Bowlby 1980).

In the time since Bowlby applied this episodic-semantic distinction, a third class of memory system, implicit (or nondeclarative), has been devised (Main 1999). Whereas both forms of explicit memory depend on the temporal lobe structures of the brain, implicit memory depends on the basal ganglia. The information in this system influences behavior but is not available for conscious recall. The implicit memory system is operational very early in life, maybe even before birth, and may explain how experiences before the age of 3 exert an influence on development, although the actual events are unknowable (Amini et al. 1996). Kelly's sense that she could never trust her mother would exemplify her implicit capacity to analyze and give meaning to early experiences without their reaching consciousness.

Bowlby (1980) uses a metaphor based on the shape of the earth to illustrate possible discrepancies in information storage. We know the earth to be a sphere, yet in our daily lives, we experience it as flat, feeling no conflict between our knowledge and perception. In contrast, family misconstructions can cause unease because of their emotional impact. We are learning from research that young children lack the cognitive development to assess certain situations logically and are more prone to early distortions of experiences. If these are not noticed and corrected, they are integrated into working models and will affect subsequent constructions and relationships. As individuals move through adolescence and into adulthood, these internal arrangements will influence the choice of romantic partners, parenting, work relationships, and one's vulnerability toward developing certain psychopathologies.

2

Attachment Relationships of Adult Life

The concept of working models implies that we have within us an elaborate and complex collection of memories, thoughts, and feelings through which we filter current and past experiences and give them meaning. They are called "working models" or representations because they are active, not static, and are capable of continually monitoring attachment-related experiences and updating expectations and plans accordingly. These cognitive-affective structures replace a psychoanalytic, orally derived theory of internal objects and explain how attachment behavior persists beyond childhood into adolescence and adult years. Adult attachment theorists, beginning with Marris (1982), Weiss (1975, 1982a, 1991), and Parkes (1991), and more recently Berman and Sperling (1994), Hazan and Zeifman (1999), and Holmes (1993a), all agree with Bowlby (1973, 1988a) that there is a behavioral system of attachment that is active throughout the life cycle and plays a part in those adult relationships that provide feelings of safety and security. The attachment system in adults consists of thoughts, emotions, and expectations about affectional relationships and is elicited when a person is under stress, injured, or frightened. Its function is essentially the same in adulthood as in infancy: to ensure the formation of enduring bonds that can be counted on for both psychological and physical protection (Berman and Sperling 1994, Bretherton 1985, Crowell et al. 1999, Feeney and Noller 1996, Hazan and Zeifman 1999, Weiss 1988).

The adult relationships that would qualify as providing bonds of attachment are with those figures who would be sought at times of danger or distress, whose presence would provide comfort and reduce anxiety, and whose loss (or fear of loss) would arouse protest and efforts to prevent separation (Weiss 1982a, 1991). These figures, considered unique and irreplaceable, are most commonly found in relationships of marriage or other committed heterosexual and homosexual pair bonds, and in relationships with parents or children (Ainsworth 1989, Scharlach 1991). Bonds of attachment may also be a component in relationships with other family members such as siblings or grandparents, therapists, teachers, close friends, pets, or religious figures (Antonucci 1994, Feeney and Noller 1996, Sable 1995, Siegel 1999, Weiss 1991).

From an ethological perspective, the presumption of a lifelong attachment system requires that the concept of protection and security be expanded to acknowledge the patterns of behavior associated with normal developmental change. For example, adults may not require the regular physical protection that is indispensable for children, but they do need to know they have a comforting base available and ready to respond if they are frightened or sick, want help with a problem, or need reassurance. They need to know someone is looking out for them, informed of their whereabouts, and willing to track them down should they not show up when they are expected. Over the course of evolution, attachment has proven to be a reliable mechanism for providing this assurance by motivating two individuals to stay together and to also vigorously object if the relationship is in jeopardy (Hazan and Zeifman 1999).

An adult's attachment behavior, similar to that of an infant, is activated by stressful conditions in the physical or social environment, conditions of threat to the relationship, or conditions within the individual such as illness or exhaustion (Feeney 1999). However, due to developmental skills such as the attainment of object constancy and the ability to make more sophisticated cognitive assessments, an adult's attachment behavior may be modified, less intense, and more flexible. Each member of a bonded pair may at times act as the available and responsive figure for the other, depending on circumstances, the nature of the relationship, and one's stage in the life cycle. Adult sexual relationships and bonds with peers allow for more subtle and varied patterns of attachment behavior. Pair bonds foster proximity, comfort, and sexual accessibility, whereas parental attachments are aimed more at protection and are most apt to be activated when the well-being of the child is threatened.

Bonds formed later in life may not have the longevity of primary attachments, existing for a more limited time or purpose. For example, psychotherapy provides the experience of an attachment relationship that may be very commanding while sessions take place, but that, following termination, may be reduced to infrequent contact or even cease to exist. However, the therapist, valued and remembered, though no longer part of an active attachment relationship, continues to be part of the patient's working models (Ainsworth 1989). Moreover, relationships such as therapy or parenting are not reciprocal, and do not have the give-and-take present in committed adult couples. Instead of mutuality, it is assumed that one person will be relied on to provide care to another. In some circumstances, as for example with aging parents, attachment behavior may be reversed, with the adult child having become the stronger and wiser figure who assists with decision making as well as physical care.

Another difference between childhood and adult attachment is that adults are more able to continually monitor and appraise the complexities of a situation and are therefore less overwhelmed when attachment is imperiled. Adults are capable of continuing to function, albeit with preoccupation and not as adeptly as usual. Also, their cognitive capacity to remember a person who is away or to maintain contact via communication techniques, such as letters, e-mail, or by telephoning, enables them to understand and tolerate disruptions like temporary separations (Weiss 1982a). Adults can internally represent expectations and beliefs, whereas young children require actual contact with attachment figures to maintain security. Adults are capable of using feedback and are more able to derive comfort from knowing they have a variety of options available, or could achieve contact if it were needed (Hazan and Shaver 1994). The dynamics and functions of the attachment behavioral system—to provide protection and security—are hypothesized as remaining the same throughout the life cycle, although the mechanisms for achieving these goals change with maturation and development (Hazan and Shaver 1994, Hazan and Zeifman 1999, West and Sheldon-Keller 1994).

For adults as well as children, feeling securely attached means feeling safe and protected. It means feeling confident in the knowledge that a chosen figure will be there and will respond appropriately if called upon for comfort and support. Adult attachment is both a mental construct that "contributes to the maintenance of an inner state of well-being" (Weiss 1991, p. 71), and also a particular type of relationship. As a relationship, adult attachment refers to emotionally significant, ongoing ties with those few, specific affectional figures who are sought, and can be relied upon, for reassurance, protection, or restoring equilibrium. These relationships are not the sole determination of adult security and well-being, but they furnish a foundation of familiarity, companionship, and communication that facilitates personal growth and exploration and reduces feelings of loss and loneliness. Bowlby (1988a) states that "throughout adult life, the availability of a responsive attachment figure remains the source of a person's feeling secure. All of us, from the cradle to the grave, are happiest when life is organized as a series of excursions, long or short, from the secure base provided by our attachment figure(s)" (p. 62).

It should be clear, however, that not all close adult relationships are considered bonds of attachment, nor can all adult attachments be presumed to be secure. In their book on adult attachment, Berman and Sperling (1994) emphasize that the only adult relationships that can be characterized as attachments are those that provide the potential for security. Thus, work or peer relationships, which may have relevance to overall functioning and may even reflect attachment history, are not considered attachments. They are not perceived as unique and irreplaceable, nor will they evoke an intense level of distress if they are disrupted. Adults have a variety of needs, from sexuality, excitement, and learning, to attachment, caregiving, and security. An attachment construct is not meant to address the complexity of adult experiences and relationships, but is limited to those particular figures who provide emotional security and foster an expectation of permanence and whose loss would have a major effect on feelings and behavior.

Berman and Sperling (1994) also identify and describe what they consider to be important dimensions of adult attachment: intensity or strength of an attachment relationship, reliability and responsiveness of the attachment figure, ease of forming affectional bonds, how readily attachment behavior is activated, and frustration tolerance. Security of attachment is defined in terms of the degree to which individuals perceive their attachment figures to be reliable and responsive. The idea that attachment behavior can be charted along a continuum of secure versus insecure is a hallmark of the theory and has implications for many areas of adult functioning, including social adjustment and psychopathology. For example, individuals who appear to be insecure about their attachments, and unsure whether those attachments will be available and responsive, have more difficulties in their close relationships, are more prone to anxiety and depression, and are more apt to seek help from outside sources. When working models are less resilient, the ease of making satisfactory bonds is affected, and the tendency for the attachment behavioral system to be activated is increased. Clinically, for instance, patients diagnosed as borderline would be expected to develop intense bonds more rapidly, react more dramatically to disappointments, and exhibit a lower tolerance of frustration than those diagnosed as schizoid.

Strength of attachment was primarily studied early in the development of the theory and was defined in terms of reactions to separation or loss or threat of separation. Because it is difficult to quantify intensity or strength of attachment, there is now greater focus on individual differences in the organization of attachment behavior and on the dimension of security versus insecurity (Crowell et al. 1999). For example, current researchers, such as Feeney and Noller (1996), Sperling (1988), Berman (1988), and Antonucci and Levitt (1984), have devised a variety of research methods, including self-report methodologies, that ask subjects to imagine the effects of separation or to describe the significance of current figures. Other researchers, such as Main (Main and Goldwyn 1984), Fonagy (Fonagy et al. 1991, 1995, 1996), and Hazan and Shaver (1987) have modified and extended Ainsworth's Strange Situation procedure and classifications of the quality of attachment in order to evaluate adults' perceptions of their relationships, both current and from childhood.

RESEARCH ON ADULT ATTACHMENT

As early as 1960, Bowlby (1960a) wrote that attachment provided a "sense of security" when it was reliable and consistent. In the volume *Separation* (Bowlby 1973), he made it clear that this criterion was not limited to childhood. "Whether a child or adult is in a state of security, anxiety or distress is determined in large part by the accessibility and responsiveness of his principal attachment figure" (p. 23). Although the statement suggests that Bowlby considered attachment an integral part of certain adult relationships, he did not develop his theoretical ideas on adult attachment in the same way he did regarding the mother–child bond (Kobak 1999, Weiss 1994b). This divergence may account for some of the difficulty and delay in measuring adult attachment and in addressing its role in various kinds of relationships or at various stages of the life cycle. In the past decade, however, research on adult attachment has proliferated, and there is mounting evidence of the benefits of these bonds for emotional as well as physical health (Hazan and Zeifman 1999). Robert Weiss (1994b), who has presented one of the more complete descriptions of adult attachment, notes that Bowlby perceived attachment behavior as the tendency to seek proximity when either the individual or the attachment relationship is threatened. However, an adult's ability to remember and reflect on experiences suggests an ongoing and complex inner construct that may enhance security even when there is no threat. Knowing that a reliable relationship is potentially accessible as a backup in times of need may of itself lead to a more relaxed mood and increase one's ability to pursue a variety of interests and activities.

Weiss (1974, 1975), along with Marris (1958) and Parkes (1969), contributed the earliest evidence of attachment in adults, with their studies on divorce and bereavement. These authors also demonstrated that adult attachment relationships, like those of childhood, could be systematically measured. Marris's (1958) influential study of seventy-two London widows whose husbands had died within the previous two years described a grief process that has become a yardstick for the experience of mourning. Parkes (1965, 1969, 1970), who was also interested in establishing a regular pattern for the experience of grief, showed that adult grief was similar to the attachment behavior displayed by children. Weiss (1994a) thinks this was one of the first empirical studies to suggest that attachment behavior appeared in the lives of adults. From his own studies of both divorced and widowed individuals, Weiss found a lingering sense of connection that the individuals were reluctant to relinquish. In taped interviews of divorced members in the organization Parents Without Partners, for example, separated spouses often felt drawn to each other despite their choice to end the marriage and get on with their lives. Weiss (1975) concluded that there was a component of attachment in these relationships, and that once developed, it seemed to persist. Even when they were furiously angry and no longer in love, many of these spouses were paralyzed with fear at the thought of leaving the marriage. Weiss documented how the appearance of emotions such as fear, anger, and sadness at the time when relationships are dissolving indicates a persistence of attachment, and emphasized that these attachment behaviors should be recognized for what they are and not interpreted as signs of weakness or overdependence. His work demonstrated that in adult relationships, attachment behavior continues to be directed toward an attached figure until the attachment bond can be dismantled; this process, like the original establishment of a bond, requires a certain amount of time.

Weiss (1974) conceptualized attachment as one of a variety of social provisions of relationships that adults require for well-being; the others are social affiliation, opportunity for nurturance, and obtaining help and guidance. Individuals maintain relationships to gain these social provisions, which can fluctuate at various times of life, and any particular bond may provide more than a single social provision. For example, because attachment relationships foster continuing proximity, they have the potential to meet emotional provisions in the other categories.

A research study designed by Kahn and Antonucci (1980) adds support to Weiss's argument that adults need both social and emotional support. In research designed to address various aspects of adult relationships over time, Kahn and Antonucci (1980) articulated a "social convoy" diagram that linked concepts of attachment and social support. The social convoy is conceptualized as a hierarchical model of three concentric circles with the individual in the center. Respondents are asked to place in the inner circle those persons to whom the individual feels "so close that it's hard to imagine life without them" (Antonucci

1986, p. 10). In the middle circle, they are asked to place those persons who are "not quite as close but who are still very important," and in the outer circle, those not included in the first two circles but who are "close enough and important enough in their life that they should be placed somewhere in their network of relationships" (Antonucci 1986, p. 11). The procedure has been given by personal interview, or mail-in questionnaire, to individuals ranging in age from 18 to 95, with varied socioeconomic, health, and cultural backgrounds. It has been used to study transitions of childbirth (Levitt et al. 1994) and the attachment needs of the elderly (Antonucci 1994). Individuals placed in the inner circle would be those with whom one has the most intimate and meaningful relationships, with the outer circles expanding to include others who are part of a fulfilling life.

The researchers concluded that relationships with individuals placed in the respondents' innermost circle could be considered functionally equivalent to attachment relationships, and that personal well-being across the life cycle was dependent on having at least one of these close relationships. In support of their argument, Kahn and Antonucci (1980) note that across age and culture the number of persons placed in the inner circle tends to be limited to three to five, suggesting that emotionally meaningful adult relationships, like those in childhood, are limited to only a significant few. Although social contacts increase with age, with new bonds such as a spouse and children added to the inner circle, the number of close relationships throughout the life cycle remains relatively constant. Furthermore, regardless of age and stage of life, individuals designated within the inner circle are usually close family members, occasionally pets and friends. A series of convoy studies of older people found the average duration of their closest bonds, predominantly with family members, to be more than thirty years. In questions given along with the convoy, it was found that those who perceived the presence of supportive confidants were more able to reach out and use health-care professionals when necessary, suggesting that a secure base of primary attachments might facilitate meeting the challenges of aging (Antonucci 1994, Antonucci and Akiyama 1987).

In contrast to those in the inner circle, individuals placed in the other two circles comprise a social network, or what Weiss (1988) calls "relationships of community." Adults require these social supports, along with "relationships of attachment," to maintain well-being. In discussing the importance of both types of social interactions, Weiss hypothesized that there are two types of loneliness: emotional loneliness and social loneliness. The former results from the loss of a key attachment figure and is only remedied by the establishment of another mutual relationship that supplies the shared understanding and emotional exchange of an affectional connection. Social loneliness, on the other hand, results from gaps in one's social or group support network rather than from loss or lack of specific individuals. This differentiation can be helpful in understanding and managing stress and emotional loneliness. For example, in my research (Sable 1989) with women who had been widowed from one to three years, those who perceived a more supportive and adequate social network reported less anxiety and depression, noting they had companionship and opportunities to share grief. But they also reported that the loss of these social ties would not lead to the grief and mourning that follows the loss of an attachment figure. The women made it clear that in that instance they felt a loneliness that was difficult to overcome; friends and family can ease that pain, but cannot replace the loss of an exclusive attachment.

ROMANTIC RELATIONSHIPS IN ADULT LIFE: THE "LOVE QUIZ"

Taken together, attachment studies from nonclinical populations suggest that attachment behavior remains essential to emotional well-being and mental health throughout the life cycle. Once a bond is established, it is not easily relinquished or redirected to others; one figure does not readily substitute for another. In the social convoy research, for instance, widowed individuals sometimes listed their deceased spouses in their inner circle; conversely, a number of mothers did not include infants under a year old, as if they were not yet fully felt to be an attachment (Levitt 1991). Weiss (1975) found that divorced individuals often feel emotionally linked to each other even while feeling misused and angry. Therapists know how reluctant clients are to have sessions with a substitute when they go on vacation. These examples suggest that it takes time to reconstruct working models to accommodate new situations or relationships, or to dissolve attachment feelings even when the desired new circumstances are present.

Ainsworth's (Ainsworth et al. 1978) research tool, the Strange Situation, was invented to identify and classify individual differences in the attachment behavior patterns of 1-year-old infants. The procedure exposes the infant to the stress of a brief separation from its mother, and then observes the child's behavior when the mother returns. Three basic patterns of attachment were identified: secure, anxious-ambivalent, and avoidant. Somewhat later, a fourth category, disorganized, was added. These categories were assumed to reflect the quality of past mother–child interactions, the child's internal representations, and expectations of caregivers' responsiveness to the child's need for proximity and contact. The pattern generally remains stable, at least until age 10, suggesting its persisting influence on later development (Berman and Sperling 1994).

Ainsworth's classifications and their various modifications have become central to attachment research and clinical practice (Holmes 1996). Hazan and Shaver (1987, 1990), for example, designed a single-item self-report questionnaire to see whether Ainsworth's classifications could be applied to the romantic relationships of adults. Their "love quiz" asked respondents to choose which of three statements most accurately described their general feelings about themselves in intimate relationships. The three choices were:

> "I find it relatively easy to get close to others and am comfortable depending on them and having them depend on me. I don't often worry about being abandoned or about someone getting too close to me." [secure]
>
> I am somewhat uncomfortable being close to others; I find it difficult to trust them completely, difficult to allow myself to depend on them. I am nervous when anyone gets too close, and often, love partners want me to be more intimate than I feel comfortable being." [avoidant]
>
> "I find that others are reluctant to get as close as I would like. I often worry that my partner doesn't really love me or won't want to stay with me. I want to merge completely with another

person and this desire sometimes scares people away." [anxious-ambivalent]. [Hazan and Shaver 1987, p. 515]

Respondents were also asked details about their most significant romantic relationships and their childhood relationships. Findings were roughly equal to those obtained with infants in the Strange Situation: two-thirds fell into the secure category, with the remainder divided almost evenly between the other two patterns. Hazan and Shaver also found a correspondence between the quality of caregiving received in childhood and young adults' perceptions of their current partner relationships. Subjects classified as secure were happier in their love relationships, were more trusting of the other's availability, and had longer-lasting relationships. In contrast, anxiously ambivalent adults tended to report distress, anger, and anxiety; they became preoccupied with their partner's responsiveness, fell in love easily, and were extremely jealous. They also had the highest rate of relationship dissolution. Avoidantly attached individuals had a fear of intimacy and maintained distance in close relationships. They tended to be pessimistic about romantic love, had problems of communication and jealousy, and had a relatively high rate of relationship dissolution.

Childhood recollections also differed systematically across the three attachment groups. Secure subjects described their parents as caring, respectful, responsive, and accepting. Adults classified as anxious-ambivalent reported that their parents were inconsistent: sometimes available, warm, and loving, but at other times inaccessible, unresponsive, and intrusive. Moreover, this group continued to be preoccupied with the type of care they had received, as well as resentful and angry about it. Avoidant adults described their parents as generally uninvolved, somewhat rejecting, and less warm and nurturing. Hazan and Shaver concluded that adult individuals rated as insecure differed from those rated secure in terms of the type of caregiving they had received as children, suggesting that adult attachment patterns do have roots in childhood attachment bonds.

In line with the opinions of Ainsworth and Weiss, who hold that attachment is a component of certain adult relationships, Hazan and Shaver also concluded that attachment has an impact on romantic love, and in fact that romantic love can be conceptualized as an attachment process. They suggest that childhood experiences produce a style of relating to others that plays a part in shaping adult relationships. Although these patterns are not fixed for life and can be changed, depending on ongoing experiences, attachment styles that originate in childhood do tend to persist and guide expectations and behavior in current situations. Moreover, styles of attachment seem to be present in parenting and work relationships as well. For example, in work-situation studies, secure adults got along better with co-workers and were more satisfied with their jobs. Avoidant adults interacted less efficiently and preferred to work alone, while anxious-ambivalent workers felt underappreciated and overinvolved at work.

THE ADULT ATTACHMENT INTERVIEW

Another approach to the study of adult attachment is the Adult Attachment Interview (AAI) devised by Mary Main and colleagues (Main and Goldwyn 1984) in an effort to assess the influence of the internal working models of parents of young children on their parenting behav-

ior. The AAI is an audiotaped, one-hour structured interview that attempts to "surprise the unconscious" and reveal "states of mind" (Main 1991, p. 141) of attachment
by asking detailed questions about the subjects' relationship and history of separation and loss experiences with
their parental figures. Subjects are asked for five adjec-
tives to describe childhood relations with their parents and
to support each adjective with actual memories. They are
asked how their parents responded to them when they
were upset, if they ever felt rejected, and how their relationship with their parents changed over time. Main, like Hazan
and Shaver, was interested in translating Ainsworth's infant categories into corresponding adult patterns. Her work
raised attachment-based research to the level of representation, rating levels of security (labeled as secure/autono-
mous or free to evaluate) according to how attachment
feelings and ideas were remembered and organized. A
secure adult is "autonomous," willing and able to speak
of attachment experiences with coherence and clarity.
Main classifies her insecure groups as dismissive, preoccupied, or unresolved/disorganized. These adults tended
to give incomplete, idealized, and/or inconsistent descriptions of their past experiences. Main also found a correlation between the attachment status of young children
in the Strange Situation and those children's mothers'
descriptions of their own relationships with their parents. Slade and Aber (1992) note that where Ainsworth's
Strange Situation measured children's patterns of behavior in relation to their parents, the AAI describes the
meaning adults give to their childhood attachment
experiences.

Although the measures used by both Hazan and Shaver
and Main, or modifications of them, have been used in
hundreds of studies, they are not without controversy.

There has been skepticism that a procedure as simple as Hazan and Shaver's "love quiz" can reliably test an attachment pattern. Respondents may be defensive and give what they perceive to be a positive response, or they may reflect the feelings evoked by a current relationship rather than an overall attitude toward attachment. One limitation of the AAI might be that it constrains people to a single style and doesn't allow for the different models individuals adopt with different people (Karen 1994); another is that it limits adult attachment to only three or four different types of adults (Crowell and Waters 1994). Clinically, the many nuances of individual differences may not be fully comprehended (Atkinson 1997). Though Hazan and Shaver (1987, 1990) focus on individuals' self-reported orientation toward their romantic relationships, while Main focuses on the coherence and defensive strategies related to remembrances of childhood relationships with parents, nevertheless, results from both tests found a correlation between adults' perceptions of their current affectional bonds and descriptions of their earlier family experiences. This suggests continuity between childhood attachment and adult psychic structure. On the AAI, for instance, secure adults describe their experiences in a coherent, consistent way, or as Holmes (1993a) terms it, with "autobiographical competence." Though their lives have not necessarily been trouble-free, they have integrated experiences into a balanced view that neither idealizes nor denigrates their parents. They value their attachments and can easily recall early memories and assess them realistically, without being overcome by past pain. There was also a relationship between the coherence of their recollections and the security of the bonds with their young children, suggesting that parents' organization of their attachment experiences affects the caregiving they give their own children. Similarly, on Hazan and Shaver's (1987) measure of young adults, there was a correlation between subjects' early experiences and the security they felt in their current romantic relationships.

ATTACHMENT QUALITIES IN ADULT LIFE

The consistency of research findings makes it plausible to hypothesize that there is an adult attachment behavioral system, which, though modified by age and experience and redirected to additional figures, is an expression of the same emotional attachment system individuals experience as children (Weiss 1982a, 1994a). As Marris (1982) conceives it, individuals learn early in life that specific nurturing figures represent comfort and well-being, and they organize their emotions and behavior around these vitally important relationships. These childhood experiences of attachment provide a model that is applied to structuring later relationships and the meaning given to them. Marris, an urban planner, recognizes the connection between emotions and attachment, and between early affectional ties and adult bonds of love. He writes, "the relationships that matter most to us are . . . [the] particular people whom we love—husband or wife, parents, children, dearest friend" (p. 185). Bowlby (1988b) puts this point in a clinical context when he writes, "For many years, sensitive clinicians have been aware that a person's mental state is deeply influenced by whether his or her intimate personal relationships are warm and harmonious or tense, angry, anxious, emotionally remote, or, possibly, nonexistent" (p. 2).

Attachment, and the behavior that accompanies it during any phase of life, evoke powerful and profound feelings. Young children require almost continuous contact with their parents to feel secure. By latency age, children can tolerate separation for longer periods of time, satisfied with the assurance that the parent is accessible. Attachment behavior toward parents declines in adolescence and adulthood and begins to be directed toward nonparental figures (Shaver and Hazan 1993, Weiss 1991). Parents are gradually relinquished as primary attachment figures, though emotional connection is maintained; attachment behavior shifts to fellow adults. A specific developmental task of young adulthood is to choose a partner with whom one can sustain an intimate and significant relationship (Antonucci 1994, Erikson 1950). The commitment of a sexual pair bond involves the integration of the attachment system with the mating and caregiving behavioral systems that ensure the biological function of species survival (Ainsworth 1989).

Marriage or an equivalent adult partnership does not meet the criteria of attachment until a couple has been together for a while. It is a central concept of attachment that, just as an infant forms an affectional bond over time, adults become attached through repeated interaction and familiarity. For this reason, Hazan and Zeifman (1999) label courtship behaviors "attachments in the making" (p. 349). If a relationship continues and becomes a reliable base, the person has an "attachment in place" (Weiss 1991, p. 74). However, because attachment develops by becoming steadier, until this attachment takes hold and is integrated into the individual's life, it is more tenuous and vulnerable to disruption.

Hazan and Zeifman (1999) contend that it takes about two years before a romantic relationship is cemented into an attachment. They administered an interview measuring four components of attachment to a diverse sample of 100 adults ranging in age from 18 to 82. Individuals who had been in their relationship less than two years were not as inclined to indicate their partner as their preferred support figure on items covering separation distress; some named friends, and others continued to name their parents. However, after two years the majority named their partner, suggesting there was a gradual redirection of attachment behavior to romantic figures.

Attachment, often the glue that bonds two adults, may be a better basis than sexuality for establishing and sustaining a romantic relationship for the time needed to raise children. At the start of a relationship, mutual attraction and sexual passion draw two people together long enough for an emotional bond to begin to develop. Research has shown that, whether for better or worse, this initial intense desire for physical contact tends to decline, as does sexual activity (Fisher 1992, Traupmann and Hatfield 1981), while the degree to which the partner is perceived to be reliable, comforting, and a secure base becomes increasingly important in maintaining what the couple considers a satisfactory relationship (Hazan and Shaver 1994). Moreover, under conditions of threat, the system of attachment is activated, that of sexual desire suppressed. Finally, sexual attraction is more easily redirected toward new figures than is attachment. An important point made by Weiss (1982a) that also helps to clarify the nature and boundaries of adult attachment is that reliable bonds can form in relationships that may or may not have a sexual component.

Adult attachment to grown children follows a pattern somewhat similar to pair bonds. Although a parental bond differs in that there is usually a lifetime commitment, parents seem to display diminishing attachment to older children and are satisfied with occasional contact unless there is an event or crisis that demands attention. Adult children, too, generally relinquish their parents as attachment figures, which may help explain Marris's (1982) assertion that adult children do not usually grieve deeply when their elderly parents die, even though they feel sorrow and miss them.

Attachment theory was originally devised to explain the biological function that is served by keeping young children and their caregivers in close proximity (Bowlby 1969a). Despite more active research with adults, it is still difficult to measure adult attachment unless a relationship has ended or been interrupted (Weiss 1994a). In particular, Weiss states that we do not yet know enough about this important bonding system, how it functions, and what happens if it is interrupted. Hendrich and Hendrich (1994) also call for caution when generalizing the attachment concept to adults. They cite a lack of data on continuity, the instability of attachment styles over time, and the influence of both parents and temperament as factors that limit drawing conclusions. Noller and Feeney (1994) note that because it is more difficult to observe attachment processes between adults we must rely more on self-report or interview. If a measure calls for a retrospective report, it may be influenced by current views of the world (Feeney 1999).

In addition to difficulties of measurement, data are still limited on specific kinds of relationships, such as those involving paternal or sibling attachments. Most of the research to date has been concerned with individual differences and the continuity of personality patterns. As a result, many inconsistencies abound. In our society, for instance, there is pressure for fathers to participate more actively in caregiving, yet we have little research on the bond between fathers and children. We have also learned about the benefits of social support, but know little about the behavioral systems underlying friendships that supply elements of attachment. Certain friends are not perceived to be interchangeable; bonds with them are enduring and provide feelings of familiarity and protection. Even more persistent than the bonds with friends are those with siblings. These relationships may be more ambivalent than some close friendships but the siblings' history of shared experience connotes mutual understanding and security (Ainsworth 1989).

Although this book focuses on adult attachment and gives less attention to caregiving, it is important to remember that the biological function of attachment is to ensure survival of the species—or, in the language of modern evolutionary theory, reproductive fitness and protection of the individual child (Belsky 1999a). Evidence exists that suggests an infant not only has a better chance of survival with two caregivers, but is more likely to prosper. In our present world, just as in the environment of evolutionary adaptedness, an extra caregiver is a buffer against the loss of the other parent. The investment of two parents helps assure infants of adequate and routine care and shelter, thus further promoting their well-being. We are currently in a period of great change in child-rearing practices and we do not yet know what the outcome will be. Fathers have traditionally been the financial support of the family, and the parent who encouraged exploration and play. Solomon and George (1999) suggest that the father's support in play and exploration may be more relevant than caregiving in fostering secure attachment in his offspring, which would explain, for example, why infants prefer their mothers for safety. Both Bowlby and Winnicott stressed that the emotional support a mother felt she received from the father was highly significant in determining her self-confidence and availability and responsiveness to her child, and there are now research findings that show that when a woman has a supportive spouse this correlates with security in the offspring (Belsky 1999b). Reality testing tells us that we will not return to this division of family responsibility in the near future, though those parents making the necessary commitment and financial and emotional sacrifices to put their "children first" (Leach 1994), for instance, by one parent staying home and not working, deserve the utmost validation and support from society. Mental-health practitioners have their own opinions and values (and defenses) about these issues, which are bound to affect therapeutic work, but if informed about the nature of attachment, they will be better prepared to acknowledge and help their clients understand and deal with their attachment feelings, especially when those feelings are troubling or in conflict with what they perceive as societal injunctions.

In concluding this chapter, it bears repeating that the concept of adult attachment is just beginning to come into its own. It has generally been left to the poets to give words to those feelings that defy definition or logical explanation—the contentment of connection, the anxiety and desperation of being alone and lonely, or the sadness and despair of loss and bereavement. Attachment theory grapples with understanding and explaining these phenomena, and shows promise of doing so. There is now research data that shows that attached individuals live longer and healthier lives and, moreover, that health decrements, ranging from an increase of disease and accidents to psychopathology, are a consequence of loss or lack of these close ties (Hazan and Shaver 1994). We have learned from therapeutic experience, and also from theorists such as Kohut (1977), that there is something very fundamental in having a relationship that validates a person's feelings and experiences. The need to be confirmed, to share the details of our daily lives, and to seek proximity and contact seems to be built into us biologically (Karen 1994). This need reflects back to childhood, to early attachment experiences, but is also a force in current attachment relationships. As the social convoy research tool has shown (Kahn and Antonucci 1980), most people have a small cluster of relationships they consider so essential that they cannot imagine life without them. These bonds may form a hierarchy with one key figure at the top, and if this person is easily accessible (for example a companion with whom one lives), such a person is in a position to supply attachment as well as some degree of the other social provisions adults require for social and emotional well-being (Weiss 1988).

Each person's attachment experiences and figures are unique. Some individuals include grandchildren and pets in their attachment circle and perceive these relationships to be emotionally significant, especially within the social provision of caregiving. Another provision, the opportunity to receive support and guidance, has particular relevance for mental-health clinicians. Therapists provide a supportive attachment relationship and guidance; like attachment figures, they are sought at times of emotional crisis. The definition of an affectional figure as someone perceived to be stronger and wiser, who will be available and responsive at times of stress, might also apply to the therapeutic alliance. The knowledge and skills of the therapist facilitate the creation of an attachment bond that can both provide the experience of a reliable and responsive relationship and offer an opportunity to understand the origin and development of distress and difficulty.

3

Psychopathology of Affectional Bonds

Attachment theory generally became known for its normative view of child development and the mother–child bond, but the framework was actually advanced to explain the origin and development of psychological disturbance. Bowlby (1980) believed that real-life experiences, such as the deprivation and separation he had observed early in his career, could arouse anxiety and distress, and that it was necessary to have a firm grasp of these variables and of how they operated, if we were to develop effective measures for treatment and prevention. He chose to focus on separation and loss experiences—unmistakable disruptions that could be systematically studied—but soon realized he first had to understand the nature of the bond that was being disrupted. Thus, he began by examining the concept of attachment, and then moved on to the problems of separation anxiety, grief and mourning, and defense. These themes form the basis of his three volumes on attachment and loss; the first applies ethological and evolutionary principles and control theory to a new theory of motivation and to the formulation of the concept of attachment; the latter two volumes explore the effects of separation and bereavement, both in early caregiving relationships and in adult years.

The concept of attachment attempts to answer some of the most fundamental questions of emotional life. It encompasses the way early caregiving experiences are internalized into representations of oneself and others, which in turn shape later responses and the ability to manage stress and trauma. Adults who have internalized feelings of worth about themselves are likely to be self-reliant and trusting, confident of the support of their attachment figures, and of their capacity to love and be loved (Karen 1998). The working models of a securely attached person are flexible and consistent, easily updated to accommodate new information and events. However, if attachment experiences have been characterized by emotional or physical abuse or neglect, threats of abandonment or withdrawal of love, disconfirmation of feelings or perceptions, or prolonged separation or loss, certain attachment thoughts and feelings may be defensively excluded from awareness, resulting in rigid and contradictory models (Bowlby 1973, 1988a, Bretherton 1988). Because mental structures tend to be relatively stable and to persist, the distortions caused by multiple conflicting models affect subsequent relationships, rendering individuals with these experiences more inadequate to function interpersonally and thus more prone to maladaptive behavior and psychological disturbance when confronted with stressful situations such as separation or loss.

From an ethological perspective of attachment, emotional distress reflects the internalization of adverse affectional experiences, both present and past, especially those that have impacted feelings of self-reliance and security. Environmental failures, such as inconsistent or rejecting caregiving, thwart healthy personality development, and introduce corresponding distortions and lack of coherence in working models that continue to affect the person as an adult. Symptoms of anxiety, depression, or anger, therefore, are responses to disruptions of personal bonds at a level that interferes with adequate functioning and satisfactory relationships with others. By noting the interpersonal nature of emotions and defensive processes, Bowlby began to reformulate Freud's concepts of anxiety, leading to a new view of separation anxiety, mourning, and depression.

When Freud advanced his ideas about anxiety in 1926, he defined it as a reaction to the danger of losing the object; grief and mourning are a response to actual loss, with defenses protecting the ego against instinctual demands threatening to overwhelm it when the object is absent. Building on this outline, Bowlby connected the stages of response to separation—protest, despair, and detachment—with separation anxiety, grief and mourning, and defensive processes. In contrast to psychoanalytic thinking, however, Bowlby pointed out that these reactions took place in adults as well as children and adolescents, and were innate responses evoked to preserve attachment. Psychopathology, then, is measured against a yardstick of healthy development, with dysfunction seen as a derailment of personality onto a maladaptive course or pathway. Rather than specific libidinal phases of development where persons may become fixated and/or to which they regress, Bowlby perceived that personality unfolds and moves forward along many possible developmental pathways, the direction determined by the interactions between existing personality and events encountered along the way. Healthy outcome does not rest on developmental progression but on the dynamics of early affectional relationships and whether they steer the person in the direction of resilience. A pathological outcome indicates that psychological development has followed a deviant pathway where defensive strategies have distorted and restricted flexible choices and behavior. Furthermore, once there are deviations in the organization of attachment behavior, they are likely to snowball so that, for instance, a child who is discouraged from grieving a loss, whether of a parent, a relative, or even a pet, may not only stifle mourning at the time but grow up to cope with emotional pain by avoidance, determined to keep a stiff upper lip and not express feelings or seek comfort (Bowlby 1977, 1980, 1988b, Karen 1994).

Thus, the effects of attachment-related trauma tend to be cumulative and may also be compounded by confusing messages and explanations from parents. Since Bowlby's original formulations, there has been increasing emphasis on the total accumulation of family experience, for example, how an event such as bereavement is handled, and less focus on the disruptions themselves (Holmes 1993a). Likewise, much of the more recent research has been on the complex of variables in this general context, and in the way they interact to influence the organization of attachment behavior and vulnerability to pathology.

PERSONALITY PATTERNS OF INSECURE ATTACHMENT

In determining the origin and development of attachment pathology, the concept of developmental pathways is one that accommodates the vast array of variables that can divert personality beyond the bounds of healthy development and toward some form of maladaptive functioning. At the time Bowlby (1977) first tried to describe individual differences in the organization of attachment behavior, he identified four patterns of insecure attachment that may develop from early caregiving experiences: *anxious-ambivalent* (or anxious attachment), *compulsive self-reliance*, *compulsive caregiving* (although I prefer the terms insistent self reliance and insistent caregiving) (Sable 1992a), and *emotional detachment*. These classifications of attachment behavior styles describe different defensive adaptions that have evolved over time to maintain essential ties. They are composed of attitudes and expectations about attachment that regulate and guide inner feelings as well as behavior toward others. It is important to emphasize that they are not equivalent to emotional disturbance; however, any of them may diminish resilience for dealing with difficulties and thus increase susceptibility to psychological distress. In addition, because the patterns reflect similar underlying experiences with attachment figures, absolute distinctions cannot be made between them, nor should they be expected to correlate with *DSM* diagnostic categories (Bowlby 1977, 1980, 1991).

Bowlby (1973) used findings from research, such as that of Ainsworth and colleagues (Ainsworth et al. 1978), when he introduced the concept of anxious attachment in the second volume of his trilogy, *Attachment and Loss*, and it has become the basis for much attachment research and refinement of theory. In Bowlby's initial conception, this was quite a broad category, as he equated it with insecure attachment and, while distinguishing it from secure attachment, declared that "the heart of the condition is apprehension lest attachment figures be inaccessible and/or unresponsive" (p. 213). The classifications were extended to include the other three insecure patterns in 1977 (Bowlby 1977), and again in 1980 (Bowlby 1980) as a way to understand individuals prone to develop disordered mourning following loss. In 1988 (Bowlby 1988a,b), the patterns were renamed to match emerging research findings, particularly those from Ainsworth's (Ainsworth et al. 1978) Strange Situation procedure and Main's (Main and Goldwyn 1984) Adult Attachment Interview (AAI).

Basically, Ainsworth and Main identified two developmental pathways of insecure personality organization, the first a tendency toward intensification of attachment behavior, and the second a deactivation and avoidance of attachment feelings and behavior. The former classification is called anxious-ambivalent or preoccupied, and the latter avoidant or dismissing. Recently, a fourth category, unresolved/disorganized, has been identified (Main 1991), and may be comparable to Bowlby's pathway of detachment; this indicates researchers' attempts to specify a more extensive exclusion of attachment-related emotions.

Anxious-Ambivalent Attachment (Preoccupied)

When individuals grow up in families that are attuned and responsive to their affectional needs, they gain confidence that others will be there for them, that they deserve comfort and kindness at times of need such as during illness or injury, and that they are capable of forming satisfactory relationships and dealing with the world. These individuals value their attachment experiences and can discuss them easily and objectively. Trust in others enables them to reach out for affection, care, and assistance, and when they suffer emotional distress it is apt to be relatively mild and of short duration (Bowlby 1988b, Dolan et al. 1993, Karen 1994, Mikulincer and Florian 1998).

In contrast to this pattern of secure attachment and coherent working models that are consistent with healthy functioning, anxiously attached individuals are worried and uncertain about whether they can count on affectional figures, and feel they must stay in close touch with, and keep a vigil on persons or places that represent safety and protection. Sometimes labeled overdependent, immature, or histrionic, these adults do not have the inner feeling of a safe base from which to venture forth, and they are prone to separation anxiety and alarm at the prospect of losing whatever support does exist. Their strategies to retain some degree of connection and responsiveness can make them appear clinging, demanding, and hesitant to pursue new activities and relationships. At the same time, they are flooded by their affects and distress and overinvolved with issues and conflicts of the past (Bowlby 1973, Dolan et al. 1993, Holmes 1993a, Sable 1994a, Slade 1999).

Bowlby (1988b) attributes ambivalence and fear of separation to inconsistent parenting, actual separation or loss experiences, or threats of abandonment. At times caregivers may have been available and responsive; at other times rejecting and unpredictable. In these scenarios, a child learns that no behavior can be automatically assumed to bring comfort; he or she is always on guard, watchful and cautious, never sure what to expect. Because thoughts and feelings in these individuals have been disconnected from the circumstances that elicited them, the stories of their lives are not logical and concise, nor are they aware of why they feel ambivalent and afraid of separation, or why a seemingly close relationship may exacerbate anxiety. Clinical manifestations of anxious attachment include agoraphobia, depression, suicidal ideation or gestures, conversion symptoms, and eating disorders (Bowlby 1977, Dolan et al. 1993, Liotti 1991, Sable 1992a, 1994a, West and Sheldon-Keller 1994).

Insistent Self-Reliance (Dismissing or Avoidant)

Rather than experiencing the uncertainty present in anxiously attached individuals, those who are insistently

self-reliant actually have almost no confidence in the availability of affectional figures. Hence they avoid and deny the
need for support and attention, defensively proclaiming a
self-sufficiency that hides their fear of trusting others. Accounts of their early years are generally brief and incomplete; they often have trouble remembering their childhood, or describe it vaguely, in an idealized manner that
contradicts perceptions of reported events. However, underneath a dismissing and incoherent narrative may be the
same yearning for warmth and affection, and the same
anger and hurt experienced by those who are anxiously
attached. In insistently self-reliant individuals, information
that would normally activate attachment behavior is defensively excluded so they do not share their feelings with
others or ask for support from them. Insensitive and unreliable caregiving has been compounded by rejection,
pressure to inhibit feelings, or ridicule for acting childish
when seeking comfort. Because the protective cover of
insistent self-reliance is precariously based, it may give
way to depression, disordered mourning, psychosomatic
symptoms, personality disorders, and alcoholism or suicide under stressful life conditions or life cycle changes,
such as marriage or bereavement (Bowlby 1977, 1980,
1991, Dolan et al. 1993, Holmes 1993a, Sable 1992a).
Bowlby credits Parkes (1973) with identifying this pattern.

Insistent Caregiving

This category was delineated by Bowlby in 1977, and
he referred to it again in 1980 as a pattern in several cases
of chronic mourning. Though it has rarely been included
in others' research, it appears to be a dynamic in certain
relationships, possibly in conjunction with one of the other
categories. Just as Bowlby connected this pattern to in-

sistent self-reliance, Kunce and Shaver (1994) saw the pattern in women identified as resistant in couple relationships. Attachment behavior is deactivated in these individuals, who give the attachment needs of others priority over their own. In affectional relationships, they divert their own attachment needs and devote themselves to caring for others. These insistent or possibly anxious caregivers engage in close relationships, but always as the one giving care, and regardless of whether this care is sought or welcomed. The childhood experience that produces this pattern may be a mother who is unable to care for her child, but who instead wants or demands this care for herself. In order to maintain proximity, the child learns to exclude and ignore her own attachment needs; an expression of attachment behavior would feel like a threat to security. In adulthood, these individuals may experience the same latent yearning for love and care as do individuals in the other categories, and feel resentment when the attention they give to others is not appreciated or reciprocated. Bowlby (1977) notes that this pattern has been called smother love, or possibly symbiotic, though he particularly dislikes the latter term because it does not recognize the pressures that were put on the child.

Emotional Detachment (Unresolved)

Recent research on attachment has found a detached style of personality that is sometimes called the "false self" (Winnicott 1965), borderline, histrionic, or narcissistic (Bowlby 1977, Sable 1983). In these individuals, affectional feelings and memories have been more extensively excluded from awareness than in individuals exhibiting the previous three patterns. There is such a fear of getting close to others that persons in this category act removed and distrustful, and may become severely anxious, depressed, and/or angry if pushed into relating. Their attachment histories are quite inarticulate, revealing traumatic, unresolved events such as emotional or physical abuse, more prolonged separations, or permanent losses. As with other patterns, there may exist an unconscious longing for affection, as well as anger for what was inflicted or denied (Bowlby 1977, Fish 1996).

Patterns of Insecure Attachment

Each of these patterns of insecure attachment is perceived in terms of how individuals relate to others. Their presence is not synonymous with emotional distress, but suggests a continuum of certain personality compromises that render adults more prone to develop disturbance at times of stress. For example, Meloy (1992) identified anxious-ambivalent attachment in individuals who act with sudden violence toward an affectional figure. The eruption of rage and violence is a reaction to fears of abandonment rooted in early attachment pathology, and is projected onto a current relationship when it appears to be in danger.

Most of the more recent research on attachment revolves around these categories or types of attachment patterns. They are the most common conceptualizations of individual differences in adult attachment patterns (Berman and Sperling 1994), and have laid the foundation for the current focus on internal representations of attachment in research and treatment (Slade 1999). Clinicians are finding them useful for conceptualizing a patient's defenses, attitudes, and behavior, and also as guidelines in managing the therapeutic relationship. Slade (1999), for example, says the patterns redefine the way we understand and frame our patients' narratives and think about transference and countertransference. It should be emphasized, however, that there is not yet full consensus on the actual categories or their particular characteristics. Nor should it be assumed that these are the only patterns of insecure attachment, or that they cover every dynamic of the attachment framework (Adam et al. 1995). Bartholomew's (1990) division of avoidance, as identified on the Hazan and Shaver (1987) test, into two dimensions, fearful avoidance and dismissing avoidance, is an indication that continued research will further delineate various patterns of insecure or anxious attachment. I agree with writers such as Brennan and colleagues (Brennan et al. 1998), who state that there seem to be two basic features of insecure attachment behavior. One, which they have labeled anxiety, is characterized by a low threshold for manifesting attachment behavior. The other, labeled avoidance, is characterized by an exclusion of attachment feeling and behavior. Brennan and colleagues point out that these two tendencies are the same two dimensions identified by Ainsworth in 1978.

I also agree with Fraley and Waller (1998) that the different attachment patterns are better thought of as having "fuzzy" or imperfect boundaries, rather than clearcut, precise ones. Not only does this fit Bowlby's (1991) descriptive approach to delineating different patterns, it is compatible with his intention that the features not be crammed into fixed categories. This approach is relevant for clinicians, who can readily observe that each patient is different, and that patients exhibit diverse feelings and behavior even when certain symptoms are similar enough to warrant the same *DSM* diagnosis. Another reason to avoid limiting features to a single classification is that individuals can act differently with different people. The same person, for example, may be insecure and clinging with an adult romantic partner but more reserved and detached in social relationships.

The concept of emotional detachment in adults was introduced by Bowlby in 1977 to describe individuals who were "incapable of maintaining a stable affectional bond with anyone" (p. 208). Although he considered the pattern as one separate from that of insistent self-reliance, by 1980 he had omitted the category; in his discussion of individuals prone to develop disordered mourning following loss, he listed only the anxious-ambivalent, insistent self-reliant, and insistent caregiver as vulnerable personality types. Bowlby did, however, continue to use the concept descriptively, as, for example, in his clinical discussion of a woman with a false self who had defensively excluded her attachment desires and feelings (Bowlby 1985, 1987). Furthermore, he suggested that individuals who were disposed to assert self-reliance fell "on a continuum ranging from those whose proclaimed self-sufficiency rests on a precarious basis to those in whom it is firmly organized" (Bowlby 1980, p. 211). That detachment may fall at one end of a continuum, depending on the degree of exclusion of attachment experiences, is supported by Main's (1995) AAI finding of a group of respondents who did not fit existing categories and whom she classified as unresolved/disorganized, and later, merely unresolved. These individuals reported traumatic incidents of unresolved loss, or physical or sexual abuse, in such disorganized or disoriented ways that Main interpreted their interviews as lacking resolution. The incoherent mental organization of their attachment experiences tends to suggest a more extensive defensive exclusion of painful memories—or what could be called an emotional detachment.

Other Attachment-Related Patterns

Main (1995) differentiated another category—"cannot classify" (or CC)—for a small proportion of respondents who alternated between categories in an incoherent manner. In this group she included individuals with severe psychological difficulties, such as having experienced abuse or psychiatric hospitalization, which could relate to certain clinical syndromes such as borderline personality disorder with its characteristic volatile all-or-nothing type of thinking (for example, people are perceived as all-good or all-bad). Adaptive strategies with respect to attachment have broken down for individuals in both the cannot classify and the unresolved categories, and in addition to an absence of coherence both groups exhibit greater inconsistencies in personal narratives. Adam and colleagues (1995) identified a similar lack of coherence and resolution of attachment-related traumas in studies of suicidal adolescents who were given the AAI in outpatient and residential treatment centers. A high percentage of the sample (82 percent) reported significant separations, losses, or instances of abuse. The finding that unresolved separations could be as traumatic as loss or abuse led the researchers to suggest that individuals with negative separation experiences also be included in the unresolved category. They explain that these experiences violate the system of attachment, which inherently expects protection and security from affectional figures.

Adam's research is significant for therapeutic work with adults because it is one of the relatively few published studies of the AAI that was done with a clinical population and that includes the unresolved and cannot classify categories. The researchers also claim it has the potential to elucidate the effects of traumas on mental constructions. They hypothesize that a combination of traumas, compounded by distorted communication from caregivers, leads to multiple, conflicting working models. This hypothesis can help therapists understand how patients construe or misconstrue past traumatic events and relationships, and offers a direction for therapeutic effort.

The conclusions of Adam and colleagues are also significant for clinicians because they suggest several "attachment-relevant dimensions" (p. 336) that may help clarify the correlation between attachment patterns and psychopathology. Psychological disorders can be understood as disturbances in the organization of attachment behavior, along a continuum of secure versus insecure. Insecure patterns would indicate an imbalance in psychological structure and affect regulation in which expression of emotion is either minimized or heightened, and access to thoughts, feelings, and memories is either limited or exaggerated and distorted (Slade 1999, Slade and Aber 1992). Attachment might also be classified along an organization–disorganization continuum, indicating a tendency for insecure individuals to become disorganized and incoherent in the face of trauma, especially when it is related to possible loss of attachment. Finally, the organization of attachment can be considered in terms of flexibility and adaptability. For example, individuals with a personality disorder, such as borderline, would be placed toward the extreme of insecurity on the continuum, identifying the presence of more disorganization and incoherence of narrative with respect to their lives and experiences. Defenses would be rigid and inflexible, hampering adaptive functioning or the capacity to resolve painful experiences of attachment.

DEVELOPMENTAL PATHWAYS: VULNERABILITY AND RESILIENCE

Near the end of his career, Bowlby (1988b) wrote one of his finest papers, "Developmental Psychiatry Comes of Age," in which he discussed the tendency of attachment patterns to persist, to be imposed to some degree upon new relationships, and to influence vulnerability to psychological disturbance. Bowlby explained that there are several reasons why the attachment patterns that form early in childhood usually continue. Not only does treatment by parents generally remain unchanged, but interaction patterns, once established, also tend to be self-perpetuating. Thus, a secure child, happier and more rewarding, elicits different responses and behavior than does the insecure, anxious child, who may be whiny and demanding. Unless there are positive alterations in the environment, the personality structure of the latter will tend to develop along a pathway that is increasingly troubled and maladaptive, undermining self-esteem and security.

Bowlby (1973) adapted the concept of developmental pathways from Waddington (1957), and conceptualized personality development as proceeding along different and divergent pathways much like the branching of a tree or the tracks of a railway system. In infancy, the pathways are close together and the child has access to a vast array of potential ones. As development progresses and working models become stabilized, the number of open pathways diminishes. Although positive experiences also alter functioning, the longer a maladaptive pattern exists, the more likely "change is constrained by prior adaption" (Sroufe 1997, p. 254). Pathology is perceived in terms of "developmental deviation" from normative patterns, with repeated failures of adaption and adjustment (Sroufe 1997). Adult pathology may be seen as a succession of experiences that divert the direction of pathways away from resilience and competent functioning and toward dysfunction.

Sroufe (1997) defines resilience as the ability to rebound to adaptive functioning after a period of maladaption. The capacity to stay organized in the face of adversity evolves and develops over time, depending on a combination of risk factors and protective factors. Early patterns of adaption serve as the prototype for subsequent development and, from the perspective of attachment theory, secure attachment functions as a protective mechanism against encounters with threat and danger. Mikulincer and Florian (1998) describe secure attachment as an "inner resource" that facilitates appraisal of and adjustment to stressful life experiences. A securely attached individual feels safe in the world, can acknowledge adverse conditions, and feels capable of coping with them. In contrast, insecure attachment acts as a risk factor that may detract from a person's resilience in times of adversity. Insecure or anxious attachment compromises the individual's developing capacities for affect regulation, social behavior, and self-image, and deflects pathways in the direction of maladaption.

This is not to say that development is determined solely by parenting behaviors. According to Bowlby (1988b), developmental pathways are determined by the interaction of the personality and the environment, especially the people in it. Acquired capacities are not static, but require ongoing adjustment to constantly occurring events

(Sroufe 1997). However, a foundation of secure attachment sets the stage for healthy development, coping, and adjustment. With positive attitudes about attachment experiences, a person is more apt to feel confident about handling the stresses of life constructively. The flexibility and self-reliance of secure attachment include the ability to turn to others for emotional and instrumental support when this is needed. Secure attachment also implies the capacity to tolerate the unpleasant emotions that generally accompany trauma and adversity without being overwhelmed by them (Mikulincer and Florian 1998). Without this security and trust in oneself and others, defensive processes may shut out certain attachment thoughts and feelings, affecting the ability to handle adversity; without resilience, both emotional regulation and behavioral flexibility are jeopardized.

Research studies of adults now exist that have found an association between insecure attachment styles and maladjustment. Some individuals inhibit emotional expression and do not reach out to others for relief and reassurance, while others are anxious and angry, exhibiting high levels of distress concerning their attachments. Either of these directions veers away from resilience and toward some degree of vulnerability, eventually leading to emotional disturbance if events or situations become sufficiently traumatic (Bowlby 1988b).

DARWIN: A VULNERABLE PERSONALITY

Charles Darwin, the outstanding nineteenth-century biologist and theoretician, was well regarded by both his family and colleagues, and nonetheless suffered from chronic ill health, anxiety, and depression for thirty years of his adult life. In a rich and scholarly biography of Darwin, *Charles Darwin: A New Life*, Bowlby (1991) makes a convincing argument that Darwin's distress was of psychological origin. Bowlby asserts that Darwin developed a vulnerable personality as a result of certain childhood experiences, most notably the loss of his mother when he was 8 years old, and that he was thus susceptible to emotional breakdown when confronted with stressful events in adulthood. Examining Darwin's psychological distress from a perspective of attachment theory, Bowlby speculates that he was discouraged from grieving for or even mentioning his mother by a busy father who turned the little boy over to the care of his older sisters. Without someone to sympathize and help a child mourn his loss, Bowlby (1991) writes,

> there is a danger that . . . thoughts and feelings will become locked away as though in a secret cupboard, and there will live on to haunt him. Then, whenever some adverse event or threat of it penetrates to that secret cupboard, with or without his realizing it, he becomes anxious and distressed and prone to develop symptoms, the reasons for which neither he nor his family may understand. [p. 77]

As an adult, Darwin was plagued by psychosomatic symptoms of pain, stomach disorders, and palpitations, as well as anxiety and panic attacks that sometimes prevented him from working for months at a time. He was preoccupied with both his own health and that of his family, and was prone to self-reproach and depression. He never overcame a timidity and fear of standing up for himself and was devastated by criticism. Bowlby postulates that Darwin was unaware that the loss of his mother had an effect on his adult behavior and that certain events, such as his wife's pregnancies, precipitated anxiety because they unconsciously reminded him of his early loss. The extent of Darwin's exclusion of thoughts and feelings about his mother is evident in a condolence note that he wrote to a friend who had lost his wife: "I truly sympathize with you though never in my life having lost one near relation, I daresay I cannot imagine how severe grief such as yours must be" (p. 78). On another occasion, while playing a word game with his family, someone added an M to the word "other" to construct the word "MOTHER." Darwin objected, "MOE-THER, there's no such word MOE-THER" (p. 78). And when Darwin mentions his mother in his writings, Bowlby notes that emotion is missing. Nothing is written about her as a mother, how she treated him, or how he felt about her.

Bowlby concluded that Darwin grew up to be sensitive to certain stressful situations as a consequence of the early death of his mother, a sensitivity compounded by prohibitions against expressing grief and by an autocratic father who often expressed anger and criticism. When an individual such as Darwin is prevented from expressing feelings during childhood or from recognizing the incidents that give rise to them, there is likelihood of problems in later years. These include difficulty both in identifying or expressing emotions, and in recognizing the causes of distress.

Bowlby's treatment plan for Darwin would have assisted him in connecting his current responses to his early loss and to the way he had been prohibited from remembering or mourning his mother. It is possible that Darwin might have recalled some of the details about his mother with which he was preoccupied, such as the circumstances surrounding her death. By discussing and sorting out his memories, Darwin might have come to understand some of the misconstructions he had made about his early life, enabling him to modify his working models of himself and his attachment figures.

In his proposed treatment plan for Darwin, Bowlby makes several important statements about psychotherapy. One is his opinion that what we call fantasy in therapeutic work is more accurately labeled *hypothesis*. When we examine clients' lives from a variety of angles, we speculate about what may have happened to them and form hypotheses about the causes of their thoughts and feelings. We may help them imagine how they were treated, but we do not imply these imaginations are fantasies with no roots in reality. The object of treatment is to trace responses to their roots in actual experiences, including what may have been "observed and misinterpreted or else heard and misunderstood" (p. 465). In the case of Darwin, one hypothesis might be that he believed he was in some way responsible for his mother's death. If he had been made to feel guilty for his behavior while she was ill, he might have construed her death as his fault.

Bowlby also explores Darwin's various and mutating array of symptoms. Clinicians use diagnostic labels to help conceptualize a client's problems and to facilitate communication with colleagues. But, as every therapist knows, it is not possible to fit individuals into methodical categories. Assessment is an ongoing process, not a one-time event (Greenberg et al. 1997). Patients, like everyone else, have a mixture of thoughts and feelings, and these change over time. Darwin suffered from psychosomatic symptoms but he also had periods of intense anxiety and quite severe depression. As early as 1977, Bowlby had written that it was not possible to make sharp distinctions between different forms of emotional distress, and in *Charles Darwin* (1991), he suggests an alternative to the traditional pattern of psychiatric classification: symptoms should be viewed as "springing from a set of closely related causes giving rise to minor variations in the expression of a common psychopathology" (p. 76).

Darwin is an individual illustration of Bowlby's framework. Subsequent findings from attachment-related research support Bowlby's basic premise that an individual's stressful life events, including those dating back to childhood—and especially separations, bereavements, and/or difficulty with attachment figures—play a major role in causing adult emotional disturbance.

ATTACHMENT RESEARCH AND ADULT PSYCHOPATHOLOGY

The research of Ainsworth and colleagues (Ainsworth et al. 1978), devised to assess brief separation and reunion behaviors in 1-year-olds, signaled a revolution in developmental psychology and showed that it was possible to measure patterns of attachment behavior (Karen 1990). Since its inception, Ainsworth's Strange Situation procedure has been used in numerous studies and also modified and applied to adults, for example by Main (Main and Goldwyn 1984) in her Adult Attachment Interview (AAI), and Hazan and Shaver (1987) in their self-report questionnaire of adult romantic relationships. As discussed in Chapter 2, the AAI is a semistructured interview that assesses adults' current mental representations of childhood attachment experiences and how they are manifest in language. The Hazan and Shaver questionnaire is a single-item measure that asks respondents to choose which of three statements most accurately describes their feelings in existing intimate relationships

Results from both tests have been remarkably consistent, finding correlation between adults' perceptions of their current affectional bonds and descriptions of their earlier family experiences. For example, Dolan and colleagues (Dolan et al. 1993) found a higher rate of insecure attachment among clients' responses to the Hazan and Shaver questionnaire in a study made at a university counseling center than among those from nonpatient samples. In addition, both anxious-ambivalent and avoidant clients reported more symptoms on the Hopkins Symptom Checklist (Derogatis et al. 1974). Similarly, Roberts and colleagues (1996) found that insecure attachment, as identified by the Hazan and Shaver questionnaire, was associated with depressive symptoms on the Inventory to Diagnose Depression (IDD) (Zimmerman et al. 1986) among nonpatient university students. And Fonagy and colleagues (1991, 1995, 1997) found that a group of inpatients who met the *DSM-III-R* (American Psychiatric Association 1980) criteria for borderline personality disorder reported a higher incidence of childhood sexual abuse on the AAI, as well as lack of resolution of the abuse. This group also had less ability to think about their feelings and experiences and make sense of them.

Another attachment-based project is Parkes's (1991) retrospective study of case notes on fifty-four adults who sought treatment for psychiatric disturbance following bereavement. The most prominent symptoms were anxiety and depression and, except where loss was sudden or compounded by other losses, there were early separation experiences that seemed to have left the bereaved individuals vulnerable to disordered grief. For instance, a small

group, classified as insistently self-reliant, exhibited delayed grief, suggesting a link to attachment problems.
Parkes posited that early experiences color adult bonds
and, together with such variables as being elderly and
alone, affect reactions to loss.

In forming hypotheses to examine the data, Parkes
included findings from studies conducted by Brown and
Harris (1978), who investigated the role of psychosocial
factors in the onset of depression. Using a large community sample, Brown and Harris found that loss of mother
before age 11, especially if accompanied by other disruptions of care, increased the risk of depression in adulthood
when there was a precipitating event such as the loss of
spouse. Furthermore, the susceptibility to depression increased with the number of vulnerability factors, such as
inadequate parenting following loss, suggesting that the
interaction of variables can combine to produce emotional
disturbance. The researchers made the significant discovery, however, that women who had an intimate relationship with someone with whom they could share thoughts
and feelings were less prone to become depressed at the
usual disappointments and losses. That adult bonds
can act as a buffer against trauma is supported by Wallerstein's (1995) study of successful marriages, which
found that these unions helped overcome the harmful effects of earlier traumatic family experiences. Likewise, the
AAI has revealed that adults rated "secure" have not necessarily had a trouble-free childhood, but have reached
an understanding of their past and are able to reflect on
both positive and negative qualities of their parents (Karen
1994, Main 1991). This research suggests that gaining
understanding through examining one's experiences, both
current and past, with a responsive, attentive person, such

as occurs during a therapeutic process, may lead to a more balanced view of relationships and help resolve feelings and reframe memories that are related to psychological distress.

CLINICAL IMPLICATIONS

In applying attachment theory to diagnosis and treatment, emphasis is put on exploring separation and loss experiences with affectional figures, and especially on the way they are perceived and how they influence clinical symptoms. Bowlby (1991) states that the role of the therapist is to act as a companion who engages clients in a "joint exploration" (p. 460) of events in their lives that may be causing stress and anxiety, with a goal of understanding and rearranging working models so that they are more in line with current knowledge and circumstances. There is encouragement to confront painful and distressing experiences, some of which parents may have discouraged the individual from remembering or having feelings about, and which clients may be reluctant to acknowledge. Once the connection between a situation and its response is grasped, symptoms can be understood as "ordinary human responses to danger or frustration" (Bowlby 1991, p. 79) that arose to sustain attachment. With more open and fluid models, defensive strategies can be replaced by perceptions and behaviors that are more likely to lead to improved relationships (Bowlby 1988a, Weiss 1994b).

Individuals are inclined to pursue psychotherapy when there is some change in the status of their closest relationships. They may be frightened about an impending separation or confronted with an actual loss. They may feel anxiety and concern about making a romantic connection, or possibly ending one. The therapist needs to understand

and clarify clients' personality styles, including how clients determine their responses to separation and loss, and also how these responses are imposed onto treatment interactions (transference) (Bowlby 1988a, Dolan et al. 1993). Contradictory and incoherent narratives point to disturbances in the organization of attachment behavior in the direction either of insecure, anxious attachment, or insistent self-reliance and detachment (Bowlby 1980).

From a perspective of attachment, defensive processes are methods to regulate negative affect and maintain proximity to unreliable or rejecting affectional figures (Holmes 1993a, Slade and Aber 1992). When certain information about attachment is defensively excluded from conscious processing, an individual may have difficulty regulating emotions or the situations that give rise to them (Bowlby 1991). Although diverted from intolerable feelings and memories, parts of personality functioning are constricted, affecting the individual's ability to cope with stressful conditions such as separation and loss. For example, individuals whose attachment style tends toward avoidant may not recognize the impact that a separation is having on them and may shut off feelings of anger and despair. Those who display an anxious-ambivalent style are likely to be hyperalert to separations, overwhelmed and angry when they are left, and preoccupied with monitoring affectional relations at the expense of engaging in the larger world (Goldberg 1997, Holmes 1993a, Karen 1994).

CLINICAL ILLUSTRATIONS

Detachment

The experience of a therapeutic attachment bond can help clients learn to communicate in ways that do not repeat ineffective strategies of the past. This relationship models a nonintrusive empathic one and helps clients reflect on their feelings and patterns of attachment behavior (Dolan et al. 1993, Karen 1994). An understanding of these patterns can also be used to manage emotional space and therapeutic activity. Dolan and colleagues (1993) suggest a matching of therapeutic technique to clients' styles, with therapists adjusting their "interpersonal stance" to clients' tolerance levels. For instance, Kelly, mentioned in Chapter 1, had such fear of closeness and attachment that early in treatment she acted distant and tense. For many months she spoke softly, carefully, and with minimal affect, and offered very little information. Bowlby (1988a) compares the therapist's work in these instances of emotional detachment to trying to make friends with a shy or frightened pony. Quiet and reserved, Kelly was reluctant to remember much of her chaotic and unhappy childhood, or to express opinions or feelings. "I think I have always been afraid to remember," she once said. Her difficulty with separation became apparent when she retreated to her home, refused to answer her phone, and became suicidal during my vacation. Over time, however, as therapy came to be a familiar and safe base, Kelly began to share and sort through traumatic incidents of her life, acknowledging sorrow and anger at her family's mistreatment of her.

A major feature of attachment-based treatment is affirming that clients' thoughts and feelings are based on real-life experiences with affectional figures (Bowlby 1988a, Gunderson 1996). Moreover, the anxiety of separation, the sadness and despair of loss, and the presence of anger are explained as inherent responses, built-in in order to attain and maintain protection and security. Attachment behavior at these times does not indicate

overdependency, but rather the presence of adaptive responses that have had to be distorted to comply with the
attitudes or behavior of others.

Anxious Attachment

Concerns about their dependency needs may be a
presenting complaint in individuals who exhibit anxious-
ambivalent attachment. This is illustrated by my work
with Megan (Sable 1994a), who came for therapy following a series of disappointing experiences with men.

> Megan would suddenly demand a commitment that
> ended the relationship, leaving her anxious and de-
> pressed, and increasingly unsure and apprehensive
> about her capacity to form secure emotional bonds.
> Megan also described herself as "overdependent" and
> a "baby" because she feared certain situations such
> as crowds, being alone on elevators, and driving on
> freeways, or because she would sometimes act impul-
> sively, such as abruptly quitting a job.
> In contrast to Kelly, Megan was outgoing and
> talkative, quickly attaching to her therapist, but at the
> same time concerned about acting appropriately; she
> would not show feelings of displeasure or anger.
> She approached treatment interruptions with appar-
> ent ease, though once they were over she tended to
> become annoyed, anxious, and irritable over many
> things.

A review of Megan's life gradually helped her to understand that her chronic anxiety and distress were the
consequence of her family experiences, that she had ex-

cluded her own attachment needs in order to comply with her parents' demands and their critical and punishing behavior. Like Kelly, Megan had been made to feel an outsider in her own family, less acceptable and loveable than others. Moreover, these hurtful patterns with family members were still occurring in the present, but were so routine and familiar that they went unrecognized until they were sorted out in treatment.

Although fear of separation and lack of confidence in the reliability of others were central issues in therapy with both Megan and Kelly, their defensive strategies were different, with Kelly minimizing and excluding attachment affect and Megan intensifying attachment behavior. Kelly learned as a young child that she could not rely on her mother and began to develop a detached pattern of attachment. Megan's frantic attempts to maintain contact suggest that she did not progress to Kelly's psychological state of avoidance and detachment but remained hopeful that she might still get love and affection. She had not given up on relationships, but the inconsistent nature of her experiences left her anxious and uneasy about attachment, afraid to separate and become self-reliant.

Insistent Self-Reliance

Barbara was a plump, edgy 60-year-old woman who entered therapy because of difficulty getting along with her young adult daughter. She stated that her daughter was reluctant to see her because she found her mother increasingly demanding and critical. Barbara said she was "depressed and feeling all alone." She complained that she had trouble sleeping, was unable to control her weight, and was not interested in being with friends. During the preceding year, three close family members had died: her husband, a chronically ill adult son, and her older brother. Barbara prided herself on being strong and independent and had handled these losses on her own. She reported that her father had died when she was 10, leaving her to care for her ill mother. When Barbara married and began raising her family, she assumed full responsibility for her home and children and did not ask for help even when one of her children had serious school and emotional problems. She found it difficult to acknowledge grief, assuming that she should handle her problems without assistance and support. She was not accustomed to reaching out to others, but had become overwhelmed by three major losses in such a short time. Her defensive strategy of self-reliance was shaken by her loss and grief and also by her underlying anxious attachment, which really made her yearn for connection. This might explain her desperation and demanding behavior with her daughter.

As with Kelly and Megan, the experience of a therapeutic attachment relationship helped Barbara compensate for lack of nurturing in her childhood and provided a secure base for exploration of herself and her interactions with others. All three women were encouraged to retrieve memories and express emotions that had been denied or forbidden in previous relationships, putting together a more unified, consistent picture of their lives. Though interpretations were a part of treatment, they were considered less important than an overall accepting relationship, which affirmed actual experiences and enabled them to revise their internal representations, and to finally feel deserving of mutually supportive, caring adult attachments.

A woman presenting herself as Kelly did might be conceptualized as having borderline, schizoid, or narcissistic personality disorder, and someone comparable to Megan as having agoraphobia, panic disorder, or possibly generalized anxiety disorder. Barbara would likely be diagnosed with a mood disorder, probably dysthymia (depression). Reconceptualizing their conditions from a perspective of attachment emphasizes the fact that personality organization, defensive strategies, and emotional distress reflect real experiences with key affectional figures, experiences that have undermined feelings of safety and self-reliance in the present.

THE ART OF THERAPY: THE SCIENCE OF RESEARCH

Bowlby (1969a, 1979) agrees with psychoanalytic and object relations theorists that childhood experiences, as in work with adults such as Kelly and Megan, are related to later emotional disturbance. However, attachment theory brings a different approach to the elucidation of clinical syndromes. Traditionally, clinical research gathered data from adult patients, and from that reconstructed earlier phases of development, inferring the events and processes that seemed to contribute to current functioning. Seeing limitations in such retrospective research, a group of clinicians, including Bowlby, Robertson, and Heinicke, undertook prospective research, the aim of which is to discern early patterns of response in later functioning (Bowlby 1980). From direct observations, for example of children throughout an entire separation experience, early phases of personality are described and, from them, extrapolated forward. This strategy does not begin with a symptom, but with a class of event, such as loss of mother in early childhood, that is potentially pathogenic to the developing child. This method then traces the processes that result from that event. Bowlby (1969a) noted that observing young children's responses to separation is "as close as we can get to observing repression actually occurring" (p. 6).

Bowlby did not discount the rich material that unfolds during therapy. In fact, at the very beginning of *Attachment*, the first volume of his trilogy, he declares that neither class of data is better than the other, and that by combining research with a clinical perspective treatment is enhanced. The process of therapy entails therapists arranging the diverse comments, behavior, and associations of patients into a theoretical schema. The schema they use will reflect the theory they espouse; thus treatment automatically involves a move from observation research to the application of theory. Bowlby's (1988a) explanation of this multifaceted process sounds very similar to the work of current relational therapists such as Aron (1996).

> What a patient tells us about his childhood and especially what an analyst subsequently reports his patient to have said are probably influenced as much or more by the analyst's preconceptions as by anything the patient may in fact have said or done; this is why I regard the systematic study by direct observation of children developing within different patterns of family care as indispens-

able for progress . . . I also believe that observations made during therapy . . . have considerable . . . potential. [Bowlby 1988a, p. 72]

In an article titled "Psychoanalysis as Art and Science," Bowlby (1979) describes therapy as an art that calls for a different mental outlook than the science of research. Bowlby's position emphasizes the value of each, but he claims that there has been confusion and misunderstanding in psychoanalysis when these two aspects are not clearly differentiated. He contrasts the roles of the practitioner and research scientist in terms of the focus of their study, their modes of acquiring information, and their attitudes of faith and skepticism. Therapists take many complex factors into account to deal with a clinical problem; scientists try to simplify by selecting a limited problem upon which to focus. During treatment, clients reveal information that remains closed to a researcher; researchers, however, can devise new methods to cross-check observations and hypotheses. For example, observing mother–child interaction or therapeutic procedure and change are types of cross checks. Finally, therapists must have faith in theory, using it as a guide; scientists are skeptical, criticizing and challenging theory.

Freud, like Bowlby, was a clinician as well as a researcher and viewed the discipline of psychoanalysis as composed of both methods. Hamilton (1987) clarifies some of the differences in the tasks of the two approaches by noting that during sessions therapists immerse themselves in their clients' lives, trying to think and feel with them and get a sense of their subjective experience. Researchers, in contrast, think and report on subjects objectively and abstractly and avoid the personal. Hamilton states that confusion over these two modes of thinking has been a drawback in translating attachment concepts into specific techniques for treatment. Attachment research has identified a range of experiences that can affect a child's emotional development; this research makes a difference in understanding the causes of distress and, thus, in the interpretations made in therapy sessions. For example, it makes a difference whether a patient is perceived as a victim of a broken attachment or as a bundle of id impulses, orally fixated from infancy, or as a narcissistic personality (Hamilton 1985).

For practicing clinicians, attachment-related research informs and augments the knowledge base they draw on, clarifying what may have happened in their patients' pasts. Along with this scientific approach to personality development and psychopathology, however, there exists an individual perspective that recognizes and respects the unique experience of each patient and strives to understand and help relieve distress at an intimate level. This is the art of therapy, an art that requires intuition and imagination, affirmation, and the capacity to bear with patients' painful emotions and experiences. The sensitivity and skills of the therapist include the ability to provide the setting and conditions in which patients can discover and recover their attachment desires and feelings, so they no longer need to shut out painful incidents and memories. The therapist encourages the patient to explore past experiences, drawing attention to relevant details, and remaining sympathetic when there is reluctance (resistance) to do so. Throughout, the therapist waits for information to emerge, careful not to move faster than the patient, or to offer more than is reasonable or professional. Finally, the therapist appreciates and accepts as final the patient's view of his life, as well as the conclusions reached with the therapist's help (Bowlby 1988a).

This personal perspective of attachment, and its application to therapy with adults, is the focus of the following chapters. It is possible that the explosion of attachment research has overshadowed clinical aspects of the theory, delaying its usage in treatment. Holmes (1996) does not see a framework of attachment as a method of treatment that stands on its own, but more as a way to define certain concepts, especially about relationships, which are shared with other theories. Farber and colleagues (1995) posit that the difference between attachment and other psychodynamic theories may mostly be one of emphasis. Similarly, Slade (1999) does not see an attachment therapy as a separate entity. Her view is that the nature and dynamics of attachment inform clinical thinking and intervention, and offer potential alternatives to the way we understand the relationship of therapy and how we think about our clients and respond to them. Hamilton (1985, 1987) states that attachment is like a background concept against which the clinician listens to and organizes patients' experiences. She writes that research on insecure attachment has advanced understanding of adult pathology, enabling therapists to imagine and reconstruct with patients what their lives have been like and to even be a part of the unfolding drama.

Attachment theory gives us a way to think about our patients' experiences and share our hypotheses about the causes of their distress. Although Bowlby acknowledged common ground with psychoanalytic and object relations theories, he also asserted that there are significant differences in emphasis and orientation, for example, in the relative priority given to real experiences over fantasy. This difference and others will be highlighted in the subsequent chapters on various clinical syndromes. It is recognized that advances in drug and behavioral therapies have made these auxiliaries in many treatment situations and, although discussion will be confined more specifically to attachment concepts, the approach described here does not negate these additional treatment methods where indicated.

Because separation is the major theme throughout Bowlby's work, discussion begins, in the next chapter, with conditions related to separation and anxiety. Attachment theory really stems from Bowlby's attempt to explain the processes involved in his observations of the protest and distress exhibited by family members when there were disruptions in the continuity of their relationships. Possibly Bowlby's greatest contribution is that he brought to light the extraordinary impact that ruptures of attachment bonds can have on our well-being. The depth of feeling connected to our relationships is at the center of Bowlby's (1977) thinking about pathology when he writes,

> many of the most intense emotions arise during the formation, the maintenance, the disruption and the renewal of attachment relationships. The formation of a bond is described as falling in love, maintaining a bond as loving someone, and losing a partner as grieving over someone. Similarly, threat of loss arouses anxiety and actual loss gives rise to sorrow; while each of these situations is likely to arouse anger. The unchallenged maintenance of a bond is experienced as a source of security and the renewal of a bond as a source of joy. Because such emotions are usually a reflection of the state of a person's affectional bonds, the psychology and psychopathology of emotion is found to be in large part the psychology and psychopathology of affectional bonds. [p. 203]

4

Separation
and Anxiety

The behavioral system of attachment is perceived to regulate proximity to affectional figures, facilitating exploration and mastery of the environment when there is no immediate threat or danger, while providing a safe haven for refuge at times of illness, fatigue, or fear. The particular threat to security of attachment that Bowlby put on the map and was interested in throughout his career is that presented by the disruption of relationships due to separation or loss. In the second volume of his trilogy, *Separation: Anxiety and Anger* (1973), he explained how a young child's temporary separation from its caregiver could elicit anxiety and anger, altering personality development and affecting later relationships with others. In this book he develops the concept of separation anxiety and, in the third volume, *Loss: Sadness and Depression* (1980), he deals with grief and mourning and the defensive processes that result from bereavement. The two titles, *Separation* and *Loss*, suggest the designation of two specific concepts, but the distinction, especially theoretically, is not so unequivocal. Bowlby (1973) wrote, "the words separation and loss . . . imply always that the subject's attachment figure is inaccessible, either temporarily (separation) or permanently (loss)" (p. 23). This distinction was not always clear in Bowlby's writing, and he did not use the words consistently. For example, in 1961, he referred to the protest, despair, and detachment phases of emotional response to separation as three phases of mourning, which he connected to loss. In addition, he recognized that it is not easy to determine the length of a temporary separation. For example, a young child would perceive an absence differently than an adult who has the cognitive skills to consider a variety of factors. Moreover, it is not often known if an event that starts out as a separation will become a permanent loss. Sometimes a caregiving person may be physically present but, if indifferent or depressed and emotionally removed, be felt as emotionally absent and unresponsive, provoking responses comparable to those that follow a physical separation or loss.

For the purpose of organizing material, I will begin discussion of attachment disorders with those that are related to separation and anxiety, and then consider those conditions related to loss, grief, and mourning. In regard to separation, Bowlby (1973) declared that a "principal source of anxiety and distress is separation from loved figures, or the threat of separation" (p. 77), which he viewed as quite a "simple formula." From an evolutionary perspective, fear of separation is a good thing. If attachment is essential to protection and even survival, separation anxiety is an instinctive response to prevent breaking of bonds. Bowlby thus recognized that anxiety and fear could be aroused during conditions such as a brief parting that were only indirectly related to what could physically hurt us. This also explains that fear can be elicited by the sheer absence of an attachment figure, as well as by the presence of certain sorts of dangerous situations. The following quotation came early in Bowlby's career. It illustrates how he saw attachment and separation at the very core of emotional functioning and marks the beginning of his reformulation of Freud's concepts of anxiety, leading to a new view of both separation anxiety and mourning and depression.

All of us find security in being with people we know well and are apt to feel anxious and insecure in a crowd of strangers. Particularly in times of crisis or distress do we seek our closest friends and relatives. The need for companionship and the comfort it brings is a very deep need in human nature—and one we share with many of the higher animals. [1960a, p. 3]

FREUD, ANXIETY, AND SEPARATION

Beginning with Freud, theorists have noted and puzzled over the relationship between separation, fear of separation, and anxiety (Bowlby 1973, Wolfe 1984). In 1926, Freud revised his thinking about anxiety, describing it as a signal of possible future dangers, especially loss of an object. In questioning how to explain the fact that both anxiety and mourning produced painful reactions, Freud delineated a sequence of responses to clarify the relation of repression to anxiety, and anxiety to grief and mourning. He defined anxiety as a reaction to the danger of losing the object, and grief and mourning as a response to actual loss, with defenses protecting the ego against instinctual demands threatening to overwhelm it when the object is absent. Bowlby built upon this outline when he identified the three phases of emotional response—protest, despair, and detachment—through which children progress when they are removed from the care of their parents and placed in impersonal environments. This outline remains a cornerstone of attachment theory, especially for conceptualizing the relationship between separation, loss, and emotional distress.

During the first stage of protest, fear and separation anxiety are dominant, indicating an attempt to search out and recover the absent person. The subsequent phase of despair is a quieter, sadder time, followed by an emotional shutting down if the separation is prolonged and/or conditions are severe. These responses occur along a continuum, and may move back and forth among various stages. Protest is connected to separation anxiety, despair to loss, grief and mourning and detachment to defensive processes that deal with the pain of loss. Bowlby (1982) defined separation anxiety as "anxiety about losing or becoming separated from someone loved" (p. 670). It reflects our "basic human disposition" (p. 671) to respond with fear and anxiety "when an attachment figure cannot be found or when there is no confidence that an attachment figure will be available and responsive when desired" (Bowlby 1973, p. 407). Whereas Freud also defined anxiety as a reaction to the danger of losing a loved person, he did not recognize that conditions such as strangeness and being alone were "intrinsically frightening," and he determined that it was unreasonable to feel afraid if there was no immediate pain or danger (Bowlby 1973). Thus, in Freud's view, becoming anxious over a simple separation, such as a spouse being away for a few days, would appear unrealistic, and therefore pathological. However, an ethological perspective of attachment explains that protest behaviors at separation are an adaptive way to protect and maintain a bond. Separation from an attachment figure, though not inherently dangerous, is one of a group of naturally occurring clues to danger that humans, as well as other animals, are disposed to respond to because they signal an increase of risk. Other natural fears that elicit behaviors intended to keep a person in a familiar and safe environment, surrounded by trusted companions, are those experienced in connection with strangeness, heights, isolation, changes in sound or light, looming objects, and sudden movement (Bowlby 1973,

Sable 1991a). Research has shown that children become sensitive to separation when they become mobile and, by the age of 3 or 4, develop fears of heights, open spaces, and darkness, conditions that would have been especially dangerous during evolutionary history (Simpson 1999). But even now, in terms of protection and adaption, it makes good sense to respond to these conditions with some type of action, as, for example, by seeking safety in the company of another person. Therefore, protest and distress about being alone, or about being separated from a potentially caregiving figure, are natural fear responses that have evolved to preserve attachment and protection.

Besides observations of young children in separation situations, research studies of different animal species have shown that separation from or loss of an attachment figure could, in itself, cause fear and anxiety, affecting both attachment and exploratory behaviors. Harlow (1958), who separated infant rhesus monkeys from their mothers and raised them on mother surrogates, demonstrated that the monkeys who had cloth mother surrogates were terrified when placed in a strange environment and did not explore their surroundings if their cloth-dummy mothers were absent. If the cloth-dummy mother was present, however, the infants would first cling to it and then begin to move about (Bowlby 1973).

These results with primates were similar to those reported by Ainsworth (Ainsworth et al. 1978) in the 1-year-old children she studied in the Strange Situation procedure. Simpson (1999) notes that her test confronts the child with two of danger's natural clues: being left alone, and being left with a stranger. When the mother was present, the children used her as a base from which to play and explore. However, when the mother left the room, a majority of the children were distressed and restricted their exploratory behavior. While the mother was away, they cried and searched for her, and also responded more intensely to frightening situations such as the entrance of a stranger (Ainsworth and Bell 1970).

Behavior following reunion, in both monkey and human studies, reflects the effects of separation. The studies of monkeys done by Spencer-Booth and Hinde (1967) found that young monkeys who have been separated from their mothers and subsequently reunited cling more to their mothers and explore less than monkeys who have not endured a separation. These monkeys also exhibited greater timidity and fear of strange situations. Heinicke and Westheimer (1966) observed that young children also became more clinging and were afraid to be left alone following a separation. Similarly, the physiologic responses such as decreased motor activity and body temperature, changes in heartbeat, and sleep disturbances that Hofer (1984) found in the despair of prolonged separation in infant rats are exacerbated in monkeys who have had prior social deprivation (Suomi et al. 1973). These research studies, which came early in the evolution of attachment theory, strengthened Bowlby's position by demonstrating that separation from a primary caregiver—whether in infant rats, primates, or human babies—leads to protest behaviors and also to intensified fear in strange situations. Attachment behavior is initiated both during and following a separation experience. Not only is it activated as exploratory behavior is deactivated, but after the experience of separation, there are also residual effects that include a greater sensitivity to any threat of another disruption, as well as a tendency for the sensitivity to persist over time (Bowlby 1973, Waters 1978).

The extensive attachment research of the past decade continues to revolve around concepts of separation and loss. Presently, there is more focus on a variety of interacting variables and mediating influences, and less emphasis on the specific protest–despair–detachment stages of response, or the specific disruptions themselves. For example, the social convoy (Kahn and Antonucci 1980) asks subjects to reflect on those figures they would miss the most if they were parted from them. And Hazan and Shaver's (1987) "love quiz" is a modification of Ainsworth's (Ainsworth et al. 1978) measure of separation and reunion behaviors, the Strange Situation procedure.

It was a significant contribution to clinical thinking when Bowlby (1973) connected observations of the responses of young children who had experienced separation or loss to the distress encountered in adult patients. For example, children who had been in the Robertsons' studies (Robertson and Robertson 1971) were prone to become acutely anxious if they sensed the risk of another separation. Bowlby noted that these kinds of

> responses and processes [seem] to be the same
> as those found to be active in older individuals
> who are still disturbed by separations they have
> suffered in early life . . . [these include] various
> forms of acute and chronic anxiety and depres-
> sion, and difficulties of every degree in making
> and maintaining close affectional bonds, whether
> with parent figures, with members of the oppo-
> site sex, or with own children. [pp. xii–xiii]

Since Bowlby pointed out the potential damage of separation, an awareness of the problem has been central to policy decisions such as arranging foster care or the hospitalization of children. Concerns about its short-term as well as long-term effects remain a key factor in the present controversy surrounding working mothers and day care. In fact, Barrett's (1997) argument that children have a greater diversity of reactions to separation than was originally perceived suggests that we do not yet know enough about their behavior following separation. According to Barrett, children, like adults, have a variety of coping strategies that fall within the range of normal behavior. At the moment of separation, children do not necessarily protest, but may try to use their usual techniques of adaptation, including a stoicism that resembles the numbness of grief and mourning. Barrett claims that even the famous "John" of the Robertson films (1971) did not initially protest, but exhibited attachment behaviors intended to get the nurses' attention. He only broke down and protested after he found he could not compete with the more aggressive institutionalized children to get his needs met.

Barrett (1997) comes to the conclusion that individual differences in children's responses to a parent's departure call for a more complex account of reactions to separation than has been generally assumed. In particular, she proposes that, in some instances, there may be an intervening phase between separation and protest, similar to the phase of numbness that occurs between loss and the commencement of grief. Interestingly, without the systematic research techniques and data now available, Bowlby (1973) wrote that the stage of protest may begin immediately or may be delayed; however the possibility of responses preceding protest has not received the theoretical attention that has been given to the identification of a period of numbness in grief and mourning.

Thus it seems there are different responses to separation, all of which are compatible with healthy functioning and development, and that reactions may be intensified or inhibited, compromising personality development and adult functioning. A major premise of attachment theory is that adults who are prone to increased responses of fear and anxiety do not have sufficient confidence in the availability of their affectional figures. Although Bowlby does appreciate the influence of genetic factors, actual frightening experiences, or cultural clues (such as being told scary stories) in generating a susceptibility to fear behavior, his focus is on the part played by individuals' relationships to their affectional figures. He contends that a client's fear that attachment figures will be inaccessible and unresponsive can be missed or hidden by defensive displacements if clinicians do not consider this fear-arousing potential in their theoretical frameworks. Bowlby summarizes his perspective on separation and fear with three propositions. First, a person who is confident that attachment figures will be available when needed is less prone to either intense or chronic fear than one who does not have such confidence. Next, this confidence (or lack of it) develops slowly during childhood and adolescence, and whatever expectations are built up tend to persist, basically unchanged, throughout the rest of life. And finally, these expectations of the accessibility and responsiveness of attachment figures are relatively accurate recollections of the experiences individuals have actually had.

ANXIOUS ATTACHMENT

Bowlby (1973, 1980) introduced the concept of "anxious attachment" to describe an adult who feels fear and anxiety over separation from attachment figures. Individuals who grow up to be anxiously attached do not have a secure base in their attachment relationships from which to move out and take part in a variety of activities and relationships. Because they are apprehensive and unsure whether attachment figures can be counted on, they are preoccupied with worry about their reliability and thus alarmed about separation from them, and act in ways that they hope will maintain some degree of assurance and security. This is reflected in a tendency to anxiety and/or panic at any threat to emotional or physical availability, which may make them appear clinging and demanding. Anxiously attached people feel afraid unless they stay close and continually monitor the behavior and intentions of those persons who represent safety. Not only are they hampered in going forth into the world, they are more apt to make adult attachments of an ambivalent and/or anxious nature and to respond with greater sensitivity to separation, loss, or stressful situations (Hamilton 1985, Sable 1994a).

When Bowlby introduced the term into the literature in 1973, he explained that the concept "anxious attachment," or "insecure attachment," was more precise than labeling the behavior overdependency or even "separation anxiety" because it avoids ambiguity or implication of disapproval. The concept of anxious attachment emphasizes the underlying meaning of the behavior, enlisting our sympathy for these individuals who have a natural desire for secure affectional bonds but who are living in constant anxiety over some aspect of their relationships. As mentioned in Chapter 3, in attachment theory the term "insecure" comes from Ainsworth's original classification of young children's responses to their mothers in the Strange Situation procedure (Ainsworth et al. 1978). From direct observations of children interacting with their mothers before and after a brief separation from them, Ainsworth and her colleagues found they could define observable patterns of attachment as either "secure" or "insecure." Bowlby (1973) later expanded the concept, equating a pattern of insecure attachment to one of anxious attachment.

Using Bowlby's framework, Lieberman and Pawl (1990) later identified anxious attachment in high-risk 2-year-olds referred to an infant–parent treatment program. These children were reluctant to approach unfamiliar but otherwise attractive objects or to interact with unfamiliar but friendly people. Affective responses were restricted, with the result that the children refrained from expressing negative feelings that might have increased fears of abandonment and helplessness. Lieberman and Pawl attributed the inhibition of both feelings and exploratory behavior to the absence of a secure base with mother.

Similarly, adults whose relationships reflect a pattern of anxious attachment are unsure about the accessibility and responsiveness of attachment figures and devise strategies to maintain some degree of proximity and responsiveness. Dozier and Kobak (1992) have called these strong activations of the attachment behavior system "hyperactivated strategies," and it is these measures that cause anxiously attached individuals to appear clinging or demanding of attention and appreciation from others. However, because their feelings and memories have been disconnected from events relevant to their fears, they are unaware of why they feel so afraid when they are away from persons or places that represent safety (Bowlby 1973, Liotti 1991, Sable 1991a, 1992a). One woman described her fear of approaching the unfamiliar as the sensation of strenuously pushing an unknown "barrier" beyond which she could not proceed. She was equally restrained in allowing her attachment feelings to surface and had sought therapy for a variety of fears as well as an inability to form an intimate adult relationship.

According to Bowlby (1973, 1988a), adults who are prone to separation anxiety have been subjected to one or more of a variety of adverse parenting experiences. These include child abuse and neglect; emotional abuse; inconsistent, intrusive, or unreliable caregiving; threats to abandon the child, withdraw love, or make love conditional; disclaiming or disconfirming the child's perceptions, feelings, and experiences; or reversing the caregiving role by demanding that the child care for the parents. There is now evidence that these kinds of pathogenic family experiences may distort personality development and dispose an individual to anxious attachment. For example, in a bereavement study of eighty-one women whose spouses had died one to three years earlier, I found that women who described a relationship of anxious attachment to their husbands were having more difficulty handling their loss and exhibited more anxiety and depression than women who had not had such relationships (Sable 1989). Furthermore, childhood experiences of separation and loss or threats of abandonment were found to contribute to more anxiety and depression in the women's bereavement. Likewise, Hazan and Shaver (1987) found similar results in two questionnaire studies of their "love quiz," one of 620 individuals from the general population and the other of 108 college undergraduate students. As mentioned in Chapter 2, Hazan and Shaver designed the measure to examine whether Ainsworth's classification of attachments as secure, avoidant, or ambivalent-anxious extended into adult relationships. Subjects were asked which of three brief paragraphs represented their manner of relating to others. Those who chose the category Hazan and Shaver had labeled ambivalent-anxious reported feelings of insecurity, in particular jealousy, emotional highs and lows, and preoccupation with their partner. Furthermore, a positive relationship was found between this adult anxiety and childhood insecurity.

Several other points are related to understanding anxious attachment. First, Bowlby (1980) writes that it is likely to result from an intermittent and partial disruption of a relationship rather than a complete loss. Intermittent and partial disruptions intensify separation anxiety but also allow some degree of hope that care and affection may still be possible. Next, in addition to experiencing anxiety regarding the possibility of separation, the individual may feel ambivalent and angry while also longing for love and support. These feelings may go unrecognized, particularly if they are "defensively excluded" due to internalization of parental injunctions against registering certain parental behaviors or threats. With later precipitating events, such feelings then develop into symptomatic behavior, such as suicide attempts, agoraphobia, conversion symptoms, or anorexia nervosa (Adam et al. 1995, Bowlby 1973, 1977, Chassler 1997).

Finally, by replacing descriptions such as overdependency and childishness with the concept of anxious attachment, we change the way we understand our clients' distress and also our approach to treatment (Sable 1979, 1983). For example, Mackie (1981) claims that concerns about overdependency in treatment affect the therapeutic relationship. Following Bowlby's view that the need for attachment is a natural part of behavior throughout life, and that adults seeking psychotherapy often lack a secure base, he notes that seeing insecure attachment solely in terms of dependency detracts from the awareness of a client's real human need for secure attachment. A therapist whose presence and accessibility bring comfort and reduce fear at times of intensified stress fits Bowlby's description of a secure base, and speaks to the therapist's "being there" when needed (Holmes 1996, Jones 1983). Helping clients understand that there is a natural inclination for attachment behavior to be evoked under certain circumstances, and that the therapist can be expected to be available at these times, is part of the process of therapy itself. This attitude promotes the establishment of a secure base from which clients can begin to explore their working models of themselves and their relationships with others, including the therapist.

Attachment-based therapy offers a distinctive perspective for organizing a client's affectional experiences. The focus is on creating a narrative of family influences that have led, for example, to feeling anxious and angry over separation. The therapist gives support and encouragement in the process of retrieving memories that have been defensively excluded, frequently helping overcome a reluctance to remember painful or frightening events. As the original nature of their anxious attachment is more clearly understood, clients are often able to develop greater self-reliance as well as security in their affectional bonds with others (Bowlby 1977, 1988a, Sable 1992a).

CLINICAL EXAMPLES

Because Bowlby saw a basic, underlying commonality in psychological distress, the first three clinical examples in this chapter will illustrate just how broad the category of anxious-ambivalent attachment is. The syndromes of agoraphobia and post-traumatic stress disorder in the following two chapters are examined in a way that is more in line with *DSM* diagnostic categories. In this chapter's first example, using the case study of Heidi, there is emphasis on illustrating the way attachment theory distinguishes anxious attachment from traditional concepts of dependency. The next two examples, the case studies of Brandon and Garrett, focus on relating family experiences to anxious attachment. Bowlby originally used the anxiety disorder of agoraphobia to illustrate the application of his concept of anxious attachment to psychological distress; therefore, the case examples in the next chapter are not unlike the ones presented here. What is important is piecing together an attachment history rather than making a precise *DSM* diagnosis. Fonagy and colleagues (1997) agree with Bowlby that there is no simple, direct relationship between attachment classification and psychopathology, and that the latter occurs when "mechanisms of defense have proved inadequate to . . . protection . . . from anxiety" (p. 246). Regardless of diagnostic category, pathology represents malfunctioning attachment strategies, either in the direction of minimizing affect in avoidant-type personality patterns or maximizing affect in anxious-ambivalent attachment (Lieberman 1997). Thus, all pathology tends to be seen as a reflection of insecure or anxious attachment, manifested by defensive attempts to maintain some measure of affectional contact and security.

Whether tending toward anxious ambivalence or toward avoidance and insistent self-reliance, individuals who are anxiously attached may develop psychiatric symptoms when faced with changing conditions such as separation or threat of separation or loss. An assessment of psychopathology depends on the person's age, present condition of life (such as recent loss), and current and past interrelationships. Once it is understood that anxious attachment is the result of real experiences within the family, especially with key attachment figures, as well as the influence of current relationships, it becomes possible to explain psychological problems that develop during adult years (Bowlby 1973, 1975, 1977).

HEIDI

The effects of traumatic events on the origins of anxious attachment and separation anxiety are illustrated by Heidi, (Sable 1979) a soft-spoken, timid, 27-year old woman. Heidi had been married to William for five years. Although he was now working as a salesman, William had been unemployed and supported by Heidi's work as a legal secretary for most of their marriage. Heidi sought therapy following a return of suicidal thoughts, increasing withdrawal at work and with friends, and a general feeling of depression. Although she said she had never been happy, she was now becoming "desperate" and "self-destructive."

Heidi reported that she was feeling trapped because she wanted to end her relationship with William. They argued continually. William could not understand her behavior, which fluctuated from demanding his attention to criticizing his lack of concern and involvement in the relationship and in chores at home. However, Heidi was dependent and lacked the courage to leave her husband because she was afraid to be alone. Her dependency distressed her because it was "childish" and "people do not come through for you anyway." An association she made to a recent dream about a visiting childhood friend was one of being a scared child, facing the world alone.

Heidi was an only child. Throughout her early years, her mother was always ill with a variety of conditions, including a congenital heart defect. Heidi had a succession of people caring for her and recalled being told to be quiet because her behavior might result in her mother's having another migraine headache or even worse. Heidi's father was an accountant who worked odd hours, and when he was home, he rested and removed himself from his family. Heidi remembered she was afraid of being alone and afraid of the dark as a child, and also that she spent much of her time isolated and without friends. She frequently missed school, being ill herself. Heidi began college but left after one year to live with an artist. As their relationship was ending, she slit her wrists. Soon after, she returned to her parents' home, where she lived until she was married.

EARLY SEPARATION EXPERIENCE

Bowlby (1973) contends that there is generally evidence of early separation trauma in adults who have a history of suicidal gestures and depression. He cites weak suicidal attempts as an expression of an unconscious yearning for love and support. Researchers such as Adam (1994) and Harris and Bifulco (1991) have found early loss or separation in individuals who exhibit suicidal behavior or depression, especially when disruption was accompanied by disorganization before the event or inadequate care in its aftermath. Similarly, depression has been produced in infant monkeys by separating them from their mothers. Viewed within the framework of attachment theory, it is possible to conceive of an accumulation of separation or threat-of-loss situations that might have affected Heidi's confidence in the availability and responsiveness of her attachment figures. These could also include her temperament or the social context surrounding early separations, for example, the familiarity and consistency of substitute care she received as a child (Bowlby 1973).

It appears Heidi grew up in a family that, in some measure, failed to provide her with a secure base. The insecure affectional behavior she displayed may be described as a condition of anxious attachment. Heidi had good reason to fear separation, as she was already subjected to interrupted care from an ill mother and threatened with greater separation if she misbehaved. She remembered how frightened she was of being deserted when she was subjected to these threats.

Bowlby writes that threats make children angry while at the same time afraid to express the anger for fear their parents might abandon them. As an adult, Heidi continued to inhibit her angry feelings: she noted that she was afraid to share her feelings with William for fear he might leave her. On the other hand, she was afraid to leave him, even though she did not feel secure with him. This situation illustrates her anxious attachment. Heidi's fear of being alone can be seen as a response to one of the naturally occurring clues to which people are predisposed to respond with fear. Young children need the actual presence of the mother to feel reassured and secure. If there is support when it is needed, as well as encouragement to move out into the world, they develop a sense of security in their interrelationships and become more able to tolerate separation in time and space. This confidence is the basis of self-reliance and it is complementary to attachment. As Bowlby (1973) writes: "Paradoxically, the truly self-reliant person . . . proves to be by no means as independent as cultural stereotypes suppose. An essential ingredient is a capacity to rely trustingly on others when occasion demands and to know on whom it is appropriate to rely" (p. 359).

Heidi lacked genuine self-reliance. Her fear of being alone was a fear of separation due to earlier caregiving failures to meet her attachment needs, and this fear represented her effort to handle her anxious attachment.

APPLYING ATTACHMENT THEORY TO TREATMENT

Bowlby emphasizes that the role of a therapist must be to establish herself as a secure base, and as someone steady and consistent whose support and understanding, and occasional guidance, help a patient like Heidi gain the confidence to explore affectional relationships, even painful and unhappy ones. The description of the therapist as a stable attachment figure is similar to Winnicott's (1965) concept of holding, and extends to include the physical setting of therapy as a place to return, away from the distractions and accountability of everyday life, and during times of stress. When attachment behavior is elicited, proximity to the therapist, in the therapeutic setting, brings comfort (Mackie 1981).

Mackie (1981) equates a child's secure base, from which he can safely explore the outer world, with the assurance a therapist provides to enable the client to explore her inner world. Acting as "a trusted companion," (Bowlby 1988a, p. 138) the therapist strives to be reliable, attentive, and sympathetic to these explorations, offering a new kind of relationship that is therapeutic in itself. The experience of "genuine emotional contact" (Fairbairn 1940, p. 16) has an intimacy and freedom of communication the patient probably has not experienced before (Greenberg and Mitchell 1983). Moreover, Mackie argues, like Bowlby, that responding to the patient's need for attachment should take priority over making interpretations. Bowlby (1988a) advocates the stance of "you know, you tell me" (p. 151), which conveys to patients that, with the help of the therapist, they can discover the nature of their working models and how they developed. Not only does this convey respect for the client's ability to make her own decisions, it avoids possible repetition of parental injunctions and distorted views about the client's capabilities.

When the experience of an attachment relationship is promoted within the therapeutic situation, past events are seen as relevant more for their influence on clarifying current activities and behavior. Where past relationships have taken on a pattern of detachment, the client has generally given up on relationships with others and may act withdrawn and afraid to trust the therapist. A client like Heidi, whose relationships tend toward anxious attachment, is unsure about the availability of attachment figures, and may act afraid, as well as ambivalent and clinging, especially when there are interruptions of sessions (Bowlby 1977, 1988a, Jones 1983). However, since implications of separation and loss occur throughout treatment, these interruptions furnish an opportunity for the therapist to explain that separation anxiety is a natural response when there is separation, threat of separation, or loss. If she is made to feel that responses such as anxiety at separation are regressive or overdependent, a client may block out the very feelings that need to be expressed. If reaching maturity implies the ability to separate and become independent, the client may feel caught between these demands, some of which come from social injunctions, and natural strivings for emotional bonds with others (Sable 1991a).

With Heidi, therapy provided a temporary attachment relationship within which she could review current and past experiences in order to ascertain how certain representational models of herself and others were formed and maintained. When experiences were misconstrued, including experiences with her therapist (transference), she was helped to recognize what may have caused these misconstructions. For example, during her time in treatment, her mother mistakenly informed Heidi that she might have terminal cancer. Even after the scare was over, Heidi was alarmed and anxious, and engaged in some acting-out behavior such as shoplifting that she had not done since beginning treatment. However, she did not become suicidal, was able to acknowledge both anger and fear, and realized her mother's illnesses and behavior were not her fault. Meanwhile, Heidi and her therapist tried to explore if something in their relationship was adding to her impulsive behavior.

Heidi's anxious-attachment pattern delayed her in attaching to her therapist and settling into treatment. She periodically canceled appointments and deliberated about terminating therapy. However, she noted that she was beginning to understand and subsequently to change some behavior. She continued to live with William, but once she realized her feeling of aloneness as a child she began to understand her insecure attachment to him. She claimed she was not as demanding of him and that they argued less. Furthermore, she began reappraising her relationship with her parents, which freed feelings that had been underground for many years. For example, Heidi became aware that it was important for her to be both married and independent, because she thought these qualities would gain her parents' acceptance.

Heidi was not treated as someone who had regressed to an early stage of oral dependence or someone who needed to mature and become independent. Instead, we discussed and attempted to sort out certain feelings, such as her wanting a secure relationship with someone. By avoiding terms like dependence or independence in the therapeutic milieu, the therapist was able to help Heidi deepen her awareness of her own natural attachment feelings. This freed both therapist and client to attempt to work toward self-reliance, without introducing interfering doubts about dependency needs being encouraged or gratified.

FAMILY EXPERIENCES
AND ANXIOUS ATTACHMENT

From the perspective of attachment, working models are composed of the conscious and unconscious inner representations that are continually used by individuals to appraise and respond to situations as they occur. Although attachment theory may overlap with other psychoanalytic and object relations theories of internalization (Kobak, personal communication), Bowlby (1969a) claims his construct of mental models, evolving out of current and past experiences with others, offers a new view. In accord with this interpersonal conceptualization, much of treatment consists of uncovering and discovering what a person's actual attachment experiences may have been and how the effects of these events have come to be part of the individual's working models (Bowlby

1973). However, because cognitive structures originate in the earliest years and are fairly automatic and stable by adulthood, the dynamics of the formation of these constructs, which are naturally resistant to major change, are often unclear. Ordinary parental care generally promotes the development of flexible and integrated models that permit the adjustment and updating of information and experience that is necessary for satisfactory adult functioning. However, where family life has thwarted security and open communication, mental structures may become distorted and conflicting. For example, if within the family children are not allowed to express, or are discounted when they do express, feelings such as anger and sadness, or are given contradictory and inconsistent messages, they may form models through which others are seen as unpredictable; such children may also portray themselves as unworthy of another's affection or not capable of having control over their lives. By adulthood, they may be preoccupied and worried about attachments, but, because of defensive exclusion, they may be unable to identify the feelings or situations that have led to their worry or suffering (Bowlby 1991, Cassidy and Kobak 1988, Collins and Read 1990, Liotti 1991).

BRANDON

The impact of an insecure family base and of defensive exclusion on personality development and adult bonds is illustrated by the account of Brandon (Sable 1994c), a young adult single man, who described difficulties with his current romantic attachment and also with advancing his career.

Brandon came into therapy to help him decide whether he wanted to remain with Niki and get married or to end their two-year relationship. Furthermore, although he was a college graduate, Brandon worked as a part-time deliveryman, a job he found unsuitable and uninteresting. In both situations he described becoming "paralyzed"—afraid to explore or think about what he really wanted. Brandon was especially alarmed about trying anything new or "unknown." Niki saw his behavior as a lack of commitment and ambition and as the source of their constant arguments. She thought his indecision provoked his angry withdrawal to a state in which he could not envision "ever getting over" his anger at her. At other times, Brandon was apprehensive of displeasing Niki and concentrated on behaving in ways that would not upset her. Brandon wanted to make changes but was afraid to let go of the "comfort zone" he felt with familiar people and places. For example, he noted that while his nondemanding work kept "the pressure off," it also left him feeling "down and hopeless."

Brandon seemed eager to get help for his distress, and talked openly and easily, but with very restrained affect. He was overly concerned about arriving on time, paying his bills promptly, and, when it was necessary for him to change an appointment hour, would apologize and ask if he had inconvenienced his therapist.

During his treatment over several years, Brandon described a family history of inconsistency, anger, and disappointments. His mother depicted herself as trapped in an unhappy marriage to a volatile, argumentative, and unsuccessful man with whom she stayed for the sake of Brandon and his two younger siblings. His father was critical and indifferent in the family, but his outbursts of unpredictable rage kept Brandon afraid to speak up for himself. Brandon came to feel responsible for his mother, maintaining frequent contact with her and even taking her on vacations. He avoided his father, and what little communication existed between them was verbally abusive and imposing on the father's part. For instance, he sometimes called Brandon to ask for money, badgering him with complaints of how family members had gotten him into financial difficulties.

It appears that Brandon, like Heidi, grew up in a family that failed to provide him with a secure base. Neither parent was able to tolerate his feelings and behavior or help him achieve a sense of competence or self-confidence. As a result of his family's injunctions to conform to their expectations, he repressed his "true self" (Winnicott 1965), and tried to comply with the wishes of others. Crittenden (1992) describes such compliance in anxiously attached adults as a way of dealing with the pain and rejection they fear will result from open expression of feelings. The detachment in the conflicted behavior that Brandon displayed with Niki could also be described in terms of Winnicott's "false self," although a Bowlbyan perspective would attribute anxious attachment more directly to actual interpersonal experiences. Brandon's outbursts of anger and recurrent anxiety reflected attachment-related experiences, while they also guarded him from distressing memories. In terms of the unpredictable anger he exhibited, Kobak (Kobak and Hazan 1991) has noted that when feelings such as anger at unmet attachment needs are disconnected from their source, they may show up later, either in exaggerations of normal responses to a partner's inaccessibility, or in angry withdrawal. Moreover, Kobak writes of several kinds of insecure attachment similar to those manifested by Brandon, including low self-worth and what Mireault and Bond (1992) call a "perceived vulnerability." Using a questionnaire study of 226 college students, Mireault and Bond have identified a perception of vulnerability in those who had lost a parent or received inadequate care in childhood. Not only did these individuals worry about future threatening events and attempt to reduce personal risk by preventive behaviors, they were also more prone to anxiety and depression than those young adults who had not had these experiences.

As Brandon came to accept his therapist as someone who would be supportive and sympathetic without needing or expecting his care, he began to sort through and reexamine his attitudes and behavior. For example, he thought that he had accepted his mother's portrayal of the outside world as dangerous and overwhelming and that he had also accommodated her subtle demands for attention and silent compliance. Being able to deal with his anxious compliance to his therapist was an important starting point for this understanding. It was many months before he could disagree with his therapist's comments, because his transference repeated his parents' prohibitions to not recognize or express angry feelings. Brandon further concluded that he had misconstrued Niki's behavior to be as demanding as his mother's, and had accumulated this anger and redirected it to his companion. In the process of examining these tendencies, not only was he able to set more appropriate patterns of behavior with his mother, but he began to feel less angry with and more committed to Niki and to pursue new options and work. At one point, Brandon called treatment his "safety net";

in response, rather than conveying that he was becoming too dependent on her, the therapist stated that he was making a firm therapeutic attachment. Regardless of how anxious attachment is exhibited, it is this quality of a secure therapeutic relationship that helps clients explore and come to better terms with their experiences (Bowlby 1988a). If Brandon's therapist had not acknowledged the significance of familiarity, affirmation, and reliability in Brandon's risking a confident attachment to her, he might have again denied his healthy attachment strivings.

GARRETT

Sometimes the natural tendency to seek emotional ties and the developmental pathway of anxious attachment are more disguised; instead of overt clinging and unrelenting worry, the individual engages in dramatic and dangerous acts. This was the situation with Garrett (Sable 1994c), another young adult single man who sought treatment for reasons quite different from Brandon's, but who also revealed feelings of anxiety and depression, as well as pathogenic family experiences dating back to his childhood.

> Garrett came for help following the breakup of a close relationship that brought to a head many years of anxiety, depression, and thoughts of suicide. He had become afraid to leave home except for work, or unless he was going somewhere nearby where people would "not be strangers." He reported regular heavy drinking, insufficient eating and exercise, and interest and participation in high-risk activities such as learning to fire a gun and skydiving.

Garrett noted that his fears and depression had occurred once before, during junior high school, in conjunction with a suicide attempt that led to therapy. This was the only occasion on which his parents gave him any confirmation of his distress. Otherwise, he remembers a childhood dominated by an alcoholic, overbearing father who was sarcastic and could be mean and punishing, as for example, by withholding a promised Christmas gift. His mother, overwrought and overwhelmed by a large family and a troublesome marriage, was usually unavailable. Garrett felt he was different from others and that his feelings were a burden to his family. He particularly noted that his parents failed to protect him from a tormenting sibling and did not respond when he complained he did not have friends.

Without encouragement, support, and protection from his family, Garrett came to see himself as "weak" and "different" and, although successful in his career, had never made a lasting adult relationship. His defensive exclusion of his emotions in difficult relation situations was apparent when, after an argument with a woman he had been seeing, he stated, "I don't know how I feel. I never know how I feel."

Collins and Read (1990) explain that impulsive, self-destructive behavior can be a distorted attempt to get hidden attachment needs met. Since his parents only responded to crisis situations, Garrett tried to get attention with life-threatening gestures. Along with this tactic, he shut off his feelings of disappointment, anger, fear, and vulnerability, and accepted his parents' view of him as a nuisance in relation to the people in his life who could have been supportive and helpful. When he had an adult relationship, it was short lived, and he chose women who themselves were not capable of intimate relationships.

Establishing a therapeutic bond with Garrett was much more challenging than with Brandon. He continually tested his therapist, by being angry or by not talking, by forgetting or canceling appointments, or by arriving late. However, although he was not conforming to customary therapeutic procedure, he was beginning to give up his self-destructive behaviors. As Garrett slowly came to trust his therapist as someone who was responsive and interested in discussing issues he was concerned about, he was able to recover memories and discover and express forgotten feelings. Garrett's therapist helped him consider whether his testing the therapeutic boundaries was an effort to be himself and still be accepted without fear of losing the relationship. Similarly, he and the therapist discussed the possibility that fears of leaving home and fears of being alone, especially with strangers in unfamiliar places (which resembled agoraphobia) might be part of an attempt to deal with his desires for personal bonds rather than indicating weakness or overdependency. Another attachment-related dynamic was Garrett's feeling that he was undeserving of being cared for. Once he was aware of how his family had contributed to these biases and to his tendency to defensively exclude his own attachment feelings and needs, he became less afraid to venture out, began to take better care of himself, and started to form more reliable affectional bonds.

ANXIOUS ATTACHMENT
AND WORKING MODELS

Working models are complex structures that cover a range of experiences and varying levels of memory and recall (Collins and Read 1990). Although Hazan and Shaver (1987) have found that adults are less influenced by their early experiences as they encounter new relationships and events in the larger world, mental models are assemblages of present and past experiences. The way parents treated their child, what they said, and the attachment patterns they modeled in their own marriages and other relationships are the basis for some of the memories and feelings that go into the formation of an individual's working models (Bowlby 1988a, Carnelley and Janoff-Bulman 1992, Kottler and Omodei 1988).

Like Heidi, Brandon and Garrett seem to confirm Bowlby's belief that inner models of attachment are derived from actual experiences with attachment figures. The two men were exposed to certain family influences that led to their forming relationships of anxious attachment in adulthood. Moreover, they both revealed anger, ambivalence, and depression, as well as anxiety over attachment. Anxious attachment is predominantly a feeling of apprehension and uncertainty about affectional bonds but also includes many other feelings. It is important in understanding the condition to remember that natural fears of danger are substantially overcome in childhood when attachment figures are consistent and reliable. On the other hand, disruption of an affectional bond can intensify natural fears. Even with someone such as Garrett, who camouflaged his fears with recklessness, the intensification of natural fears was indicated in his discomfort with unfamiliar people and his fear of going into strange areas alone.

Experiencing secure attachment in treatment can help anxiously attached adults restructure their inner working models to feel less afraid. Brandon and Garrett were able to use a therapeutic relationship to understand and connect their feelings to the original family experiences that produced them. That anxious attachment can, and often does, exist in males should be noted by clinicians, since traditionally terms such as dependency and neediness have usually been attributed chiefly to females (Lohman 1981, Sable 1991a). Attachment theory has expanded our understanding of human behavior by showing that the security of knowing that attachment figures are available, responsive, and reliable frees individuals—whether men or women—to live their lives with confidence, participating in the outside world without worry of what might happen should they become frightened, injured, or ill.

5
Agoraphobia

In the musical, *Les Misérables* (1987), there is a song, "On My Own," in which a female character sings "When . . . he is gone, the river's just a river. Without him the world around me changes. The trees are bare and everywhere the streets are full of strangers." These words might be poetically describing the feelings of someone with agoraphobia. After the loss of a loved one, or when one is unsure about the reliability of attachment figures, one indeed may feel alone, on one's own, in a world that suddenly feels less safe and familiar; the strange can seem more ominous and threats of danger become intensified.

Listed in *DSM-IV* (American Psychiatric Association 1994) as an anxiety disorder, where it is classified in forms with and without a relationship to panic attacks, agoraphobia is defined as fear of leaving familiar surroundings, especially when alone. Symptoms vary from person to person, with the fears of venturing out alone and into strange and distant areas the two most dreaded situations. These symptoms are frequently part of a cluster of fears that may include going into public places such as crowded theaters or shopping centers; traveling in a train, bus, or car; and being in open or closed spaces or in high places. Fear tends to be associated with specific situations such as standing in line, being on a bridge, or driving on the freeway, where a quick escape to a familiar location is difficult or impossible. The person may fear that something dreadful will happen while he or she is away from home, something such as dying or becoming helpless. Moreover, the more anxious a person becomes, the more fears of leaving home are magnified. Sometimes the feared situations are social, such as fear of visibly trembling or being stared at.

Along with the presenting fears, there are usually accompanying complaints of depression, depersonalization, or psychosomatic disturbances, as for example a pounding heart and dizziness. Panic attacks, an intensification of physiological responses accompanied by a sense of impending doom, occur in many individuals and often precede onset of the condition. These attacks are especially frightening because they mimic symptoms of serious, life-threatening physical conditions such as heart attacks. Also, because of their unpredictability—panic attacks can occur at any time—some people restrict their lives, fearing they will experience an attack if they pursue daily activities or even leave the house (American Psychiatric Association 1994, Ballenger 1989, Barlow 1988, Bowlby 1973, Buglass et al. 1977, Clarke and Wardman 1985, Davison and Neale 1990, Frances and Dunn 1975, Frustaci 1988, Liotti 1991, Marks 1970, Michelson 1987).

Agoraphobia occurs mainly in married women. It generally begins in young adulthood, but it may last many years, eventually becoming so severe that a person becomes housebound. It is considered to be the most prevalent and distressing phobia in adult patients (Dozier et al. 1999). The term, first used by Westphal (1871) and later advanced by Freud (1926), originally referred to fear of open spaces, but the condition is now generally characterized as a fear of leaving home, or of being separated from some person or place that represents a feeling of security. Within a framework of attachment, agoraphobia is conceived as a condition of anxious attachment, related to an absence of attachment or fear of separation from those with whom one has formed affectional bonds. Because of fear and anxiety over the availability and responsiveness of attachment figures, the person is preoccupied with maintaining proximity and is thus prone to separation anxiety and clinging behavior; confidence to explore the world or deal with stressful situations is constricted (Bowlby 1973, 1988a, Marrone 1998, Routh and Bernholtz 1991, Sable 1991a).

Bowlby attributes agoraphobia to earlier separation or loss experiences or threats of separation. Instead of an internalized security of attachment, inadequate parenting or traumatic events generate uncertainty about the accessibility of affectional figures. The bond of attachment that develops in treatment offers an opportunity to internalize the comfort and security of a reliable relationship and to explore and understand the effects of past fears and experiences in order to develop more self-reliance and improved relationships with others.

Although therapists now recognize fear of leaving a safe base as the main symptom of agoraphobia, the influence of close personal relationships in the development and treatment of the disorder has been relatively neglected or unclear. For example, Buglass and colleagues (1977), in a study of thirty married agoraphobic women, found no differences between the women and a matched control group other than the agoraphobic symptoms themselves. By way of contrast, Holmes (1982), in a study of twelve agoraphobic patients, found both childhood experiences and a current adult relationship relevant to understanding agoraphobia, and, furthermore, that treating the couple together reduced agoraphobic symptoms. Although there is support for this technique (see Barlow et al. 1981) Cobb and colleagues (1984) found that including the spouse in treatment was not helpful. The mixed results of couple treatment led Barlow to conclude that the dynamics of each couple must be assessed individually. The inconsistencies of the findings, including those related to the influence of a current partner on developing symptoms or affecting the outcome of treatment, suggest there may be other factors involved in understanding the behavior and its treatment.

Although much of the current psychodynamic formulation on agoraphobia follows in the tradition of Bowlby (Ballenger 1989), treatment is increasingly directed toward immediate symptom relief by medication and/or cognitive-behavioral therapy (Alfin 1987, Frustaci 1988, Routh and Bernholtz 1991), even though the results of these techniques have not been substantiated (Ballenger 1989, Barlow 1988, Liotti 1991). Thus, while agoraphobia is acknowledged to be a complex disorder that can be difficult to treat (Alfin 1987, Bennun 1986, Mathews et al. 1981), more attention is being given to the panic aspects of the phobia and less to the underlying dynamics (Liotti 1991, Parad 1988).

This chapter applies a framework of attachment to understanding and treating the symptoms of agoraphobia. There is particular consideration of Bowlby's formulation of separation anxiety in conceptualizing agoraphobia and an examination of the points that distinguish it from traditional theory. Discussion begins with a review of the relation of separation to anxiety and psychopathology.

SEPARATION AND FEAR

When Freud revised his thinking about anxiety in 1926, he noted the distress of young children separated from their mothers and concluded that "missing someone who is loved and longed for . . . [is] the key to an understanding of anxiety" (pp. 136–137). However, Bowlby (1973) notes that though Freud had defined anxiety as a reaction to the danger of losing the object, he never applied this theory to agoraphobia. Instead, Freud perceived the inability to walk in the street unless accompanied by a trusted companion as regression to infancy, with repression and projection or displacement of sexual and aggressive impulses. As late as 1933, Freud wrote of the "feelings of temptation that are aroused . . . by meeting people in the street. In his phobia he brings about a displacement and hence forward is afraid of an external situation" (p. 84).

Subsequent to Freud, object relations theorists Suttie (1935), Winnicott (1952), Fairbairn (1952), and Mahler (Mahler et al. 1975) recognized the significance of separation in anxiety, but because their only theory of motivation was drive theory, they continued to opine that the urge to stay home represented "a regression to unresolved dependency needs" (Weiss 1964, p. 8). Winnicott (1965), for example, saw the capacity to be alone in terms of independence and maturity.

In contrast, Bowlby's ethological-evolutionary framework replaces drive theory and conceives an adaptive function in separation anxiety, one that is related to a natural inclination to recover or restore an attachment relationship that is in jeopardy. From detecting the distress family members exhibited when separated or threatened with separation or loss, Bowlby conceptualized an instinctive disposition for a baby to seek proximity and form an affectional bond to its caregiver. When attachment is reliable and consistent, it serves the biological function of protection and security. As previously discussed, with a "secure base," children move out and explore the world, expanding their experiences and relationships, increasingly able to tolerate separation in time and space. Lacking security, exploratory behavior is stunted (Karen 1990). Sooner or later, the child begins to respond with fear in strange or unexpected conditions and is driven toward the attachment figure (Bowlby 1973, Bretherton 1985).

Furthermore, using direct observation studies of children and the reactions of animals to unwilling separation from a figure to whom they had become attached (see Bowlby 1973, Heinicke and Westheimer 1966, Robertson and Bowlby 1952), Bowlby outlined his sequence of responses to separation, which begin with protest at the parent's departure, and are followed by despair and detachment. These responses occur on a continuum, with attachment behaviors such as crying or angry outbursts particularly evident during the protest phase, and suggest a vigorous effort to bring back the missing figure. Later research has shown that even very brief separations elicit these acute reactions (Schore 1994). When the parent does not return, hope begins to fade and there is the withdrawn and subdued mood of despair. Finally, if the separation is prolonged or the experience severe, defensive processes may deactivate attachment feelings and behavior, leading to an emotional detachment, which can persist into adulthood.

The existence of inner working models of insecure attachment with misattuned caregivers explains a young child's ambivalence after reunion as well as his alarm if another separation is suspected (Bowlby 1973). By adulthood, the complexity and flexibility of working models enable understanding of circumstances, hence separation may be tolerated more easily, or at least for a longer period of time (Weiss 1982a). In understanding agoraphobia, however, it is important to note that these early disruptive experiences have a lasting effect on an adult's personality and make such persons prone to feeling anxious and afraid when alone and when conditions are strange and frightening.

SEPARATION ANXIETY AND AGORAPHOBIA

According to Bowlby (1973), separation anxiety describes "how we feel when our attachment behavior is activated, and we are seeking an attachment figure, but without success" (p. 405). This behavior, exhibited by animals as well as by children, adolescents, and adults, is a natural instinctive response to threatened ruptures in attachment. The effects, moreover, are cumulative, and they persist. Children exposed to repeated experiences of separation are likely to grow up more sensitive than others to any kind of separation or loss. In addition, they may be frightened and anxious in a variety of situations that do not appear alarming to others.

Bowlby's view of the function of attachment makes it possible to explain how someone can fear certain situations that appear to have minimal danger. Through evolutionary development, humans have become biologically predisposed to react to the natural clues of an increased risk of danger, such as darkness, unfamiliarity, or being alone and isolated. Open spaces can be a threat in certain situations, which may be why Freud saw agoraphobia as fear of open spaces. There are animal studies that show that animals will cling to edges of a space and avoid running in the open. I had a dog who played frisbee by going out of his way and trotting along the side of the house, rather than cross the open space of the yard. Alfred Hitchcock understood the precariousness associated with open space when he placed Cary Grant alone in an open field, as he tried to dodge an airplane swooping down on him in the film *North by Northwest* (1959). Hitchcock escalated the tension in the scene by isolating the actor in the wide-open space with no safe haven in sight while endangered by a moving, large, noisy object (the airplane). In ethological terms, the presence of multiple natural clues compounds the potential for danger and intensifies reactions of fear. Ohman (1993) noted, moreover, that most of the fears reported by adults are elaborations of natural clues—such as fear of darkness, heights, spiders or snakes—and not of contemporary menaces, such as bombs or automobiles. Recent brain research is suggesting that there may even be specialized structures that have evolved to specifically register fear, assuring that danger does not go unrecognized.

Separation from an attachment figure is another of the natural clues that warn of a possibility of peril; human beings are genetically biased to respond with feelings of fear and separation anxiety at these times of threat so that measures will be taken to maintain security. However, although separation anxiety is an adaptive response to disruption of attachment, certain pathogenic family experiences, such as emotional or physical maltreatment, repeated rejection, threat of abandonment, or actual separation or loss can exacerbate reactions.

Persons who display agoraphobic feelings and behavior are acutely anxious and uneasy about the reliability of attachment figures. Due to real experiences that have undermined their sense of secure attachment, they have lost the ability to tolerate the usual separations of daily life (Liotti 1991) and are afraid to be away from whatever sense of safe base exists with another person or a specific place (Parad 1988). Moreover, agoraphobics are unaware of the basis of these feelings, having excluded certain memories and the connections between events (Alfin 1987, Liotti 1991, Sable 1991a).

As he does for the conditions discussed in the previous chapter, Bowlby (1973) describes the personality pattern of adults who exhibit chronic anxiety over the availability and responsiveness of their attachment figures as an anxious attachment. Because of their uncertainty and fear of desertion or worry that they may not be cared for, agoraphobic individuals seek to maintain proximity to assure contact with attachment figures. The apprehension about their relationships hampers their going forth into the world and also their ability to cope with the inevitable challenges of life when they occur. Adults who suffer agoraphobia symptoms do not have the sense of a secure base that would have enabled them to overcome the natural fears of unfamiliar people and places. Instead, they feel anxiety and/or panic if they go far from attachment figures or familiar surroundings and can maintain security only by staying close and clinging to whatever base they have (Guidano and Liotti 1983, Parad 1988).

Besides being subjected to one of a range of pathogenic family experiences, anxiously attached individuals may have been required to act as caregivers to a parent (usually mother), reversing the typical order. Often this feeling is reinforced when children are made to feel incapable of doing much on their own or when an impression is created that the outside world is dangerous (Bacciagaluppi 1985, Bowlby 1973, 1977, Parad 1988, Sable 1992a). For example, Liotti (1991) found instances of reversal in his personal-interview study of thirty-one agoraphobic patients. I found (Sable 1994a) that every client in an outreach community treatment group for agoraphobia described mothers who demanded care and in other ways failed to be "good-enough mothers"

(Winnicott 1965). Likewise, in a questionnaire study comparing forty agoraphobics to individuals suffering social
phobias, Parker (1979) discovered that the agoraphobics
reported insufficient maternal care. And, on an individual
basis, Ruderman (1992) reports that in psychotherapy
sessions with a woman afraid to leave home, the client
described her mother as physically abusive, as well as
emotionally absent.

These findings tend to confirm Bowlby's position,
which is consistent with Freud's early awareness of pathological parental behavior (Bowlby 1988b, Hunter 1991),
that actual experiences with caregivers influence the development of fear and anxiety. Psychotherapy offers the
opportunity to experience an attachment relationship, and
to explore and understand the effects of separation experiences in the development of agoraphobic fear behavior
patterns. The client is assisted in recovering memories,
as well as responses to them, and is thus able to connect
feelings to the situations that may have evoked them. As
these are understood within the therapeutic relationship,
it is possible to modify inner working models of oneself
and one's interpersonal relationships, leading to tolera-
tion of separations with less anxiety, an increased ability
to move about alone, and more self reliance in relationships with others (Liotti 1991, Sable 1991a).

PSYCHOTHERAPY: MEGAN

The account of Megan, the young adult single woman
whom we met in Chapter 3, illustrates the application of
attachment theory to psychotherapy for agoraphobia. It
also demonstrates that anxious attachment can occur in

various types of adult relationships, from a romantic bond to relationships with a parent or sibling.

An attractive, effusive, and energetic woman who worked as a freelance artist, Megan came into therapy because she was feeling anxious and depressed over her relationships with her family, as well as with men with whom she became involved and envisaged a potential for forming emotional bonds. She became increasingly apprehensive and unsure of herself whenever she began to like someone, and would either pull away by acting "bitchy and sarcastic," talk incessantly, or make unreasonable demands for a commitment. In every case, the relationship soon ended, leaving Megan lonely and discouraged.

Megan further described herself as "overdependent" and a "baby" because of certain behaviors and fears. She was afraid to move about in crowds, to be in social situations, or to drive great distances from home on freeways. Elevators were a particular ordeal, and she only managed to use them by deliberately avoiding eye contact with other occupants. She also complained of frequent headaches, "sick, tight feelings" in her stomach, and panic attacks. At times she would act impulsively; when she suddenly quit a job, for example, it left her frightened, as though she was losing control.

When therapy began, she lived at home with her mother, who was divorced from her father when Megan was 19. Megan claimed that she and her mother were very close, "just like sisters, not like mother and daughter." Although Megan had lived away from home for periods of time, it was convenient to remain with her mother, as both women were afraid to live alone. In addition, her mother did not know how to drive and relied on Megan to take her places.

During therapy, which covered four years, the narrative of Megan's life and relationships emerged. The older of two children, she reported that her mother was warm and attentive, while her father was a self-centered, fun-loving traveling salesman, who, for no apparent reason, could suddenly become very angry. Her sister seemed to be her parents' favorite, escaping some of the mistreatment Megan received. This mistreatment included severe spanking by her father, and criticism from both parents, who humiliated her by telling her she was "too fat" or "not capable" of doing competent work. When Megan was a teenager, her mother told her it would "break their hearts" if she were ever to get pregnant before marriage; she interpreted that to mean that she would "lose" her parents.

Megan had not done well in school and had relatively few friends, finding it difficult to get along with others her age. By the time she was a young adult, she had been labeled the "strong one" of the family, because she could do things without asking for anyone's assistance. She went to work right out of high school, but there were frequent job changes. She remained close to her family, continually trying to achieve some approval and acceptance. For example, she attempted to be helpful to her sister, who was now married, but found the relationship difficult because they argued constantly and because the sister called Megan "crazy and paranoid."

ANXIOUS ATTACHMENT AND AGORAPHOBIA

From an attachment perspective, Megan grew up anxiously attached in her relationships with others. Her mother wanted care from her, reversing the usual parenting order, while her father was self-centered, short-tempered, angry, and frequently away from home. Her parents' pathogenic behaviors left Megan feeling her attachments were not reliable or available to her. She attempted to maintain proximity because she was afraid of losing whatever support she had. She was afraid of being abandoned if she shared her feelings, such as disappointment or anger, or tried to make attachments outside her family.

Bowlby (1973) alleges that experiences of separation and loss are prominent in the development of fearful feelings and behavior. He explains that young children require the actual presence of a caregiver, the confidence of a secure base, and encouragement to move out into the world in order to develop the ability to tolerate separation in time and space. The inherent tendency to feel afraid of unfamiliar people and surroundings is thus overcome within the security of attachment. In Megan's situation, however, these natural fears were intensified by experiences that undermined her confidence that others could be relied upon or that she was deserving of comfort and protection. Megan's agoraphobic fears can be seen as manifestations of her fears of separation resulting from insecurity over attachments.

Due to the uncertainty of her family situation, Megan defensively excluded her own attachment thoughts and feelings and accepted her parents' behavior, perceptions, and comments. This led to both anxiety and anger, which had to be redirected away from their true source, her family, and made her view herself as unworthy or incapable of forming satisfactory bonds with others. She then carried this self-image into her adult attachments, including therapy. She quickly became attached to her therapist, but was concerned about acting appropriately and not showing feelings, such as anger. She said things such as "you don't know what I'm really like when I get angry." She also acted calm and unconcerned before vacations, sometimes noting that she'd completely forgotten there was going to be a separation. But, once the separation was over and she was reunited with her therapist, she tended to be anxious, irritable, and annoyed about many things unrelated to therapy.

Attachment and the Process of Therapy

In applying the theory of attachment to treatment, Bowlby (1977, 1988b) emphasizes that the role of the therapist is to establish the sense of a secure base within which clients' representational models of themselves and their attachment figures may be explored. Assured of a reliable therapist who is sympathetic, interested in them, and available, especially at times of stress, clients have the courage to begin to examine their experiences, both current and past.

The therapeutic experience of an attachment relationship has been equated with the sense of security a child receives from a consistent caregiver (Casement 1991, Osofsky 1988, Weiss 1991) and also with Winnicott's concept of holding (Bowlby 1988b). An example of the former is given by Osofsky (1988), who notes that each type of bond promotes self-esteem and feelings of safety when maintained with intuitive responsiveness. With regard to holding, Casement (1991) and Cassidy and Kobak (1988) describe the therapist's ability to both manage and encourage the expression of clients' feelings that had previously been discouraged or denied expression in earlier relationships.

When children are prohibited from expressing anxiety, anger, or sadness, they may selectively exclude experiences or feelings that would elicit attachment behavior (Cassidy and Kobak 1988, Lieberman and Pawl 1990). As a consequence, an adult client may not only have difficulty identifying and expressing emotions, but also identifying the family situations that may have produced them (Bowlby 1991). This defensive exclusion manifests in treatment when clients are reluctant to rely on their therapists or have difficulty communicating their feelings. A crucial part of therapy, then, is for the therapist to become a trusted companion whose skills help the client feel "really heard and adequately understood" (Casement 1991, p. 115).

An attachment experience, moreover, takes priority over interpretation and allows the client to lead the process (Bowlby 1988b, Casement 1991). With agoraphobia, it is important for the client to have freedom to examine inner memories of past relations and also aspects of the outer world that are frightening (Liotti 1991). When distress intensifies, as it is likely to do with anxious attachment, proximity to the therapist, as well as the physical setting of therapy, reduces fear and anxiety (Bowlby 1988b, Jones 1983, Sanville 1991).

> Fear of separation and anxiety about the reliability of others were central issues in my work with Megan and in my attempt to help her discover the nature of her family experiences. Her feelings of anxious attach-

ment in relationships led her to impose certain expectations on her therapist that were clarified as they were elicited in the transference relationship. For example, Megan worried about displeasing her therapist, and tried to accommodate to what she thought might be demanded of her. She also tried to be the strong one by excluding her own feelings. It was suggested that she might be afraid she would lose the support of her therapist if she let her know she was sometimes angry with her.

As therapy progressed and Megan began to feel secure with her therapist, she could look at her responses, such as the fear and anger that were evoked upon threat of separation or disappointment in relationships. She brought her mother, sister, and two different male friends with her to sessions, which made it possible to directly observe their behavior and their interactions with Megan. Her therapist proposed that this might also be a way for Megan to expose the way she was treated by others so that her therapist would then validate her impressions. This also helped show Megan how difficult it was to simply express herself to her family. When her mother attended a session, she proclaimed her affection for Megan amid a mixture of complaints, for instance, that Megan needed to be "less childish" and "more independent."

Subsequent to this hour, Megan had begun to see that in spite of what her mother said, she had held her daughter in the position of caregiver for herself. Her mother's confusing messages, which conveyed that Megan was strong but also dependent, became apparent. Megan began to understand how she had misconstrued her mother's caregiving behavior and to comprehend the origin of her anxious attachment to her mother and to others. She was more able to retrieve and review experiences and feelings that she had excluded for a long time. For example, she thought she provoked conflict in relationships because she feared the other person would stop seeing her and because she wanted reassurance. About this time, Megan moved into her own apartment. She also began to have steadier attachments with men, though at first with men who did not treat her well. One of them, Steven, attended several sessions with Megan. She had decided he was not the kind of man with whom she wanted a committed relationship and wanted to leave him, but found she had become afraid to be away from him, afraid to be alone, and that her driving problems had returned. These were all indications of her anxious attachment.

Gradually, Megan's real attachment experiences became clearer to her and she came to understand how her family had affected her confidence in forming satisfactory relationships. She ended the relationship with Steven and changed some of her behavior with her mother.

The therapeutic relationship of attachment provided Megan with a safe base from which she began to examine and sort out a lifetime of experiences. It was significant for her that she was not made to feel overdependent, but that her behavior was seen as a reasonable response to the way she had been treated in her family, not only in the past but also in the present. This enabled her to overcome her reluctance to retrieve memories and feelings she had excluded for many years without fearing that her therapist might think she was childish, which would have been a repetition of how she had been viewed by her family. Megan did not know how to reconcile her mother's injunctions to be more independent with her own intrinsic desire for close attachments. In a Bowlbyan framework that distinguishes attachment from dependency, the natural inclination for secure affectional bonds is acknowledged and respected, avoiding the pejorative connotations of dependency (Bowlby 1973, Sable 1979).

How the therapist responds to communication outside of sessions is important in dealing with clients' anxious attachment. With Megan, the confidence of knowing she could call her therapist if she wanted to promoted a secure base in therapy and rarely led to extra contact. Likewise, termination is handled in a way that allows for a gradual parting, and does not repeat painful separations of the past. Now with a secure therapeutic bond, previous separation experiences are reexamined, making the impending one less upsetting. As her therapy was ending, Megan stated she knew she could touch base with her therapist, and occasionally she did. The internalization of a secure attachment relationship led to greater self-reliance and the ability to leave treatment, but because of the exclusive and enduring nature of attachment, there is also a natural desire to retain a link to the therapist. Sanville (1991) calls this new attitude and flexibility about resolving transference and termination an "open door policy."

ATTACHMENT RESEARCH, NARRATIVE, AND CLINICAL APPLICATIONS

Eagle (1997) notes some typical difficulties in applying research to understanding and treatment that seem especially relevant to clients like Megan who lack self-reliance and trust in others. According to attachment theory, the foundation of therapeutic change is the relationship that forms between therapist and patient. With support, sympathy, and insight from the therapist, patients are able to review experiences and revise the narrative and structure of their working models, eventually achieving improved relationships with others. However, Eagle cautions against equating the ability for self-reflection and "autobiographical competence" (Holmes 1993a, p. 82), as defined on the Adult Attachment Interview (AAI), with secure attachment. Eagle points out that while "secure attachment" is defined on the AAI as the ability to tell a coherent and plausible narrative, this is not how insecure and secure attachment were originally conceptualized. The AAI finding is significant since it may be that the ability to revise working models may facilitate the capacity for and development of more adaptive behavior, including breaking the repetition of maladaptive patterns between parents and children. But the measure has not shown that remembering and coming to terms with negative experiences necessarily indicates secure attachment. If secure attachment is defined in terms of the characteristics of a narrative, the meaning of the concept is arbitrarily altered to a focus on reflection on experiences rather than on the ability to make and maintain satisfactory affectional bonds with others.

Eagle sees important therapeutic implications in this distinction, because it affects how the process and outcome of treatment are perceived. People seek treatment for distressing symptoms, generally centered on troubling interpersonal relationships. They may come to construct a more plausible narrative of their experiences but this is a by-product of therapeutic change and does not automatically indicate secure attachment. Bowlby referred to secure attachment as a "confident expectation" (Eagle 1997, p. 224) that attachment figures would be accessible and responsive if a need for them should arise, coupled with a feeling of worthiness about receiving another's care and comfort. Megan, for example, constructed new versions of her life story that helped promote her self-reliance. And, from Bowlby's perspective, she also internalized a reliable relationship with her therapist, and became more confident of her ability to explore the world and have stable relationships. Moreover, Megan now felt deserving of these improved aspects of her life.

LIZZY

Some patients seek treatment for agoraphobic symptoms; others describe a variety of complaints such as anxiety or depression, but then begin to reveal patterns of agoraphobia. Until the past decade, agoraphobia was not readily recognized by mental health professionals. As a result, therapists sometimes did not know what behavior to look for or how best to conceptualize it. People suffering from the syndrome cannot usually understand what is wrong. Thus, achieving a grasp of the meaning of this cluster of anxiety symptoms can be relieving and enlightening. Often the patient feels understood for the first time.

The account of Lizzy, a 32-year-old, very thin, pale, and highly anxious woman (Sable 1991b), demonstrates how the confusion of intensive anxiety is relieved by the therapist putting a framework of understanding around the symptoms. It also shows how the disorder affects the interaction of all family members, restricting and altering the behavior of each of them.

Lizzy came into therapy because she was suffering from anxiety, depression, and a series of fear symptoms that were affecting her relationship with her family. She had become anxious if separated too frequently from her husband, which upset him, and was afraid to drive alone beyond certain precise boundaries, because she would "have no one to count on." In order not to feel afraid, Lizzy expected the oldest of her three children to accompany her. This daughter had herself become a behavior problem.

During therapy, Lizzy described a painful childhood in which her family had moved, sometimes abruptly, from city to city because her father had difficulty keeping a job. She had found it hard to make friends, and remained close to her family. Even now her parents lived nearby. Her mother was described as afraid to be alone or to drive a car; she relied on Lizzy to take her places and to stay with her when the father traveled. Lizzy was an attachment figure to her mother, and their relationship suggests a pattern of reversal that had existed since Lizzy's childhood. Her mother also passed on cues about what Lizzy should fear, such as moving too far away from her. Lizzy had the impression that her mother thought Lizzy could not manage on her own.

Lizzy's anxious attachment and fear of separation can be connected to real experiences. As the therapy relationship furnished her with a familiar and secure base, she was able to share fears and feelings such as her fear of being alone, without having them seen as childish and inappropriate. It also enabled her to link anxiety over separation to actual events with her parents and her husband. As Lizzy came to understand her behavior as a response to family experiences, she was able to release her daughter from the reversed caregiving situation Lizzy had previously sought to maintain. She and her husband worked on their relationship, examining whether Lizzy's alarm at being apart from him reflected some concern about his support, or whether it was more related to her early experiences. As she came to see that she had expected him to behave in a certain way, she was able to let him be a more reasonable attachment figure for her. Eventually her symptoms subsided.

CHERYL

Cheryl (Sable 1991b), a 36-year-old, pleasant, soft-spoken woman, who came into therapy because she was feeling depressed and sad, provides an example of agoraphobia occurring in combination with feelings of grief and mourning. Cheryl moved and spoke slowly, with little emotional expression, and had difficulty talking about herself. She had been married to Jim for fifteen years; they had three children.

Cheryl reported she was feeling troubled by recent changes in her moods and behavior. For no apparent reason she would suddenly want to cry. She frequently felt tense and upset or angry. At social gatherings, she saw herself as an "outsider" looking at others. Sometimes she awoke in a panic in the middle of the night with a premonition of doom, frightened but not knowing what she was afraid of. In addition, she had become increasingly afraid both to walk about "in the open" or to be in a car. Driving on the freeway especially frightened her; she worried that a car might cross the centerline, smash into her, and she would die. She noted that she feared death, and that she had never realized how final it was until her mother's death eight years before.

Additionally, Cheryl had always been afraid to fly and was only able to do this and certain other activities if accompanied by a trusted companion, such as her husband. However, she stated that her confidence in Jim had become "shaky" due to marriage and work problems, and she no longer saw him as "strong and independent." This left her feeling misunderstood and alone. An upcoming vacation with him, which involved flying, also precipitated treatment.

In therapy, Cheryl recounted her life experiences. She was the younger child of parents who did not get along. Her mother was silent and submissive to a controlling and critical husband. Neither parent approved of Cheryl's friends. Her father was himself fearful (for example of flying), and was overprotective and restrictive of Cheryl's activities. Her mother, although usually at home, was withdrawn from the family, and did not take care of her appearance or of the house. Cheryl saw her mother's life as empty and was determined not to be like her, but instead to become strong and independent. She left home at 18, resolved to work and not marry, but, once married, was devoted to her family and successful in her part-time work for a sales company.

It appears that Cheryl grew up anxiously attached in her close relationships with others. She wanted to be loved and cared for but had not been made to feel deserving of love and care. Instead, she sought to be independent, stating that she would be "weak" and overly dependent if she relied on others or shared her fears and feelings. These mixed emotions, which seem to contain societal biases about independence, confused Cheryl and led her to concoct reasons to justify receiving support. Her struggles to make sense of feelings and experiences were further compounded by unresolved mourning for her mother. It is noteworthy that Cheryl reported feelings of dissociation and that she also had unresolved grief in connection to her mother. The link Liotti (1995) makes between early loss and adult dissociative disorders in studies of psychiatric patients suggests that Cheryl's mourning for her mother was diverted by some painful experiences with her that probably dated back to very early years.

> After six months of therapy, Cheryl had completed some grieving for her mother and reappraised her family experiences, including her fears of separation and the pain of loss. This work enabled her to reassess her relationship with Jim. The therapist helped her understand how earlier experiences of insecure attachment were being imposed on her adult relationships. Her marriage improved, and her fears of moving about and her panic attacks ceased. Therapy concluded when she and Jim prepared for the plane trip. A final comment to her therapist revealed Cheryl's trust in therapy as a secure base as well as her understanding of her fear behavior: "I know I could call and you would talk to me all the way to New York."

ANXIOUS ATTACHMENT AND THE SECURE BASE OF THERAPY

The attachment histories of Megan, Lizzy, and Cheryl suggest that a person may develop anxious attachment and a fear of participating in the world if exposed to certain traumatic experiences. Each of the women discussed in this chapter had experienced repeated threats of separation and/or actual separation in their early years, as well as reversed parenting. All described pathology in their parents. A current problem with an attachment figure (or difficulty making affectional bonds) precipitated treatment. In addition, these women felt social pressure to appear independent, and were unable to resolve this demand with their desire for secure attachment. Treatment with Lizzy and Cheryl was shorter than with Megan, but a connection was established with all three that led to relief of their distress and greater awareness of their attachment needs and feelings. The women were helped to understand that feelings of anxious attachment are basically an adaptive response to a signal of danger: separation, threat of separation, or unreliability in attachment relationships. On examining their experiences, with the support and confirmation of the therapist, the women began to reconstruct their working models of relationships, as well as their attitudes about deserving affection and care, and were able to let go of agoraphobic behavior.

The approach of the therapist was to be reasonably available (that is, to accept phone calls between sessions), but generally just having the confidence that the therapist could be relied upon if needed was enough to reduce the client's anxiety or panic. Cheryl did not call before taking the plane trip, but she had conveyed to her therapist that she knew she could call without being seen as childish or overdependent.

A secure therapeutic bond is central to providing the conditions for this confidence and also for retrieving memories and reworking inner working models both of attachment figures and self to correspond more closely to current experience (Bretherton et al. 1990, Osofsky 1988). Freud (1919) noted that attachment to the therapist is used to encourage the agoraphobic patient to venture forth, with the knowledge that there is a base upon which to rely. It is the feeling of safety in therapy that frees the patient to explore both her inner and outer worlds, and it takes time for a trusted attachment to develop and to change long-standing patterns of behavior. Sanville (1991) cautions that when sessions are limited in number, such as we see occurring under the HMO pressures for cost-effective services, the nature of the therapeutic experience will change. She also cites a type of therapist, one who is directive and gives advice, as reinforcing the premise that answers lie outside the person. It follows that cognitive-behavioral and/or medication treatments, because they are time limited, structured, and do not deal with the complexity of underlying dynamics, are particularly ineffective with anxious attachment, where a primary goal is to help individuals develop a feeling of enduring attachment as they learn to take charge of their lives.

Two symptoms that are especially important in treating agoraphobia are fear of being alone and fear of strange places. A frequent complaint of agoraphobic patients is that they feel childish and overdependent because of their fear of being alone in strange situations or even in a setting such as a supermarket, which common sense says is not dangerous. When it is recognized how the presence of a trusted companion reduces anxiety, especially under strange conditions, one can appreciate that the absence of such security may increase fear. If an individual feels an attachment figure cannot be counted on for emotional support or actual help, he is more prone to be afraid when conditions are strange or frightening than if he confidently knew there were others on whom he could depend. Moreover, when parents have prohibited their children from appraising parental behavior accurately, it is more likely that the children will omit, suppress, or falsify painful experiences (Bowlby 1973). For instance, a mother might have reinforced a child's fear of leaving home and going to school, rather than acknowledging that the mother herself had elicited anxiety by threatening to desert the family or behaving cruelly to the child.

Therapists may have to probe for these recollections and connections because clients may not realize their significance and think to mention them. To accomplish this, therapists need to be informed of the range of separation experiences that could be engendering their clients' anxious attachment and know that these painful memories may be concealed from conscious awareness. In a systematic study of thirty-one agoraphobic patients, Liotti (1991) found that patients were helped as they became more aware of the childhood experiences that may have been a factor in the development of their fear behavior patterns.

Besides uncovering and reviewing actual events, early attachment experiences surface in treatment, reenacted in the transference (Casement 1991), and furnish an opportunity to explore working models and defensive distortions in order to understand the events and memories that may be related to anxious attachment. Sanville (1994) points out, however, that patients organize their external experience into their particular "psychic reality." She questions whether attachment theory's emphasis on real experiences pushes us to look for a definitive cause of disorder that we can never actually know. As she perceives experience, it is intermediate between external reality and psychic constructions; thus, working models represent the client's perceptions of events, mediated by an internal process traditionally called fantasy. However, Fox and

Card (1999) suggest that there could be an affective core to memories that reflects security or insecurity, and that would set the tone of the reconstructions of earlier experiences. Such affective charge would also influence behavior even if particular past events, such as a parent threatening abandonment, are not accessible to conscious recall.

ANXIOUS ATTACHMENT AND WOMEN

Attempts to explain why more women than men are diagnosed as agoraphobic remain controversial. Reasons given for the higher incidence of agoraphobia among women range from biological and cultural factors to how the condition is defined and reported. Dumont (1991), for example, posits that fear and worry are women's legacies from the eras of hunting and gathering, where an error could result in toxic death for an entire tribe. Others have suggested that men are taught to be tough and to master their fears, whereas women are socialized to be "helpless" and "dependent" and are also allowed to say they feel afraid and to withdraw from frightening situations (Barlow 1988, Fodor 1974, Wolfe 1984). It seems pertinent that the condition is usually precipitated by disruption of a key relationship (Ballenger 1989, Liotti 1991, Ternan et al. 1984, Wolfe 1984), a connection that points to the interpersonal nature of the disorder. Gilligan (1982) has addressed the difficulties created for women when society fails to acknowledge the significance of emotional and social well-being in their relationships. It is possible that cultural biases about their sex pressure women to exclude attachment feelings and behave with an uncomfortable independence. Furthermore, society may also be forcing women to minimize the value they put on their home base (Gelfond

1991), with the result that some attachment behaviors are attributed to a clinical syndrome of agoraphobia. That attachment behavior is adaptive is evident in the transient, agoraphobic-type fears that occur at times of stress, such as hospitalization or bereavement (Holmes 1982). I know of several women who had fears of leaving home for a period of time after their husbands were killed in airplane crashes. As I will explain later in Chapter 11, "Pets and Attachment," this activation of the attachment behavior system also occurs in animals. An example is reported by a veterinarian (Cardona, personal communication) that dogs cling more intensively to their owners when the pets have cancer.

There is some evidence that attachment behavior is more readily activated in female children (Liotti 1991). And, though modeling as well as cultural factors may influence behavior, girls are less encouraged to explore and generally know less about their surrounding environment (Fodor 1974, Gelfond 1991). Each of the women discussed in this chapter was told the outside world was dangerous and each had a parent who modeled fearful behavior. Parental behavior and injunctions, therefore, added to a natural inclination to feel afraid in certain situations, rather than providing a secure base that could diminish feelings of fear.

As the woman singing the song "On My Own" in *Les Misérables* knew, a person alone, on her own and without attachment, does not feel self-reliant and independent but instead rootless, isolated, and more easily frightened. The feelings and fears, however, are not due to a struggle to repress unacceptable sexual or aggressive drives as early theory suggested, but to a sense of being unprotected and vulnerable without a secure base of attachment. Self-reliance reflects a balance between attachment and exploratory behaviors, and is only possible when one has confidence in one's attachment figures, and knows that they are readily available and responsive should they be called upon. This tendency does not end with childhood, but "throughout life, being alone is a condition that either stimulates fear or greatly intensifies fear aroused in other ways. Concomitantly, being with a companion greatly reduces fear" (Bowlby 1973, p. 166). This statement also explains why the desire for secure attachment must not be construed as overdependency or secondary gain, and may enable us to better understand the higher incidence of agoraphobia in women. It is likely that society needs to change certain attitudes about relationships—in regard to men as well as women—and must further be organized to ensure its members stable and predictable affectional bonds in safe environments (Gelfond 1991, Marris 1991). For example, recognizing the importance of place to women has implications for dealing with events in their lives such as divorce or homelessness (Gelfond 1991). Throughout life, coping with separation is an inevitable challenge. But an ethological view of attachment accounts for the security that anyone, at any age, finds in affectional bonds. The following quotation (Lewis 1994) describes the way security of place enhances attachment. It shows there is a natural inclination to shorten a lengthy separation by beginning to feel an absence and a desire to regain contact. Also, it is noteworthy that it was written by a man: "I feel better when I am at home than when I am not at home; when I am away from home too long, my distress at not being there increases, as does my desire to be home" (p. 47).

As therapists, we needn't worry that we are making our patients overdependent when we convey that we are available at times of heightened stress and anxiety. Regardless of whether we label certain fears agoraphobia or simply anxious attachment, we are dealing with fear and anxiety induced by faulty attachment relationships in our patients' lives. This is not to say that frightening experiences, or hearing frightening stories, cannot also intensify natural fears. But even as we move to consider post-traumatic stress disorder in the next chapter, where breakdown in mental functioning can be directly related to a traumatic incident, the influence of affectional bonds should not be discounted or forgotten. As I found in both professional and informal discussions with individuals following the severe Northridge earthquake in California in 1994, people found it very significant, especially those closest to the terror of the epicenter, if they were alone, without the assurance of attachment, at the time the earthquake struck.

6
Trauma

Anyone can be exposed to a terrible life event that upsets psychobiological and social equilibrium, and stresses one's ability to cope with usual routines and relationships. Most people are distressed and suffer intrusive thoughts after an unbearable ordeal, but eventually affects and memories related to the incident will be accepted, worked through, and integrated into mental models. Their lives go on. In some victims, however, emotional wounds do not heal with time; the tyranny of the experience haunts the present, and they are unable to adjust to changed circumstances. Instead of modifying the meaning of the experience and making it part of the past, they go on to develop symptoms that meet the diagnostic criteria for the anxiety condition known as post-traumatic stress disorder (PTSD) (van der Kolk and McFarlane 1996).

Whether it is due to the improved understanding of the impact of real experiences, or to the devastation resulting from the proliferation of handguns, terrorism, and random brutality, the diagnostic assessment of post-traumatic stress disorder has increased, and clinicians are finding many of their patients are overwhelmed by symptoms related to trauma, either of recent occurrence or that took place years before. Although it has long been recognized that traumatic incidents such as military combat may lead to intense psychological distress, it was not until 1980, when the *Diagnostic and Statistical Manual of Mental Disorders* (*DSM-III*) (American Psychiatric Association 1980) made PTSD a specific diagnostic category, that it was given formal recognition. Listed as an anxiety disorder, PTSD refers to a cluster of symptoms that may follow "exposure to an extreme traumatic stressor . . . that involves . . . threatened death or serious injury (to one-self or others)" (American Psychiatric Association 1994, p. 424). These stressors consist of accidents, violent crimes, and disasters, as well as war experiences or historical incidents, such as concentration camp internment or loss or threatened loss of loved ones (American Psychiatric Association 1994, Barlow 1988, Davison and Neale 1990, Horowitz 1993, Janoff-Bulman 1985). The PTSD reactions are characterized by two basic responses: an emotional numbing or feeling of detachment from others, alternating with times when the trauma is relived or re-experienced, usually through recurrent, intrusive recollections or dreams. Additional symptoms may include sleep disturbances; irritability or outbursts of anger; difficulty concentrating; memory impairment; survivor guilt; elevated autonomic activity, such as exaggerated startle response or hyperalertness; and/or a domino effect, an intensification of symptoms when the individual is exposed to events that resemble or symbolize the traumatic incident (American Psychiatric Association 1994, Barlow 1988, Green et al. 1985, Janoff-Bulman 1985, van der Kolk and McFarlane 1996).

PTSD can be acute, chronic, or delayed and is known to occur in children as well as adolescents and adults (Durkin et al. 1993, Eth and Pynoos 1985, van der Kolk 1987, van der Kolk and McFarlane 1996). There is still a lack of consensus, however, as to whether the variety of stress-related responses represents a single clinical condition or whether it is necessarily an anxiety disorder (Barlow 1988, Davidson 1994, Varkas 1998). In support of a PTSD classification, van der Kolk (1987, 1994) claims that the response to uncontrollable and overwhelming life events, from war, concentration camp experiences, rape, and civilian disasters to child abuse and neglect, is remarkably consistent, even when controlling for the variables of age, type of trauma, community responsiveness, or predisposing personality. Moreover, evidence that these kinds of traumatic life events do affect individuals' identities and proneness to psychopathology has led to concern about the impact of certain experiences on mental health. In fact, it has been argued by van der Kolk (1987) that public consciousness and growing concern about child abuse and neglect have been instrumental in pointing out the influence of early mistreatment on adult disturbance, gradually shifting attention away from intrapsychic determinants of personality and distress, and toward perceiving etiology in terms of actual stressful experiences.

Likewise, attachment theory's emphasis on the impact of real events offers a distinctive theoretical perspective for understanding and treating PTSD. Conceptualized as a continuum of response related to preserving attachment; PTSD represents the exaggeration of a basic tendency of human nature—an attempt to ensure protection, security, and actual survival. Features such as anxiety and intrusive imagery are perceived as heightened attachment behaviors that are automatically evoked upon disruptions or trauma, while numbing and avoidance of others indicate an attempt to conserve effort and prevent being overwhelmed during the process. Treatment needs to help patients regain a feeling of safety in themselves and in their world, and can begin with the therapist providing a secure therapeutic relationship. Besides uncovering and reviewing memories, the meaning connected to them has to be explored, modified, and placed in its proper context.

It is also crucial to help individuals give words to frightening experiences, and to make sense of their sensations and emotions, or the intensity of their reactions could cause them to feel alone and crazy (Bowlby 1988a, Siegel 1995, van der Kolk and McFarlane 1996, Varkas 1998).

PTSD AND ATTACHMENT BEHAVIOR

Freud (1920, 1926) defined trauma in terms of the terror and helplessness felt by the ego when it is overwhelmed by an instinctual excitation that usurps its defensive functioning. According to van der Kolk (1987), the subjective feeling of helplessness and threat occurs when one loses the sense of a safe base within oneself or in relationships with others or lacks a place of retreat from which to deal with frightening experiences or emotions. The collapse of confidence that there is order and continuity in life leads to feelings that one's actions cannot control or influence what happens. Siegel (1995) adds that an experience can turn traumatic when the threat of injury or death to oneself or another is deliberately perpetuated by another human being or involves betrayal by someone who would normally be assumed to be trusted, for example, a parent. Other factors that may compound distress are the meaning assigned to the event, and the inability to escape from continued threat or harm. Casement (1994), interested in the influence of overwhelming emotions, defines psychological trauma as "that which can't be managed alone." In terms of attachment, the posttraumatic stress reaction is a response to the possibility that one could lose protection or even one's life. As a result, a surge of attachment behavior is called for, such as is typical in the protest stage of separation. Along with this are the aforementioned moments of numbing and avoidance that conserve affective and physical resources. The excessive anxiety of PTSD may reflect a heightened tendency to attachment behavior, an intensified effort to preserve or restore attachment. As Bowlby (1980) writes,

> Since the goal of attachment behavior is to maintain an affectional bond, any situation that seems to be endangering the bond elicits action designed to preserve it; and the greater the danger of loss appears to be the more intense and varied are the actions elicited to prevent it. In such circumstances all the most powerful forms of attachment behavior become activated—clinging, crying and perhaps angry coercion. This . . . phase of protest [is] one of acute physiological stress and emotional distress. [p. 42]

PTSD may be one of the possible outcomes when responses to experiences such as threatened separation or sudden loss become distorted and dysfunctional, when defensive processes shut out painful feelings and perceptions beyond what would be adaptive. Using concepts from information processing, Bowlby (1980) perceives defenses as the methods individuals use to deal with thwarted needs for protection and security. Maneuvers such as the exclusion (repression) of attachment-related emotions and material result from aversive affectional experiences or threatening situations. Holmes (1993a) suggests two basic patterns to these strategies, one being an avoidance, where attachment feelings are suppressed and the person remains on an "emotional periphery of relationships" (p. 150), and the other an ambivalent defense, where the person clings and insists on whatever support is possible to obtain. When the strategy is avoidant, aggression and anger are defensively excluded and/or redirected to other sources, whereas with ambivalence exploration is held back. PTSD's combination of symptoms may be equivalent to those that fluctuate throughout the stages of separation responses—protest, despair, and detachment—and also include the physiological and emotional responses described in the delineation of grief and mourning, in particular numbing, followed by yearning and searching for whatever is lost. The interpersonal nature of the symptoms differs from the traditional view of defenses as intrapsychic (Holmes 1993a).

The circumstances that lower the threshold of attachment behavior can range from natural disasters to sudden frightening experiences, to the chronic stress of living in an abusing and/or neglectful home environment. For example, chronic PTSD in adults has been attributed to early child abuse and/or neglect (Fischer et al. 1997, van der Kolk 1987). Other potential stressors include fear of losing key attachment relationships or losing one's familiar, personal environment when, for example, a home is no longer a safe refuge due to a catastrophe such as an earthquake. A disaster may be seen as a sudden and unexpected situation that threatens separation of family members from each other. The more severe the disaster, the more serious the threat and the greater the chance of actual separation or loss. Moreover, the desire to remain close to family members will probably persist for days or weeks after the disaster is over (Bowlby 1973, Sable 1981).

Bowlby (1973) has noted the alarm experienced by people who are alone during a disaster, and the possibility of an intensification of basic fear responses. "Throughout life, being alone is a condition that either stimulates fear or greatly intensifies fear aroused in other ways" (p. 166).

Citing research findings on a tornado that struck a town in Mississippi in 1953 and the Los Angeles earthquake of 1971, Bowlby states that the presence of companions at times such as these is reassuring and reduces fear, even if the companion cannot really do anything. Viewed ethologically, being alone and apart from someone with whom one has an affectional bond might not actually prove to be dangerous, but being isolated and alone, especially if conditions are strange and alarming, does increase the risk of danger and harm. Bowlby (1982) has identified these conditions as part of the group of natural clues that signal an increase in the risk to biological survival. In addition to strangeness and isolation, these natural fears include darkness, sudden movement or sound, or looming objects. Separation from an attachment figure is also a natural clue of possible danger and compels some type of action in an effort to attain protection. Because these responses are adaptive, it is misleading to label them as regressive or immature.

There are several reasons theory has tended to overlook this built-in, adaptive fear of being alone. Besides the fact that this fear occurs in combination with other natural clues, our culture's attitudes toward independence often make a desire for closeness and comfort difficult to admit; it may only show when situations are acute (Bowlby 1973). During the aftermath of a severe Los Angeles earthquake (January 1994), I noticed that the first comment people made, when they had been alone during the quake, was to state that this had been the case. They clearly recognized that they felt an absence of others and seemed to be implying that this increased their feelings of vulnerability.

Besides expressions of the fear felt at being alone at the moment of the earthquake, many expressed lingering fears of being alone, for example, being on a different floor of the house than other family members, or going into their homes alone. Afterward, everyone seemed to be staying closer to home. Streets were less traveled. Absenteeism at work increased. Activities were curtailed, and there were fears of entering parking structures or going to shopping centers because some had been severely damaged and had become the media's prominent images of earthquake damage. The severity of the earthquake, therefore, compounded the natural clue of separation and also evoked an array of separation and loss responses.

The first descriptions after the earthquake were of feeling "numb," "spacy," "dazed," or "disoriented." One seriously injured man reported that the emergency hospital administered to him immediately but that no one had ever asked his name, possibly showing the confusion and numbness of hospital personnel. There were complaints about the inability to concentrate, and sleeping difficulties. Some people had earthquake-related dreams. Others woke up at the same time every night; one, for instance, woke at a time that corresponded to an hour before the earthquake had struck. Others were afraid to sleep in the dark, or to continue sleeping alone, and made arrangements to stay with friends or family at night. Some wanted pets in their beds, stating that this made them feel safer. One puzzled, "Who's being protected, the cat or me?"

Throughout the first weeks, aftershocks brought fresh terror and apprehension. From my observations, there was a connection between geographic location and subsequent distress. Two families in the Valley area, which was the hardest hit, felt that the area was being attacked by enemy forces. One of these family members thought that her house was going to "turn over." These people remained "jumpy," reacting to minor noises (a truck, an airplane, a barking dog) ignored by others, and took precautions such as placing tennis shoes under their bed and keeping flashlights, clothes, and money nearby. One person considered relocating to another state.

An evolutionary approach explains the adaptiveness of both emotional numbing and distress (such as difficulty sleeping) in terms of protection and survival. Bowlby (1980) describes the usefulness of numbing in bereavement as providing a way to allow the reality of devastating loss to be slowly integrated into working models. Without this kind of protective shield, individuals could be overwhelmed by affects, which would seriously threaten their ability to process information or cope without becoming physically and emotionally exhausted (Schore 1994). In Los Angeles in 1994, the local media reported that several people who died of cardiac arrest at the time of the earthquake may have been scared to death, which suggests there may have been insufficient numbing, coupled with defenses inadequate to diminish the potential of lethal terror. Similarly, not sleeping can be adaptive, keeping one alert and ready to move if necessary. Frequent review and discussion of the event, or the occurrence of persistent intrusive thoughts about it, may reflect an attempt to put the experience into some meaningful context or a yearning and searching to restore what is lost.

Ethological principles can also be applied to understanding the spectrum of responses to trauma when these persist for at least one month and become PTSD. There is now evidence that stressful situations such as separation can alter heart rates, sleep patterns and body temperature of both human and animal infants, and these responses can have long-term effects on the ability to modulate anxiety and aggression (Gabbard 1992, Krystal 1990, van der Kolk 1987, 1994). Schore (1994) explains that a young child internalizes the caregiver's regulatory function, which in turn "indelibly influences the evolution of brain structures responsible for [affect regulation] . . . for [the] rest of the life span" (p. 540). An attuned parent generates sufficient levels of positive feeling to induce the development and organization of a psychic structure that is capable of adaptive socioemotional functioning. In contrast to optimal conditions, childhood experiences of trauma or misattuned affective interactions are associated with insecure attachment, dysregulation, and inhibition of cortical processing of memories. Such misregulations are stored in permanent unconscious memory, interfering with the organization of psychic structure and affect regulation, thus impairing the capacity to regulate heightened levels of anger and distress. Persons with such experience are more susceptible to anxiety and emotional disturbance at the time of later trauma.

Within the Bowlbyan framework, someone whose attachment behavior is constantly primed is described as anxiously or insecurely attached. It is possible that these individuals are more prone to PTSD but, as with any psychological disturbance, it is not clear why some individuals develop PTSD in the course of time after trauma while others do not. However, for those who do, rather than the usual lessening of fear and despair, there is a complicated, disordered outcome (Barlow 1988, Horowitz 1993, van der Kolk 1987). Reasons given for the outcome include the circumstances and severity of the stressor, age, prior traumatization, social support, current and past experiences with others, and the working models the individual brings to the incident (Boman 1986, Bowlby 1980, Holmes 1993a, van der Kolk 1987). When the trauma is great, when the person is closer to the impact zone, when there is injury to oneself or injury or death to loved ones, there is greater likelihood of pathological adjustment (Bowlby 1973, Raphael and Wilson 1993, van der Kolk 1987).

Holmes (1993a) lists three distinct but interrelated instances where attachment difficulties could influence emotional dysfunction: when a bond is broken or disrupted, when inner working models of attachment are such that there is more vulnerability to stress, or when individuals' perception of the reliability of relationships makes them more vulnerable to breakdown in the face of adversity. Holmes cites the relation between spousal bereavement and actual death of the surviving spouse in the year following loss as an example of one of these factors affecting adjustment to a stressful life experience.

Treatment for traumatized individuals involves reviewing current and past experiences, as well as the trauma itself, in order to help the person make sense of the event and put together a scenario of how it happened. For resolving crisis states, the provision of a safe setting, with a trusted therapist, is fundamental. Persons who have been emotionally hurt by trauma, or betrayed by those with whom they should feel the most protected, must first feel they have a secure base of empathy, support, and understanding if they are going to marshal the courage to process distressing events and readjust their working models to accommodate changed circumstances.

TREATMENT FOR TRAUMA

What distinguishes those who develop PTSD from those who do not is an inability to resolve the trauma, but instead their tendency to organize their lives around avoiding its painful reminders and affects. Since the past cannot be undone, the goal of therapy is to help clients confront the memories they are reluctant to face, and to help them reconstruct the events in a meaningful way (van der Kolk et al. 1996). Although the PTSD literature talks about reliving a traumatic event, Marris (personal communication) points out that most people do not want to go through the experience again, but rather want to explain it. The therapist helps the client examine and reflect on the experience and its internal repercussions, including the retrieval of details of the trauma that until now have been unavailable. Together they assemble emotions and perceptions of the past, forming a narrative of the client's condition in the present (Holmes 1993a, Siegel 1995).

Siegel (1995) defines narrative as "the telling of a series of events" (p. 100). Such a narrative is constructed out of interpersonal experience and requires the ability to retrieve memories that have already been encoded and stored in the mind and brain. Cognitive research has shown that trauma can disrupt the encoding and storage of information, inhibiting and distorting later recollection and the coherence of narrative. For example, a person may focus on a limited portion of a traumatic situation or something in the environment that was not directly threatening or related to the event. Although this reduces the risk of emotional flooding during the time of the trauma, memory processing, as well as later access to information about the event, is impaired and disjointed; the trauma itself and its emotional effects are left in limbo, disconnected from the usual complex associations of experience.

When a therapist helps a traumatized patient organize a personal history, the patient's inhibitions in the ability to tell a coherent story are revealed by the way memories are recalled and also by the expression of affects. The facts of an event may be remembered and recounted, but the sense of time may be absent, or certain interpersonal details and emotions missing. There may be intrusive memories and/or feelings of depersonalization. However, now the therapist is present to assist in processing events and feelings. Siegel (1995) warns that if affects and sensations are retrieved without emotional and cognitive processing of dissociated memories, the person may feel the trauma is happening "all over again." The process of resolution includes desensitization, self-reflection, and the formation of a coherent narrative that gives psychological meaning to having been abused or made to feel helpless. Being able to reflect on experiences, along with an abreaction that brings disparate pieces of memory together, puts the painful event in the past instead of its being mistaken for happening in the present, such as occurs in a flashback. As Siegel (1995) writes, "the symptoms of unresolved trauma are themselves traumatizing" (p. 117) until they are clarified and controlled.

Schore's (1994) contribution on affect regulation adds to an understanding of the therapist's role in resolving trauma and consolidating narrative. The establishment of an affective attachment bond describes a working alliance in which the therapist is attuned to the patient's internal states, and verbally expresses interventions that regulate affect and induce comfort. The shared affective experience with a trusted therapist is indispensable for counteracting traumatic events, learning to tolerate painful memories, and regulating emotional reactions to them. Schore has described how treatment actually rewires the connections of the right frontolimbic cortex of the brain, replacing toxic representations with more benign ones.

The application of attachment concepts to the therapeutic work of a shared narrative has several notable features. One is the belief that the internal world is primarily shaped by the effects of real experiences rather than fantasy. Bowlby (1991) asserts that when we speculate with clients about their feelings and the meaning given to actual events as they have been processed through and woven into working models, we are trying out various hypotheses. Thus, an event such as an earthquake happens in the outer world, but is construed and dealt with according to the mental structures the client brought to it. Moreover, attachment theory emphasizes that these formulations of experiences are constructed from clients' own histories and must be seen in this context; otherwise, clients may feel misunderstood and discounted as they have in previous relationships. Pynoos (1994) points out how complicated it can be to dissect the interaction between personal meaning and external reality. Because an experience sets in motion a continuum of responses, numerous emotions and memories are connected and must be pieced together to understand how reactions originated and developed. It is important that responses be affirmed as they are discovered and recovered. Pynoos (1994) reports that the symptoms of trauma victims improve when a perpetrator is arrested and/or sentenced. This societal confirmation of the reality of the experience could be a significant validation for the victim.

An example of validation on a personal level was evident in the film *Good Will Hunting* (1997), when the therapist kept repeating to the patient who had been abused in childhood that it was not his fault. Although portrayed with the Hollywood flair of an instantaneous breakthrough, the scene showed how the affirmation of the injustice the patient had been subjected to was more important than any interpretation that the therapist could have made at that moment. The phrase was insightful because it reminded the young man that mistreatment had been done to him;

it was something over which he had had no control and for which he was not to be blamed. Acknowledging the impact of an event, either at a societal or personal level, helps clients feel that they have been heard and that their feelings are justified, and this affirmation is more crucial than making interpretations (Bowlby 1988a). Listening to details of some experiences may not be easy; the therapist may have to hear some pretty gruesome facts, and resist the temptation to discourage what may feel like too much abreaction.

Another feature of attachment appears in Bowlby's (1991) suggestion that what clinicians call empathy is frequently the offering of sympathy for reports of unfortunate life experiences. Finally, it is recognized and conveyed that although they may be unusually intense, emotions such as protest, anxiety, and anger are basic human responses to threatened separation or loss and are not indications of overdependency. Bowlby's (1973) distinction between attachment and dependency respects the natural desire for relationship without the negative connotations of dependency (Bowlby 1973, Golden 1990, Hamilton 1985, Sable 1989, 1994a). The therapist fulfills an inherent need for attachment, a concept compatible with Kohut's (1977) concept of providing an empathetic selfobject. If the therapist conveys that the desire for comfort and reassurance is somehow childish or a symptom of overdependency, not only may clients feel that they should have outgrown the need for others, they may feel the therapist will not sympathize with them and that the therapeutic situation will only repeat the way they have been unsupported in the past.

Helping clients understand the natural inclination for attachment behavior to be evoked at times of stress is part of the therapeutic process (Bowlby 1973, Sable 1991a,

1992a). Not only do therapists encourage expression of feelings, but they tolerate them as family members may not have (Casement 1991, Winnicott 1965). If they were once told to inhibit emotions or suspicions of family secrets, patients may have defensively excluded memories and feelings from awareness. PTSD is itself often a secret stigma (Pynoos 1994). Clients may further falsify, omit and suppress information based on family messages (Bowlby 1973).

Techniques specific to dealing with disasters include helping the person confront what has happened and express feelings associated with the event. As feelings are connected to the stressors that elicited them, including what may have been said in the past to distort reaction to subsequent trauma, working models can be reappraised and reconstructed. Treatment can be short- or long-term, depending on the time it takes to process information and rearrange models; it will take longer when the event is major, sudden, or unwanted (Bowlby 1980, Horowitz 1993).

ALEXIS

It may also take time for experiences of trauma to surface. Presenting complaints of PTSD range from anxiety and depression, substance abuse, physical health problems, and disordered grief to difficulties in work or personal relationships (Raphael and Wilson 1993). Unless the client has experienced the trauma recently, the extent of its effects may not be evident.

This was the situation with Alexis (Sable 1994b, 1995), a tense, pale woman in her late forties whose presenting complaints did not suggest or reveal a PTSD condition until local events, which did not affect her directly, turned into a crisis. As I look back, I find Alexis sought treatment in the period before the second Rodney King verdict was to be announced in Los Angeles, a time when tension was building throughout the city. At the time, she expressed concern about recent crying spells that seemed to occur abruptly and over which she felt no control, and an overreaction to the demands or misfortunes of others, even strangers. The death of a casual acquaintance from heart disease had upset her and even caused her to wonder if she might have done something to prevent the sudden loss. Alexis was also concerned over outbursts of anger toward her husband, Andrew, for seemingly minor incidents, such as a disagreement over a television program. She complained that Andrew had been "imposing" on her, delegating chores that would pile up; Alexis felt she hardly had time to get them done. Instead of telling him that she was angry, she tried to "contain" herself so he would not be "overwhelmed by [her] negative mood" and so she would not lose him, a possibility that seemed quite real since their relationship had grown more distant over several years. Having few friends and long-standing troublesome relationships with others, Alexis felt that Andrew was the only person on whom she could rely. She attributed her inability to get along in interpersonal relationships to her tendency to "take over" and tell everyone what to do. Besides being easily frustrated by the performance of others, she found it hard to ask for help or accept suggestions.

Alexis's determination to be self-sufficient could be traced to the expectations placed on her in her family of origin. She was the second oldest of five children, and both of her parents were alcoholic, frequently unfit and unavailable to their children. At these times, Alexis was made responsible for the care of her siblings and would be severely reprimanded for mistakes that were beyond the comprehension of a young child. An incident of significance occurred in a motel room, when trying to care for a younger sibling while her parents were deep in a drunken sleep. Her father's response, when Alexis later proudly related having called room service for food, was to criticize his daughter for failing to give a tip. Another time she was blamed for a sibling's serious injury even though a parent was present. When she was in her twenties, her mother developed cancer. Alexis returned to her family, and assumed primary care for her mother until she died. She continued to reproach herself for not being able to save her mother.

As a result of these kinds of expectations, Alexis came to question herself in difficult situations, wondering "What did I do wrong?" By the time she completed college, she was drinking heavily and, once married to Andrew, one of the few men she ever dated, they both became alcoholic. It was only years later, when she was being fired from a managerial position and where counseling was recommended, that Alexis acknowledged her alcoholism. She and Andrew subsequently stopped drinking. She equated her inability to "turn off" her drinking to her not being able to turn off her tears.

Neither Alexis nor Andrew wanted children. Their social life was limited, with Alexis devoting most of her time to a small business venture, where she could "be [her] own boss." However, her difficulties with others, including an unwillingness to ask for help, were proving to be roadblocks to success.

WORKING MODELS OF INSISTENT SELF-RELIANCE AND TRAUMA

It appears that Alexis grew up feeling responsible for the well-being of others. She also had the need to keep her own attachment feelings and behavior defensively excluded from awareness or activation. Due to their own inadequacies, Alexis's parents reversed caregiving responsibilities, pressuring their daughter to feel responsible for others; they also belittled and humiliated her with criticisms and a demeaning nickname that her siblings continued to call her on the rare occasions she had contact with any of them. She proclaimed a self-sufficiency that diverted attention away from her attachment strivings and from asking for affection or occasional assistance for herself.

Bowlby (1977, 1980) describes the personality pattern of individuals who act as if they do not want or need the consideration or protection of others as compulsively self-reliant. This proclamation of independence, or insistent self-reliance (Sable 1991a) hides an underlying yearning for love and care, as well as anger and frustration for not having received it. As shown by research, this is one of the insecure attachment styles where an individual's coping is likely to crumble under excessive stress (Mikulincer and Florian 1998).

Alexis's assertion of self-reliance, together with symptoms of tenseness, short temper, difficulty sleeping, outbursts of tears, and a history of alcoholism and depression can be a sign of post-traumatic stress disorder, but these can also be indications of delayed or suppressed grief, as for a loss that was never fully resolved (Bowlby 1980, Lindemann 1944). Although she described herself as sad and depressed, Alexis thought she had recovered from and was unaffected by the loss of her mother, and expressed confusion and surprise at her preoccupation with her mother now that she was in therapy.

With her working models of unavailable and unresponsive attachments, along with expectations of rejection or punishment, Alexis could neither acknowledge any disappointment in her mother nor grieve her loss. Several current events then converged with these cognitive biases to produce Alexis's anxiety and depression: she was approaching the age that her mother was when she had become terminally ill, and she felt less secure in her marriage and unsuccessful in career pursuits.

The strenuous attempt to maintain her self-reliance was further shattered when the second Rodney King verdict was about to be announced in Los Angeles at a time during which her husband was out of town. Alexis noticed a return of her crying spells, which had begun to diminish, great apprehension and fear of being alone, and difficulty sleeping or concentrating. One day she started to recount two extremely dangerous and frightening incidents in her adult life, both of which had occurred in foreign countries, where non-English-speaking soldiers held guns to her head. As she recalled the episodes, she cried uncontrollably, sobbing that, in both instances, she feared she was going to die. However, she had never told anyone of her terror and had never discussed the events.

After this dramatic session, Alexis began to deal with other past experiences. Bottled-up memories and feelings surfaced, such as guilt over not being able to keep her mother alive, and Alexis was able to finally grieve her loss. An example of handling disparities in a patient's working models was the therapist's suggestion to Alexis that for parents to impose parental demands could feel like a tremendous burden to a young child. This illustrates how the common tendency for traumatized individuals to blame themselves is instead based on parents' treatment and perceptions that the child is at fault. The therapist's comment was also sympathetic, intended to show that Alexis would receive acceptance and support in the therapeutic relationship. It is also helpful for the therapist to point out that parents distort information because of their own difficulties. In such instances, therapeutic awareness is best directed not to a condemnation of the parents, but toward understanding the patient (Bowlby 1973). When Alexis examined her argumentative tendencies, she decided that her family's injunctions had permitted her no opportunity for seeking support. Not knowing where leadership should begin and end, she assumed full charge, which estranged others from her. She stated, "Before, I used to ask myself what did I do wrong. Now, I say, What help didn't I get?" Alexis was eventually able to be more open with Andrew and to realize she misconstrued some of his behavior based on her fear of loss or expectations of being rejected and/or treated badly. Their relationship improved, as did her work situation. Dealing with traumatic incidents, as well as family experiences that may have undermined secure attachment, was vital to helping Alexis understand her current feelings and distress. This also relieved the effects of the frightening events she had carried secretly and silently for years and which she had not previously realized had continued to impact on her behavior.

ATTACHMENT THEORY AND POST-TRAUMATIC STRESS DISORDER

Using an ethological-evolutionary framework of attachment, it is proposed that post-traumatic stress symptoms can be conceived of as intensified attachment behaviors that are elicited at the time of separation, threat of separation, or loss of people or places that represent safety and survival. The anxiety of PTSD is perceived as a type of separation anxiety in which fear and anxiety are so intense that attachment behavior is urgent and demanding. Holmes (1993a) has compared attachment behavior to an invisible pull, not unlike the force of gravity, which motivates movement toward or away from a secure base. This force depends on conditions of the moment, such as the location of an attachment figure. When security is shaken by separation or loss, or threat of separation, responses of alarm and anxiety are elicited. These responses are intrinsic to human nature and essential for forming and maintaining affectional bonds, especially in the face of danger. Thus, separation anxiety can vary in degree from a response that is healthy to one that is maladaptive.

Raphael and Wilson (1993) divide disasters into personal traumas and community traumas. When elicited suddenly and without warning, such as during natural disasters or crimes, the urge for protection is particularly fierce. However, regardless of the cause, the underlying dynamic is the same: people want safety and protection and the care and comfort of attachment figures when there is a feeling of apprehension or uneasiness. There is significant survival value in responding to possible life-threatening events, and current thinking seems to agree that PTSD symptoms are similar regardless of the trauma (see van der Kolk 1987, Weisaeth and Ettinger 1993). Similarly, lengthy avoidance and withdrawal from others might also be related to protection, with affective detachment a defense against the hurtfulness of past rejection or inadequate support. In this scenario, owing to adverse experiences, attachment behaviors are defensively excluded from awareness, and the need for others is not acknowledged. In terms of the stages of response to separation—protest, despair, and detachment—an extended lack of emotional involvement could indicate more severe and/or prolonged mistreatment, possibly lengthy discontinuities of care, or physical or emotional abuse. The scars that chronic childhood mistreatment can leave are now well documented, but adults too can have ongoing stress and trauma that drastically alters and undermines their sense of security in the world. In fact, Herman (1992) suggests that the diagnostic formulations of PTSD do not do justice to the complexity of the symptoms or personality changes that can result from more recent repeated trauma. She claims that chronic abusive conditions, such as maltreatment of a romantic partner, can erode an adult's existing personality structure. Krystal (1978) noted the constriction of emotional sensations in Nazi concentration camp victims who surrendered to the helplessness and hopelessness of their situation. Even with an internal world more capable of sustaining comforting images or confidence of competent functioning than a child's, an adult's assumptions about her feelings of safety or the ability to control her life can unravel when traumatic experiences occur. There then develops a "frightening awareness" that security, trust, and hope are only illusions (Varkas 1998).

One major contribution of attachment theory that is particularly relevant to PTSD is the appreciation of the effect of real-life experiences, both current and past, on personality development and vulnerability to psychopathology. Because treatment for psychological distress evolved out of Freud's psychoanalytic approach, techniques for dealing with actual stressful incidents have lagged behind a focus on fantasy and the internal world (Bowlby 1988a). However, the continuum of response set in motion by loss or threat of separation or loss can be seen as a promising way to further explain reactions to trauma. Concerning the activation of attachment behavior in PTSD, the emotional numbing, which alternates with hypervigilance and activity, may be a conservation-withdrawal state, permitting expenditure of effort to reach attachments but also limiting psychological excitement or strenuous muscular behavior beyond what is adaptive (Schore 1994, van der Kolk 1994). Furthermore, if not only emotional well-being but survival as well is felt to be connected to the reliability of familiar attachments, PTSD might reflect the trauma of separation from, or loss of, a loved person or essential relationship. In support of this suggestion, Barlow (1988) writes that "severe grief reactions comprise a special instance of PTSD" (p. 530). The account of Alexis's treatment shows the link between attachment, grief, and PTSD. Insistent self-reliance, and also insistent caregiving, were her defensive maneuvers to avoid the disappointment that engagement with others had brought in the past; in her case, working models of unresolved grief and inaccessible attachment figures were finally overwhelmed by societal events.

Another contribution of attachment theory is the evidence it has provided on resiliency and adjustment to trauma. Early secure bonds are a primary defense against development of vulnerability, and thus offer protection from responses to trauma turning into psychopathology. Secure attachment acts as a protective factor, promoting resilience and the ability to recover from or adjust to sudden misfortune or chronic life stress. Conversely, individuals with childhood histories of abuse or severe neglect have a poorer prognosis than those who had more secure bonds as children. Early disruptions of attachment reduce the individual's long-term ability to cope with stress, or to modulate physiological states of arousal. For example, a child may constrict her emotional responses at the time of trauma, a response which, though adaptive to the crisis at hand, may spill over into other realms of development. This kind of spillover, resulting in a generalized numbing, may explain the PTSD symptoms seen in children who witness domestic violence (Logan and Graham-Bermann 1999). Furthermore, acknowledging and dealing with the early traumas of attachment have been shown to affect therapeutic outcome (Osofsky et al. 1993, van der Kolk et al. 1996).

Bowlby (1980) writes that we may never completely get over a major loss. Thus, therapists need to find out about and pay attention to the influence of past traumas on current problems. The poignant statement made by Elie Wiesel (1995), the Nobel Prize–winning author and concentration camp survivor, when he visited Auschwitz on the fiftieth anniversary of its liberation, attests to the abiding effects of trauma: "As I walk to the gate, I have the same fear as I had fifty years ago. It is in me. It is still the same fear." Recently, in television interviews of people injured in the 1994 San Francisco earthquake (*Prime Time*, February 24, 1999), those affected said they were not yet over the trauma. They still had many fears generally related to the circumstances of their experience. The Northridge earthquake in Los Angeles united the community and provided much opportunity to share feelings and receive the social support of others, factors known to reduce the stress in crises (Raphael and Wilson 1993). At the same time, there was an unprecedented demand for mental health counseling services in Los Angeles County, which suggests the seriousness of risk of psychological distress.

Although it is now known that a substantial proportion of individuals exposed to extreme stress become symptomatic, post-traumatic stress disorder is still a new and not yet clear-cut category of psychopathology. More research is needed to clarify what constitutes a stressor and how to improve our therapeutic techniques. We now know that dissociation at the moment of the incident seems to predict PTSD (van der Kolk 1997). We also know responses to trauma can become chronic and impair affect regulation and interpersonal functioning for many years; yet on the other hand, we know that not everyone exposed to a disruptive event develops PTSD. Also, we do not fully understand the tendency of traumatized individuals to re-expose themselves to situations that are reminiscent of the original event. Nor are our training and skills for working with real experiences fully developed. For example, it is unclear at what rate a person can best deal with the events of a past trauma, though we know that premature exploration of the past can exacerbate symptoms. Perhaps the current trend of rushing mental health

personnel to the scene of a disaster may not be particularly useful and may even be detrimental. In the immediate aftermath of trauma, there is need for action to establish safety and predictability. To force abreaction could
threaten such emergency defenses as numbing, which
protect the person from being overwhelmed by an awful
experience (Baum et al. 1993, Green 1993, Raphael and
Wilson 1993, van der Kolk et al. 1996).

Van der Kolk and colleagues (1996, 1997) question
whether traditional therapy alone can psychologically
process the biological changes that result from trauma.
They explain that advances in research on the biology of
PTSD confirm the existence of dysregulation on physiologic, neurohormonal, and immunologic levels. Also,
neuroimaging studies of patients with PTSD are documenting structural and functional abnormalities in the
ability of the brain to filter and process information. In
particular, these authors note that trauma is registered in
the right hemisphere of the brain, the hemisphere that
regulates the autonomic and hormonal responses to emotional stimuli. In contrast, the left hemisphere manipu-
lates words and images, and puts information into categories of meaning. At moments of high arousal such as
trauma, activity in the left hemisphere decreases, curtail-
ing the ability to analyze the situation or give words to
it. From an ethological standpoint, this promotes survival
at the time of trauma because an immediate emotional
response to danger provokes lifesaving reactions of fight
or flight. However, in the disorder of PTSD, heightened
emotional arousal is continuous, and the part of the central nervous system responsible for categorizing experience and generating sequences does not function properly.
This malfunction affects the capacity to process subsequent information. For example, a sensory cue such as a

sudden loud noise, now dissociated from the traumatizing event, can make victims feel as if the trauma has returned, and that they are being traumatized all over again. Although van der Kolk and colleagues acknowledge that it is necessary to identify the triggers and connect words to the somatic experience, they feel that individuals experiencing PTSD are unable to understand the situation, and can neither communicate the emotions they are experiencing nor take the steps necessary to deal with what is happening. Van der Kolk alleges this circumstance may have therapeutic implications and that we need further investigation to elucidate the degree to which putting traumatic experience into words can reverse actual biological changes.

Attachment theory suggests directions for both research and therapy with patients suffering from PTSD. The Adult Attachment Interview (AAI) has shown that it is not trauma per se but its resolution that seems to be associated with insecure patterns of attachment. This suggests the significance that reviewing and restructuring the meaning of events in treatment can have on overcoming the effects of trauma (Fonagy et al. 1996). After the Northridge earthquake, I noticed how often I applied the theory to reassure individuals and explain that anxiety such as fear of being alone was natural and adaptive. This application respects clients' feelings, reduces self-blame, and gives them the freedom to further express their concerns and fears without compounding the alarm they feel. Further implications of the approach include helping individuals in a variety of situations, such as dealing with the pain of separation anxiety in immigration, or in treating the PTSD exhibited by children who are exposed to violence (see Pynoos and Nader 1993). Another implication of the theory is its understanding that a therapeutic bond, within which the experience of trauma is shared, promotes feelings of safety and security.

Marris (1982) writes that our main affectional bonds provide a "structure of meaning" upon which we plan our lives and find significance. When we lose attachment, or experience a threat of losing it, we feel distress and anxiety and try to restore balance and security. The present increased attention to the concept of trauma and to the diagnostic category of PTSD may reflect the growing uneasiness, uncertainty, and violence in our society. If we can better understand the depth of our attachment needs, and the way traumas of relationship experiences impact on a basic human desire for security, we may be better able improve our ability to help clients who are dealing with frightening or distressing life experiences.

7

Loss, Grief, and Mourning

In the previous chapter on trauma, it was pointed out that the loss of a central attachment figure can be one of the most traumatic events any person can have to endure. Anyone who has lost a cherished relationship knows the wrenching and unrelenting pain of loss, especially when it is irreversible. Permanent loss can be excruciating, unleashing an emotional upheaval of grief and mourning that lasts some period of time, and that can feel absolutely unbearable. The process is characterized by intense and fluctuating feelings that range from fear, anxiety, and anger to sadness and loneliness. There may be difficulty coping with even everyday activities. Not only is grief painful to experience, it can also be hard to witness. There seems to be so little someone else can do to bring comfort and relief since the only thing bereaved persons want is what they cannot have—the lost attachment returned. Any efforts short of accomplishing this impossible task are therefore bound to be seen as off-target, basically unwanted and unappreciated (Bowlby 1980).

According to attachment theory, the bonds we form with main affectional figures are felt to be unique, irreplaceable, and essential to both social and emotional well-being. Adult attachment is considered a product of an attachment behavioral system that began to develop in childhood, with a primary caregiver, and later with other close persons. Though modified by age and experience, and directed to new relations such as romantic and sexual partners, adult attachment remains crucial to maintaining security and a sense of meaning throughout life. Thus, there are sound biological reasons for attempting to recover attachment figures if they are missing, and there is almost an automatic expectation that with effort recovery is possible. The breaking of a bond, for instance, through divorce or when a spouse dies, will set the process of grief and mourning in motion, but where traditional theory saw the function of grief as a deliberate detachment of feeling and connection, Bowlby contends that it is really just the opposite. There is, instead, a strenuous effort, especially in the first stages, to do everything possible to retrieve attachment and only gradually and reluctantly is this effort eventually given up. Like the early attachments on which they are patterned, adult bonds form slowly, with proximity and interaction, and only dissolve gradually as ties weaken and undergo change (Ainsworth 1982, Marris 1982, Weiss 1975).

The capacity to resist giving up or replacing attachment is part of what makes the mourning process so intense and painful and also liable to give rise to both psychological and physical disturbance. It has been estimated that up to one-third of bereaved individuals need professional help (Sanders 1988) and Bowlby (1980) asserts that some of the anxiety and depression, as well as the personality disorders seen in clinical practice, may be an expression of mourning that has become pathological.

This chapter applies concepts of attachment to understanding and treating the processes of grief and mourning when they take a maladaptive course. The discussion begins with a brief look at the development of theories on loss and pathological grief, followed by an attachment perspective on understanding and treating disordered outcomes. Two clinical examples illustrate treatment.

The first, Mary (see Sable 1992b), examines spousal loss; and the second, Elizabeth, demonstrates how childhood loss can be a significant dynamic in an adult client's depression and difficulty in relationships. Following Lindemann's (1944) position, Bowlby conceived pathological mourning on a continuum, varying only in degree from that experienced in the normal process. Clinical manifestations include chronic mourning, with intensified and prolonged grief responses, or an absence of conscious grieving where mourning is avoided and inhibited. These disordered patterns reflect an interaction between the personality of the individual and certain circumstances of loss, such as the relationship to the lost figure, suddenness of death, or adequacy of social support. Treatment provides a person with whom to explore those attachment and loss experiences, both current and past, which may be related to difficult adjustment. Once it is understood how these kinds of experiences have impeded dealing with loss, it is possible to see them in a new light, leading to a more satisfactory completion of grief and mourning.

DEVELOPMENT OF THEORIES ON GRIEF AND MOURNING

Bowlby first connected the loss of attachment to emotional disturbance in 1942. By 1980, when *Loss* was published, attachment theory had come to be seen as a distinct theory, and in this final book of his trilogy, he applied an ethological perspective to understanding the relationship of attachment to loss. Observational studies that had been done by Marris (1958) and Lindemann (1944) as well as Parkes (1972), who had joined Bowlby at the Tavistock Clinic in 1962, supplied scientific data on adult bereavement, extending ideas on the subject beyond Robertson's work with children. And, though an attachment framework can be applied to losses other than actual death, the bulk of the literature on adult grief has tended to focus on spousal bereavement.

Freud, too, recognized the suffering involved in bereavement, and attempted to explain its connection to mental illness. His influential paper, "Mourning and Melancholia" (1917), introduced the terms of grief and mourning into the psychological literature, with grief described as an intrapsychic process in which libido is withdrawn from the lost object. Although he was puzzled as to why the struggle of "grief work" should be so painful, Freud concluded it was a normal process that lasted up to one year and required no medical attention. Freud further noted that an adult who has a "pathological disposition" from childhood trauma can develop pathological mourning or melancholia when there is ambivalence toward the lost object. He identified this outcome as depression, wherein feelings, especially anger, are turned against the self.

In the final pages of "Inhibitions, Symptoms and Anxiety" Freud (1926) made another attempt to understand and explain the painful process of grief when he suggested a connection between separation and loss, and anxiety and depression. He wrote that anxiety was a reaction to the danger of losing the person, and that the pain of mourning occurred following loss, with withdrawal of libido from the object. Freud, and the classical psychoanalytical theorists who followed him, considered pathological outcome as an internal conflict rather than one due to interpersonal factors, or to real-life experiences such as separation or loss. Furthermore, there is now evidence that certain conditions Freud considered to be pathological, such as anger, ambivalence, and a sense of the continuing presence of the lost figure, occur in the majority of those who recover from grief. Freud also gave minimal attention to the compelling urge to seek out and recover the lost person, which is now seen as a dynamic in both healthy and pathological mourning (Bowlby 1961, 1980, Glick et al. 1974, Sable 1989).

Later theoreticians, especially those interested in object relations, began to expand on Freud's work and to look at a variety of experiences with others (Bowlby 1969a). Suttie (1935) for example, wrote that an infant had an innate need for love and companionship which, when thwarted by separation or loss, produced a variety of adult difficulties. Likewise, Melanie Klein (1940) connected pathological grief in adults to childhood experiences, in particular how the child responded to its fantasized separation experiences with mother. Although she is credited with recognizing the relation between early childhood and later responses to loss, Klein's emphasis on fantasy, to the exclusion of real events or how parents actually treated their children, was challenged by Bowlby. He thought neglect of real experiences was a serious omission in psychoanalytic theory, and, moreover, that these actual events were directly related to the outcome of the mourning process.

THE FOUR PHASES OF GRIEF
AND MOURNING

Bowlby's (1980) view of grief is basically an extension of his description of the separation responses, which were presented in Chapters 1 and 4. One departure is that in grief there is an initial "emotional shutdown" (Holmes

1993a, p. 90), a feeling of numbness and disbelief, which protects the griever from becoming overwhelmed by the suddenness of a loss (Parkes 1972). This numbing phase gives way to the phase of yearning and searching—the pronounced protest, worry, and anger of separation distress and anxiety. Even though the affectional bond cannot be recovered, this early grief consists of intensified attachment behavior and separation anxiety, originating in a preprogrammed tendency to attempt recovery. The two final phases are delineated as disorganization and despair, and reorganization. The responses of these four phases of mourning occur on a continuum, fluctuating back and forth over a period of weeks and months, and vary from person to person because people grieve differently (Bowlby 1980, Parkes and Weiss 1983). The processes may be conscious or unconscious, and the outcome may be either healthy or disordered. When mourning proceeds to a healthy resolution, individuals accept that a change has occurred in the external world, with subsequent changes in their internal world, and they are able to reorganize their patterns of interaction with others and develop new meaningful relationships. If mourning becomes disordered, defensive processes have diverted its course, exaggerating or distorting normal responses to some degree (Bowlby 1980, Brown 1982, Horowitz 1988, Lindemann 1944, Marris 1974, Parkes 1972).

The first phase, numbing, usually lasts from a few hours to a week. The bereaved person feels stunned and has a sense that life is unreal. The individual may have outbursts of distress or anger, but mainly exhibits a sense of distancing in an effort to absorb the shock a little bit at a time (Bowlby 1980, Parkes 1972). "I can't believe it" is a remark typical of the numbing reaction, which prevents registering a painful and perhaps inconceivable loss.

The following phase of yearning and searching for the lost figure lasts from a few months to years. As the reality of the loss begins to register, the bereaved experiences moments of intense distress and searches restlessly for reunion with the lost loved one, even when doing so is acknowledged as irrational. The individual may be preoccupied with memories and events leading up to the loss, combined with a sense of the mate's actual presence. The bereaved person is alert to any clue in the environment, such as the sound of familiar footsteps, that might signal the person has returned. Sometimes the bereaved person actually calls out, hoping to be answered (Bowlby 1980, Parkes 1970, 1973, Raphael 1975).

During this stage, physical difficulties such as insomnia and lack of appetite may be evident. A range of intense feelings or vivid dreams in which the person is still alive or present may occur. Separation anxiety reflects feelings of danger and distress; sometimes it intensifies to panic. The person may feel he is losing his mind or control. Anger is directed toward overcoming obstacles to reunion and/or reproaching the person for leaving and discouraging her from "leaving" again (Bowlby 1961, 1980, Parkes 1972).

A deep and pervasive sadness accompanies mourning, especially during the third phase of disorganization and despair. The bereaved person is more withdrawn, needing time to reconcile the urge to recover with the recognition that reunion is not possible, a realization that comes with reorganization, the final phase of the grieving process (Bowlby 1980, Parkes 1972).

The pain of loss heals slowly and involves both the expression of grief and the ability to tolerate it, a cognitive process that accommodates the changed circumstances while retaining an inner sense of the bond (Bowlby 1980,

Fraley and Shaver 1999, Hamilton 1987). Mourning has no clear ending, although sometimes a turning point occurs, perhaps in dispersing the person's possessions or clothing (Parkes 1972). Gradually, manifestations of distress and despair become less frequent, until finally only an occasional resurgence of grief occurs (Marris 1974). This gradual lessening of grief helps explain the overall difficulty of observing and defining successful adjustment. Because mourning may last months and years, no accepted time limit can be defined. It may take two or three years to recover a sense of well-being, to examine new situations, and to organize attachment behavior for new experiences and people (Baker et al. 1992, Bowlby 1980, Weiss 1988, Worden 1982). If therapists underestimate the duration of grief, they may place unreasonable expectations on their clients. A comment such as "You learn to live with it, but never get over it" indicates that individuals probably never fully get over a major loss (Bowlby 1980). At some point toward the end of the first year, however, most bereaved people feel they are on their way to recovery. If the bereaved person shows no signs of moving toward adjustment by this time, it is possible that mourning is taking an atypical course. Pathology, however, can also manifest itself before this juncture anytime during the first year of mourning.

DISORDERED MOURNING

Disordered mourning is considered a variant of the normal grieving process. It is characterized by difficulty making and maintaining satisfactory relationships, difficulty in revising life plans, and/or poor physical health. In its more common clinical form—chronic mourning—

responses to loss become intensified and prolonged, with symptoms of anxiety, depression, or anger. These symptoms may be expressed as intense guilt or self-reproach over the loss, social withdrawal, agoraphobia, psychosomatic symptoms, or substance abuse (Bowlby 1980, Conway 1988, Gut 1989, Horowitz 1988, Jacobs and Douglas 1979, Marris 1974, Parkes and Weiss 1983, Prudo et al. 1981, Selan 1982, Worden 1982). Along with presenting complaints for seeking treatment, clients will mention the loss and the sadness still connected to it (Worden 1982).

> For example, David, a 50-year-old man, sought therapy around the first anniversary of his wife's death because he no longer had any "zest for life" and did not want "to get out of bed and face the day" without her. She had died after a lengthy battle with cancer, and David found himself still brooding over her illness and blaming himself for decisions related to her care that both he and the doctors had made. He continually cried, felt hopeless, and was uninterested in any activities, preferring to return home after work to what he called a "shrine" to his wife. He maintained their home and his wife's clothes just as she had left them—"in case she might return."

Gorer (1965) identifies this preservation of a home or even a room as it existed when the person was alive as "mummification."

Worden (1982) noted that protracted grief, as in the case of David, is fairly easy to assess because the person usually tells you about it. Often, however, bereaved persons describe a range of psychological and physical complaints, such as depression, difficulty getting along with others, dissatisfaction with life, disturbing dreams, or substance abuse, that are not immediately connected to the loss. In contrast with chronic mourning, grief may be inhibited, delayed, or manifested in what Bowlby calls the absence of conscious grieving (Bowlby 1982, Horowitz 1988, Lindemann 1944, Worden 1982). In such circumstances, bereaved persons have suffered a loss but claim that they were either not deeply affected or have recovered from it. Weiss (1988) refers to this avoidance of grief as a compartmentalization, whereby loss is recognized but the person refuses to attend to it. Events such as another loss or the anniversary of a death that was not mourned may precipitate symptoms, usually depression (Bowlby 1980, Volkan 1970, Worden 1982). Bowlby (1991), in his biography of Darwin, postulated that Darwin's physical ill health, anxiety, and depression, were related to the inhibition of grief over the death of his mother, when he was 8 years old. Barbara, who was mentioned in Chapter 3, became depressed, with sleeping and eating disturbances as well as difficulty getting along with an adult daughter, as she inhibited grief over three recent losses. Because she was unused to relying on others, her insistent pattern of self-reliance precluded access to her sadness and grief. She thought she should be able to handle the deaths of her husband, adult son, and older brother by herself and could not admit or express the pain of loss. Nor could Barbara reach out to others to share her grief. Her symptoms, including anger at her daughter, were signs that she was not coping as well as she claimed.

Although bereaved persons may exhibit a mixture of chronic and inhibited grief responses (Weiss 1988), these two opposite forms of grief both indicate failed mourning. The loss is believed to be reversible, whether there is awareness of this or not. Thus, there may be a strong urge to seek out and recover the departed person, together with anger and/or self-reproach, but an absence of sorrow and sadness (Bowlby 1980, Volkan 1970). Other features of disordered grief that may occur on their own or in combination with other adverse reactions include insistent caregiving redirected from the lost figure to others, exaggerated elation as a result of refusing to acknowledge death, and taking on the symptoms of the deceased's illness (Bowlby 1980).

Healthy mourning is distinguished from disordered mourning by the length of time the process persists and the extent to which it influences functioning. Pathological processes occur in various degrees of severity (Bowlby 1980, Marris 1974, Parkes 1972, Weiss 1988). Because grief can last a long time and is apt to intensify at times such as the anniversary of the death or under conditions of stress or change, pathological mourning, or some of its features, may not be immediately obvious to the practitioner. For example, David had ambivalent feelings about his marriage, and felt an underlying anger and guilt that became apparent only after a few sessions. In order to recognize and deal with his complicated grief, it was necessary to understand the range of conditions that contributed to his disordered mourning.

FACTORS AFFECTING THE COURSE OF MOURNING

Research suggests that disordered mourning reflects an interaction between the personality of the bereaved and circumstances of the loss (Bowlby 1980, Horowitz 1993, Sable 1989, 1991a, Worden 1982). It is critical to assess the type of loss and the events surrounding it, as well as the adequacy of social support. If the death was sudden and unexpected, such as from cardiovascular disease, an automobile accident, violence, or suicide, the bereaved person's grief is more likely to be compromised (Carey 1977, Levinson 1972, Lundin 1984, Parkes and Weiss 1983, Sprang et al. 1989, Welu 1975, Zisook 1987). The abruptness of a tragic event can seem like the cruelest kind of loss, precluding the opportunity to say good-bye or resolve relationship issues and problems (Parkes 1975). Moreover, unforeseen loss cannot be explained and seems to make no sense (Weiss 1988). Levinson (1972), using Bowlby's stages of grief, declared that sudden and un-timely loss causes complications in both the numbing and yearning and searching phases of mourning since such a tremendous blow puts the bereaved person into a state of suspension. Davidson (1981) described the state as being left with a feeling of incompleteness and a sense of shock, which compounds and precedes an extended or prolonged mourning process. When there is a feeling that the death need not have occurred, such as in suicide or an accident, there is also more likely to be self-reproach, guilt, or an-ger at the self or lost person. Moreover, with suicide there is an added social stigma (Bowlby 1980, Sanders 1988, Welu 1975).

The nature of the relationship with the lost person is also related to the outcome of mourning, especially if it involved ambivalence or insecurity. Events that occurred prior to death, such as those surrounding the final ill-ness, the death itself, and whether multiple losses have occurred, all affect the grieving process (Bowlby 1980, Sprang et al. 1989). Barbara, for instance, had lost three close family members in the year before seeking therapy, compounding other risk factors.

With regard to social networks, the important fac-tor is whether the bereaved person perceives the people around her as helpful, and whether they allow her to express her thoughts and feelings. It is important to share grief, even in our culture that emphasizes independence and suppression of feelings. Also, people do not generally recognize how long the mourning period can last. Thus, friends and family may act awkwardly or provide little support, and only for a short time, leaving the bereaved confused and uncertain of what to do with her grief (Parkes 1972, Parkes and Weiss 1983, Simos 1979).

In addition to the circumstances of loss, the personality of the bereaved and her experiences, especially related to attachment, separation and loss, affect mourning and the forms it takes (Bowlby 1980, Parkes 1991). Bereaved persons who have experienced childhood separation or loss, rejection, or unstable family conditions are apt to establish adult relationships with some distortions in the patterning of attachment behavior, and this can influence their responses and adjustment to loss (Bowlby 1977, 1980). When working models of expectations, feelings, and behavior take a pathway of insecure attachment, access to attachment-related information and emotions has been defensively excluded, or possibly exaggerated and distorted (Slade 1999). These individuals are more prone to make adult attachments of an ambivalent and/or anxious nature, and also to have greater difficulty dealing with traumatic experiences such as bereavement (Bowlby 1980, Parkes 1972). Main (1995), for example, found the majority of mothers whose incoherence classified their attachment personality pattern as unresolved/disorganized on the Adult Attachment Interview (AAI) had experienced earlier unresolved losses. In my study (Sable 1989) of eighty-one women widowed for one to three years, some of the women described their previous relationship with their husband in a way that would qualify as anxious attachment. These women also reported more child-hood experiences of separation and loss and experienced more distress during bereavement. Conversely, those who reported happier marriages and early security in their families handled bereavement better. Likewise, Parkes (1991), in a study of bereaved individuals seeking psycho-therapy, found that depressed individuals were more likely to have lost a parent in childhood or been subject to re-jecting or inconsistent caregiving. Parkes concluded that early separation events made these individuals vulnerable to later bereavement difficulties, especially when the griev-ing process was complicated by a troubled relationship with the spouse. His findings point out how important it is for clinicians to look for early disruptions of attachment in their client's history and to encourage discussion of them during treatment. The therapist provides a safe set-ting for exploring, remembering, and sorting through these experiences and the meaning attributed to them. A sym-pathetic, reliable, and attentive therapist helps clients feel "sure of an understanding response" (Bowlby 1991, p. 77), and thus willing to examine the past with its painful ex-periences and feelings, and the present with its unsettling bereavement.

TREATING DISORDERED MOURNING

Once the client is assured of a secure therapeutic re-lationship, the goal of treatment for disordered mourn-ing is to understand what has impeded adjustment so that the process of mourning can be more satisfactorily com-pleted (Gut 1989, Parkes 1972, Simos 1979, Worden 1982, Zisook 1987). When mourning has become chronic, such as occurred with David, expression of feelings is apt to be quite intense and may be compounded by transference of feelings toward the lost loved one onto the therapist (Parkes 1982). Clients are relieved when their therapist reassures them that their feelings and behavior are typical of grief, and that their distress will not overwhelm the therapist (Parkes 1972, Shuchter 1986). However, ongoing and extreme expressions of emotion, without change, are gently discouraged in chronic grieving (Parkes 1972, 1982). David, for example, was encouraged to express his grief in a supportive atmosphere, but also to explore some of the reasons behind his distress, guilt, and anger.

Bowlby (1980) defines defensive processes as the "defensive exclusion" of information or emotions that occur as a result of relationship experiences. Past events or threatening situations may be continuing to affect adult behavior and working models (Bowlby 1991). For example, David was not only angry with his wife for dying and abandoning him, he was still enraged at his own mother for the inadequacies and hostility of her care. He had imposed that anger onto the doctors for not saving his wife, and guilt onto himself for not supervising her medical attention more judiciously. The therapist's role with David was to connect his earlier disappointments to his current loss and grief and to help him become aware of how they were influencing his current mood and behavior, including his reluctance to move out into the world and explore new relationships.

While clarifying issues related to the defensive exclusion of painful memories, therapists need to convey that the desire for close relationships is natural and does not mean the client is weak or overdependent. Anxiety, anger, and yearning are part of a mourning process, part of a desperate attempt to maintain attachment. Thus, they should not be seen as childish or a sign of overdependency but as an outgrowth of instinctive responses that may have been heightened by real experiences. Effects, moreover, seem to be cumulative, even in adulthood. For example, Barbara sustained three losses in the year before she became acutely depressed. A therapist uninformed about the nature of attachment behavior might not have seen her edginess with her daughter as a sign of inhibited grief.

For clients such as Barbara, who do not seek treatment for chronic mourning, it may take some time before unresolved grief begins to surface. Worden (1982) lists a variety of "clues" to unresolved grief, such as a fervent response to a subsequent loss or recurring themes of loss during treatment sessions. In such instances, the therapist should pursue a discussion related to the particular loss: How did the person die? Does the client feel that the grieving process has been completed? Is the client still preoccupied with the loss? When did the presenting symptoms begin in relation to the loss? What is the nature of current and past relationships with others? What separations and losses have occurred in the past and what were the client's responses to them (Gut 1989, Melges and DeMaso 1980, Shuchter 1986, Zisook 1987). Barbara, for example, wanted help for difficulties with her adult daughter but did not realize how her grief and her anger toward both childhood figures and adult experiences were causing her to impose much of her distress onto her one remaining close family member.

With either inhibited or chronic grief, the use of an attachment framework for forming a narrative about these kinds of affectional experiences has been found to be effective in treatment of disordered mourning. Parkes (1991), in his study of bereaved individuals who sought psychotherapy, described the therapeutic bond as a base from which bereaved individuals can examine their loss and their view of the world. Podell (1989) used similar guidelines in work with adolescents who had lost a peer in a disastrous fire. Attributing prolonged and complicated mourning to unresolved early losses that left the adolescent vulnerable to dealing with later trauma, Podell's treatment focused on connecting current distress to the earlier losses, and to the subsequent difficulties these had caused.

There has been some recent speculation that suppression of grief, when it is not forced on an individual, such as happened for instance to Darwin, may not be as harmful as Bowlby thought. Fraley and Shaver (1999) suggest that there may not be a failed adjustment when the bereaved has the opportunity to share grief to the degree she feels necessary, or if there is a dismissing style of attachment. Though Bowlby (1980) warned that a protective shell of avoidance may make a person seem "immune to mourning . . . but at what a price!" (p. 240), Fraley and Shaver say that suppression may actually be helpful for individuals with an avoidant attachment style because their defenses are organized in such a way that they can shut off feelings of loss. On the other hand, Fraley and Shaver seem to support Bowlby's basic premise when they qualify their suggestion and state that suppression may be detrimental to recovery if the missing person was an attachment figure. Consequently, inhibited grief carries a risk of disordered outcome and thus a possible need for therapy even in avoidant individuals. Treatment for pathological mourning may be focused and either short-term or more extended. The following case history of Mary describes clinical work with a woman who entered therapy at approximately the first-year anniversary of her husband's death. Treatment lasted six months.

SPOUSAL BEREAVEMENT

Most people spend their adult years in pairs, deriving much of the meaning and security of their lives from a close affectional relationship. If it is a lasting relationship, such as marriage, it is inevitable that eventually, one member of a bonded couple will die, leaving his partner bereft. This loss represents a devastating disruption of attachment and there is evidence in the literature that spousal bereavement constitutes a major threat to both psychological and physical health (Glick et al. 1974, Maddison and Viola 1968, Schmale 1971, Weiner 1978). Loss of spouse is related to altered immune functioning, a higher incidence of psychiatric hospitalizations, and premature death, including suicide (Bunch 1972, Carr 1970, Jacobs and Ostfeld 1977, Lynch 1977, Parkes et al. 1996, Raphael 1977, Rees and Lutkins 1967, Stein and Susser 1969, van der Kolk 1997). Indeed, one can die of a broken heart. When loss is compounded by difficult circumstances surrounding the bereavement, such as a tragic accident, inadequate social support, and/or painful attachment experiences, the risk of disordered adjustment increases. In Mary's situation, both early experiences and a troubled marriage contributed to her escalating distress, resulting in a condition of chronic mourning, as well as a recurrence of agoraphobia.

MARY

A 60-year-old, slight, nervous woman, Mary sought help because she was having "a terrible time giving up" her husband. Mary complained of various psychosomatic disturbances, such as eating and sleeping difficulties, and also anxiety and fear when she was alone or driving too far from home. Although she reported that she felt sad and depressed, she would not let herself cry because she had "cried so long." She wanted to work but was too upset to follow through on job interviews.

In addition to these disturbances, Mary was drawn to ideas of reincarnation. She attended a séance with the intention of communicating with her spouse (she reported that she did not). She found comfort visiting the beach because, at his request, her husband's body had been cremated and his ashes strewn in the ocean. She felt guilty because she had not been at the hospital when he died. When she arrived, she could not bring herself to look at his body. Later Mary visited the hospital and felt she "brought him home" with her. She also found it difficult to watch television because it reminded her of the many hours her husband spent in front of the television when he was sick and suffering. Often she found herself wandering aimlessly, unable to concentrate, waiting and watching for a "sign" from her spouse.

Much of the physiological and emotional distress Mary reported, including her perambulations to find her missing mate and her interest in reincarnation, which Volkan (1975) points out is not unusual among bereaved persons, also occurs in healthy mourning. However, the late onset of her interest in reincarnation as well as the persistence and intensity of her distress suggested prolonged, disordered mourning. Furthermore, Mary's fears of being alone or too far from home seemed to reflect anxious attachment exacerbated by the loss of her spouse, but possibly also connected to earlier life experiences. Her anxiety symptoms suggested that she was still in the yearning and searching phase of mourning.

The therapeutic relationship provided Mary with an alternate base of attachment from which she could explore her experiences, both with her spouse and her early parental figures. She had cared for her ailing husband during the last six years of his life, as she had previously cared for her mother who was ill for many years when Mary was an adolescent. The early loss of her mother left her "afraid of death" as well as confused about its meaning. She tried to keep all her "crazy thoughts" to herself, because she was afraid of what others would think. The week after she told her therapist about bringing her husband "home with her," Mary stated that she could now laugh about this and that she did not want to be "among the dead" anymore. She also commented that she had mixed feelings about her marriage but that expressing negative thoughts made her feel guilty and disloyal. Her therapist tried to convey that attempts to understand experience are intended to clarify the effects of past relationships, not to find fault.

As Mary recalled her life experiences, information that had been defensively excluded was gradually retrieved. For instance, she was able to see that her childhood experiences had caused her to be anxious and an insistent caregiver in her close relationships. Rather than misconstruing her tendency to cling in certain fearful situations as a condition of dependency, the therapist considered whether certain situations of separation or loss or threat of separation had undermined Mary's natural desire for love and care. The impact of having a sick mother who eventually died was examined; Mary told the therapist that she could now mourn her mother, for whom she had "never shed a tear." She also acknowledged her anger and disappointment in some areas of her marriage, such as her having been left with no financial security because her husband had not wanted her to work. Mary's spiritual interests and fears diminished. She got a part-time job and began dating a man she had known previously.

Therapy offered Mary a temporary attachment that allowed her to deal with her separation and loss experiences in an affirming and accepting atmosphere. She was able to express her grief, explore her relationships, and achieve an understanding of the effect of her earlier experiences on her adult relationships and grief responses. Mary was ready to say a final goodbye to her spouse, to stop grieving, and to pursue new plans and relationships.

EARLY LOSS, UNRESOLVED GRIEF, AND DEPRESSION

Bowlby's (1980) argument that young children do mourn, once a controversial subject in psychoanalysis, is now supported by research and clinical experience. The following example of a pleasant, likeable young adult woman, Elizabeth, illustrates how the early loss of a parent can be related to detachment, depression, and difficulty in attaining secure attachments in adulthood. This is especially true when the child is not reassured or helped to mourn. The example also shows how the exploration of real experiences can be pivotal in therapeutic change.

ELIZABETH

Elizabeth entered treatment because she was worried that she was "having a breakdown." She complained that she was "totally depressed" and "lonely," continually "on the verge of tears" and unable to cope with a responsible job that was less and less satisfying. Although Elizabeth had a romantic relationship, it was troubled, because Tony wanted commitment and marriage while Elizabeth was "nervous and frightened" and claimed she didn't know "what a relationship [was]." She explained that she didn't want to be hurt, and that she really didn't trust people enough to get close and share her feelings. Elizabeth also mentioned that her father was terminally ill, but several sessions later she began to cry, and divulged that he was not her "real father"; that her real father had died when she was 6 years old. Elizabeth had hardly any memory of her actual father, and never found out how he died or where he was buried, as her mother refused any discussion of him. Her narrative of her early family situation was that her mother soon remarried, and that their life went on as if her father had never existed. She remembers having trouble making friends, "not trusting easily" and, as an adult, being more comfortable in relationships with partners who did not pose the possibility of developing a "real personal relationship," such as married men. She reproached herself for being easily upset, quick to anger, and overly sensitive to the reactions of others. This latter feature, she noted, had existed since her father died, but Elizabeth attributed it to her own inadequacies, such as an inability to "control" her emotions.

From the outset, Elizabeth expressed positive feelings about therapy, for example, that she was able to talk about experiences she had never shared before and that she noticed she was feeling much better. However, she was easily upset during sessions or at any change in scheduling hours. What was notable was that she would become just as angry on those occasions when she initiated the interruptions as when her therapist had a vacation or illness. She would also get a return of psychosomatic symptoms, especially severe headaches, which had diminished since beginning treatment.

With her therapist's support and encouragement, Elizabeth approached her mother with some of her unanswered questions. Explaining her own trepidation at the time of her husband's death, her mother now was able to tell Elizabeth how her father had died and where he was buried. She admitted she had not been available to her daughter because she had been distressed by the sudden loss of her spouse and by having to go to work with no substantial skills. Elizabeth reported that finding these missing pieces of her early life made her feel "more [her]self." We were then able to connect how her stepfather's terminal illness, as well as difficulties with Tony and her job worries, triggered her unresolved loss and mourning of her father. Not only did Elizabeth become less angry with her therapist, she also became more tolerant of her mother and of the deficiencies in their relationship that she had carried since childhood. She became less afraid of intimacy, and decided to discontinue the relationship with Tony because their problems could not be resolved in a way that would meet her needs. Elizabeth felt more confident and worthy of a better bond. She also improved her career by accepting a promotion that was more in keeping with her interests and abilities.

ANXIETY AND GRIEF

Although it was not as pronounced with Elizabeth, who was impaired by a childhood loss, both she and Mary described symptoms of fear and anxiety that were directly related to their bereavements. Because loss and mourning are more frequently associated with tears, sadness, and depression than with panic and anxiety, these latter affects have tended to be overlooked in the literature on grief (Sable 1989). For instance, Freud seemed to view anxiety in relation to threat of separation rather than to real loss; in 1926 he identified anxiety as a "reaction to the danger of a loss of an object" (p. 83), but professed uncertainty about its connection to mourning. Nor did he relate it to the process of yearning and searching for the lost relationship that Bowlby has made central to his conceptualization of grief. Within the stages of grief and mourning delineated by Bowlby, there is emphasis on the bereaved's attempt to recover the lost figure, and on the influence of separation anxiety in the process. Bowlby (1982) defines separation anxiety as "anxiety about losing or becoming separated from someone loved" (p. 670). Following loss, it alerts the bereaved to the possibility of danger and also acts as an attempt to ensure protection by bringing back the figure who is now missing. As a young child cries and desperately tries to bring back its mother when she leaves, so too do adult grievers instinctively concentrate all their efforts and energy, all their hopes, on recovering the lost person. The propensity to seek out and retrieve an affectional relationship is a chief dynamic in grieving and is reflected in feelings of fear, anxiety, and panic. Anxiety is elicited and fear is intensified when an attachment figure's availability is uncertain. Relevant to this, a person is less afraid if there is confidence that attachment figures will be accessible for aid or comfort when needed (Bowlby 1973). Bowlby has explained the connection between anxiety, fear behavior, and loss, by noting that the presence of a trusted companion reduces alarm in frightening situations whereas being alone when conditions are strange intensifies fear. As an attachment figure, by definition, is one who is essential to security, the loss has left the bereaved in a world that is suddenly strange and frightening, and where the individual is left alone to deal with it.

Using a conceptual framework of attachment, I found confirmation of Bowlby's position on grief and anxiety in an interview study of eighty-one women whose husbands had died one to three years before (Sable 1989, 1991a). In particular, I found that fear and anxiety were present throughout the first three years of bereavement, and, moreover, that those women who were identified as anxiously attached in their relationships reported a more distressful adjustment. The women in the study ranged in age from 26 to 82, with a median age of 63. The length of time married varied from one to fifty-three years, with an average of thirty-five years. The majority had been in long-term relationships. Data were obtained by semi-structured, face-to-face interviews, followed by two existing questionnaires, which were filled out by the subjects. The interview and questions explored general functioning and feelings since loss, relationship with the spouse, social support systems, details of the loss such as the mode of death, and early life experiences. The interview questions were derived from bereavement studies done by Marris

(1958) and by Parkes and Weiss (1983); they also included parts of the Attachment History Questionnaire (Pottharst 1990) to assess early life experiences and questions that Arrindell (1980) found comparable to symptoms of agoraphobia, and that fit Bowlby's concept of anxious attachment. The last part of the study involved two standardized, self-report scales, which were filled out by the women: the Texas Inventory of Grief (TIG), a twenty-nine item self-report scale, devised to elucidate the grief process (Zisook et al. 1982); and the Brief Symptom Inventory (BSI), a fifty-three item test that measures current psychological distress and can be used with nonpatients (Derogatis and Spencer 1982).

Results of the research showed that fear and anxiety were related to grief in a majority (58 percent) of the women, who noted increased worry, panic, and fear since their husbands' deaths. Prominent were fears of being alone, reported by thirty of the eighty-one women, (37 percent); physiological manifestations of panic and anxiety, such as palpitations, reported by thirty-one (38 percent); and fear in strange situations by sixteen (20 percent). Twenty-nine (36 percent) became more afraid to go out alone, though sometimes this was qualified in terms of urban crime. An example of intensification of fear is reflected in the responses of a woman in her early sixties, who was quite anxious; she reported heightened fears of being alone, being in strange places, traveling, and enclosed places. One of the younger women, bereaved twenty-one months, gave expression to her anxiety in a manner that reflects panic as well as fearfulness:

> It was very hard the first year. [I'm] doing pretty good now. [I'm] scared of certain things ... [there's] an emptiness, loneliness. It's worse than physical [pain].

I've been through a Middle East war and was never scared. The first three months I was in shock. [I] kept busy. Then I began waking in the middle of the night. My chest hurt, my heart was pounding. I felt I'd die from a heart attack. [I] felt claustrophobic. . . had to go outside to breathe. So I became scared at night. I went to a psychiatrist. He said I had a panic disorder. . . I still worry I'll die tomorrow. I'm still scared at night.

The subjects themselves made various connections between fear, anxiety, and being alone. For instance, one woman responded to the question, "How has your bereavement changed you?" with "Now I know what fear is." Although some noticed a decrease in fearfulness after the first year, much fear remained. Sixty-nine percent of those afraid to be alone remained so; 75 percent continued to feel panic; and 85 percent were still more alarmed in strange situations. Thus, besides confirming the prevalence of fear and anxiety in bereavement, the study found a lasting effect that suggests a risk to successful adjustment.

Further associations between attachment experiences, anxiety, and grief were supported by the study's findings that women who reported having had a more satisfactory and happy relationship with their husbands were less anxious and afraid. Likewise, those women who described more secure early attachment were handling bereavement better; they had less distress at the time of loss and showed better adjustment for both outcome factors, depression and anxiety. Conversely, childhood experiences of separation and loss or threats of abandonment were found to contribute to more anxiety and depression in bereavement. Furthermore, the women whose real experiences had resulted in the uneasiness and insecurity of anxious attachment had more difficulty adjusting to their loss. This finding suggests that when working models do not perceive attachment figures to be reliably accessible and responsive, fear and anxiety may linger, even as sadness wanes. This was the situation with Mary, presented earlier in the chapter. Her heightened attachment behavior and chronic mourning were an indication that an anxious-ambivalent pattern of attachment had impeded her recovery. Another implication of this finding is the added support it gives to the concept of anxious attachment as a personality pattern that influences reactions to stress. It also helps clarify that fear and anxiety are part of the mourning process and points to their key role in certain types of disordered outcomes.

LISTENING TO LOSS

The permanent severing of a bond around which thoughts, emotions, and behavior have been organized can throw the individual into a depth of despair and crisis where nothing in the world any longer seems certain or reliable (Marris 1982, Parad et al. 1976). According to research that has followed Bowlby's (1980) original propositions, there is now evidence that grief runs a predictable course but one that lasts longer than people expect. Because it is such an arduous and difficult process from which to recover, mourning may well precipitate a pathological outcome. With either chronic grief, such as that exhibited by Mary, or inhibited grief, such as that which hampered Barbara and Elizabeth, dealing with disordered adjustment involves a therapist's ability to listen to clients' experiences of loss and help infuse them with meaning. This task can be complicated if a therapist's past experiences begin to stir up his own painful memories. The feelings of loss can be potent and overwhelming, but only as therapists help clients to express the depth of their distress and relive the history of the relationship can working models be rearranged to accept the finality of bereavement along with a comforting image of the person who is now gone.

An important implication in applying attachment concepts to therapy is the recognition that the loss of affectional bonds affects both the clients' inner and outer worlds (Harris 1997). With spousal bereavement, for example, even when adjustment is proceeding well, loneliness is clearly felt to be a major problem. In the study that I conducted, those women who perceived a supportive and caring social network of family and friends reported a better adjustment than those who did not. They explained that though these alternative persons do not replace a close, exclusive attachment, they make grief easier to manage because they provide companionship and an opportunity to share feelings (Sable 1991a). Another kind of substitute attachment that appears to reduce loneliness and promote adjustment to loss is the company of a pet. As will be discussed further in Chapter 11, the women in my bereavement study who owned pets, in particular dogs or cats, reported significantly less loneliness than those who did not have pets. I have proposed that pets provide an element of attachment that offers proximity and comfort to many adults (Sable 1995). In bereavement, pets can counteract isolation and loneliness, acting as a buffer against feelings of emptiness and giving a sense that life goes on. They are a reminder that the person is not alone.

A woman in my study of spousal bereavement said, "It is difficult to describe the feelings of bereavement. I believe it is the most powerful feeling one can ever feel." The intensity of the reaction to the loss of a loved one and the length of time it persists attest to the fundamental part attachment plays in the lives of us all, not only when we are young, but throughout the life cycle. Our innate capacity for attachment leads us to form lasting affectional bonds with others, and to grow up looking for meaningful adult relationships around which we organize our lives. If we lose one of these exclusive bonds, the world around us seems to collapse. Gradually, after much time and sorrow, the relationship, as it was, is relinquished, and interest becomes renewed in future experiences and relationships. Working through grief does not mean forgetting the lost person. "I have very happy memories of my spouse," a woman who was adjusting well wrote on a questionnaire in my bereavement study. Through the process of grief and mourning, a painful loss is eventually made a part of treasured memory. When bereavement becomes disordered, clinicians can apply attachment concepts to understanding and treatment, helping clients restore meaning to their lives.

8

Emotional Detachment

In this and the following chapter, the discussion will focus on those individuals whose degree of disturbance classifies them within one of the *DSM* categories of personality disorders. The *DSM-IV* defines a personality disorder as a stable, pervasive, and inflexible pattern of behavior that leads to significant impairment and distress across a broad range of personal and social situations (American Psychiatric Association 1994). Though both the *DSM* and attachment theory assume that disorders are characterized by difficult interpersonal relationships, attachment theory does not make the fixed distinctions between psychological disturbance that are included in the *DSM* classifications. Instead, all levels of distress tend to be seen as having the same underlying dynamic: there is some distortion in working models due to adverse family experiences, both present and past. In this vein, personality disorders would suggest a greater degree of defensive exclusion of attachment thoughts and feelings, and thus more pronounced distortions of behavior as well as greater difficulties in affectional relationships with others.

This chapter will discuss those who exhibit an emotional detachment, namely the withdrawal and restraint in relationships that is exhibited in diagnoses that resemble schizoid or avoidant personalities. Those with more volatile and unstable moods who would be classified as having a borderline personality disorder are discussed in the next chapter.

The concept of emotional detachment refers to individuals who have a fear and avoidance of close relationships. This fear leads them to distance themselves from others, and to also shut away their basic desires for closeness and affection. According to attachment theory, individuals who defensively limit access to affectional thoughts and feelings have been subjected to severe and/or prolonged experiences such as lengthy separation, permanent loss, or chaotic home lives, often involving physical or emotional abuse. Their remote and unresponsive style of relating developed as a protection against painful experiences and memories, and indicates a defensive strategy to sustain a relationship that was crucial to security and maybe actual survival.

Bowlby (1944) first identified an incapacity to form close and satisfactory relationships in the paper "Forty Four Juvenile Thieves." The paper was based on case studies of children and adolescents referred to the London Child Guidance Clinic (where Bowlby worked early in his career) for problems of stealing and delinquency. He coined the phrase "affectionless character" to describe fourteen of the young thieves who were found to be indifferent to showing or receiving affection, and he identified two causal factors that were statistically significant. All but one of the children had had a prolonged separation (six months or more) from his mother during the first five years of life, which led to an "inhibition of love by rage and the phantasies resulting from rage" (p. 123). Bowlby noted that clinicians could be confused by a superficial sociability, but that even when the offenders appeared to have ties with others, "there were no roots in their relationships" (p. 38), and no real concern for others.

Bowlby (1960a,b) further developed the concept of detachment through his association with James Robertson at the Tavistock Clinic, in their attempt to explain observations of the responses of young children who had been removed from their mothers and placed in institutional care with strangers. Bowlby (1960b) noticed a lack of attachment in the final emotional detachment phase, which succeeded the phases of protest and despair when the separation from the mother continued.

Children who are detached may appear interested in pursuing their daily activities and behave in an outgoing, friendly manner, giving the impression that they have successfully adapted to their changed circumstances. But closer inspection reveals a new self-centeredness regarding food and material things, and an absence of attachment behavior toward others. When reunited with mother, these children are unresponsive and undemanding. They may act as if they do not recognize her, and, though possibly tearful, will turn away and refuse efforts of closeness and comfort. The chilling stare of detachment and distrust that a child can give a parent is demonstrated in the Robertsons' film, *John* (1969), when John first looks at his mother upon her return after a nine-day separation. As he had explained earlier in regard to the young thieves, Bowlby saw John's affective withdrawal as a defensive stance, a deactivation of attachment behavior to avoid the pain and longing for someone who is unattainable. John's look indicates that his trust in his mother has been shaken, and that underneath his detached manner is anxiety and hostility over a painful experience. Fraley and Shaver (1999) suggest the child may also be unsure of how to manage conflicting feelings, or may be punishing the parent for abandonment.

How entrenched detachment is, and whether and for how long it continues, depends on the length of separation and conditions of substitute care provided the child during that time, as well as the nature of the relationship with the mother before and after. Under favorable conditions, such as the presence of a sympathetic and familiar substitute caregiver in a familiar setting, detachment is less apt to occur, or, to the extent it does occur, is more likely to be easily overcome when the mother returns. The bland and shallow response generally gives way to a renewal of the bond. When conditions are less favorable, however, the influence of the separation on young children can persist for longer periods; sometimes they may even remain in a phase of attachment indefinitely (Bowlby 1960a, 1980).

DETACHMENT IN ADULTS

The phases of protest, despair and detachment are responses along a continuum and all parts of a separation process. Bowlby (1973) links these phases to adult forms of anxiety, depression, and emotional detachment, relating experiences of separation or loss in childhood to adult psychopathology. Used descriptively, detachment in an adult refers to a pattern of personality development that represents a severe disruption or absence of affectional bonds, and describes a person unable to make and maintain genuine relations with others. In contrast to a secure or anxious-ambivalent affectional style, attachment behavior is absent, replaced by an "aloof, noncommittal" attitude (Bowlby 1973). A detached adult may exhibit a smooth, seemingly friendly exterior and appear composed and less afraid than others. But the apparent good adaptation is superficial, and underneath "the springs of love are frozen and . . . [the] independence is hollow" (Bowlby 1960a, p. 109). Such an adult is thus conceived as being emotionally detached, both outwardly from people and inwardly from feelings and memories. This defensive strategy prevents the activation and processing of information relevant to attachment, especially information that would elicit feelings of longing or of the distress of abandonment. Bowlby (1979) writes that a person who uses detachment as a defense is "afraid to allow himself to become attached to anyone for fear of a further rejection with all the agony, the anxiety and the anger to which that would lead. As a result, there is a massive block against his expressing or even feeling his natural desire for a close trusting relationship, for care, comfort and love" (pp. 11–12).

Bowlby (1977) identified a personality pattern of emotional detachment in adults when he expanded the concept of insecure or anxious attachment behavior to include four different categories. The other categories of insecure attachment were anxious-ambivalent attachment, compulsive (or insistent) self-reliance, and compulsive (or insistent) caregiving. Although subsequent attachment research often equates defensive detachment with insistent self-reliance, Bowlby seemed to see a difference as well as a need to explain that there are varying degrees of avoidance and defensive exclusion.

By 1980, in *Loss*, Bowlby had reduced the four categories of insecure attachment to three, eliminating detachment. However, he continued to use the concept descriptively. "The deactivation of systems mediating attachment behaviour, thought and feeling, appears to be achieved by the defensive exclusion, more or less complete, of sensory inflow of any and every kind that activate attachment behaviour and feeling. The resulting state is one of emotional detachment which can be either partial or complete" (p. 70).

ATTACHMENT RESEARCH

The quotation above suggests that Bowlby perceived emotional detachment as a partial or complete deactivation of the attachment behavioral system. Subsequent research on attachment in both children and adults, as well as findings from cognitive science, have supported a personality pattern of detachment and also advanced our understanding of the defensive mechanisms involved (Fraley et al. 1998). Ainsworth (1984) identified a pattern of avoidance in some 1-year-olds in the Strange Situation procedure who did not exhibit distress when their mothers left the room, and who also turned away and ignored them on reunion. The children stayed within sight, maintaining proximity in case of emergency, but defensively concealed their attachment behavior and emotions. Ainsworth found that the inhibition of affective expression was related to previous experience of parental rejection, lack of responsiveness, or rigidity in the home environment. By deactivating attachment behavior, the children did not experience negative feelings such as anger, which could annoy and further alienate the caregiver. Moreover, Main's (1981, 1991) finding that a majority of the parents of these children exhibited avoidance on the Adult Attachment Interview (AAI), classified as dismissing, suggests the parents have deactivated their own attachment behavior in a way that impacts their children's security of attachment (Cassidy and Kobak 1988).

Kobak (Cassidy and Kobak 1988) also found a correlation between avoidance and lack of family support in his study of fifty-three first-year college students who were given self-report measures and also rated by their peers. Avoidant individuals were rated as less resilient and more anxious and hostile by their peers than secure individuals, even though the subjects themselves did not report more distress. Not only does the study suggest that these avoidant individuals minimize acknowledging distress or difficulty, it shows that behavior that was originally adaptive in one's family may be inappropriate and maladaptive when transferred to other contexts. The study also supports the idea that a personality pattern of avoidance or detachment, once formed, tends to persist, influencing behavior in later relationships and situations.

Kobak's conclusions are supported by another study of college students (Florian and colleagues 1995), who were given a questionnaire including the brief Hazan and Shaver (1987) self-report measure. The researchers found that individuals classified as avoidant perceived less social support from both family and friends, and sought less emotional and instrumental support than secure individuals. They concluded that a person's attachment style was significant enough to affect an overall orientation to his or her social world.

Hazan and Shaver's (1987) quiz measured adults' perceptions of themselves in their romantic relationships. In contrast, Main's (1991) Adult Attachment Interview (AAI) probes for adults' representations of their childhood experiences with their parents. Both measures, however, modified and extended Ainsworth's classifications to adults, examining attachment organization at the representational level. Main (1995) classified transcripts on the AAI as "dismissing" when they seemed aimed at minimizing the importance of attachment experiences. Dismissing adults often could not remember much about their childhood, or gave vague or idealized accounts that were not supported by autobiographical details. For example, someone might claim having an "excellent mother," but later relate "I didn't tell her I broke my arm. She would have been really angry" (Main 1995, p. 440). This lack of coherence would then continue across the interview. Sometimes replies might be short and guarded, or imply a dislike of or lack of interest in the topic. Emotional experiences would not be described with any depth of feeling or insight, making it possible to evade painful memories. These same inconsistencies were present in the unresolved group, the difference being a greater degree of confusion. This distinction could be relevant to conceptualizing both borderline personality disorder and emotional detachment.

On Hazan and Shaver's (1994) measure, adults categorized as "avoidant" also revealed a fear of intimacy and tended to keep a distance in their close relationships. These adults were pessimistic about romantic relationships in general and had a relatively high rate of relationship dissolution. In an attempt to further elucidate these dynamics of avoidance, Bartholomew (1990) proposed expanding the concept of avoidance on Hazan and Shaver's quiz into two categories: one category, which she labeled "dismissing," indicates a defensive insistence on self-sufficiency and invulnerability to rejection. The choice appears on the self-report measure as "I am comfortable without close emotional relationships. It is very important to me to feel independent and self-sufficient, and I prefer not to depend on others or have others depend on me." Bartholomew labeled the other category "fearful," indicating a conscious fear of intimacy due to anticipated rejection. This choice appears on the self-report measure as "I am somewhat uncomfortable getting close to others. I want emotionally close relationships, but I find it difficult to trust others completely, or to depend on them. I sometimes worry that I will be hurt if I allow myself to become too close to others" (Bartholomew and Horowitz 1991, p. 244). Although both groups showed problems becoming close and relying on others, they differed on some measures, for example with regard to their sense of self-esteem. In the dismissing category self-esteem was rated high, whereas in the fearful category it was rated low. Moreover, the negative self-image in the fearful group was related to higher levels of interpersonal problems, lack of assertiveness, and social inhibition. Though both categories showed an avoidance of intimacy that could make it difficult to establish close relationships or update working models, there were gender differences. Females tended to subscribe to the fearful category, whereas more males identified themselves as dismissing. This finding may reflect cultural biases that allow women to more freely acknowledge fear; men are generally compelled to profess self-sufficiency and independence.

Further support for a concept of detachment comes from two studies conducted by Fraley and colleagues (1998). In one study, adults were asked to write about their reactions in their most recent romantic relationship where someone had broken up with them. Using Griffin and Bartholomew's (1994) Relationships Styles Questionnaire (RSQ) for scoring the results, the researchers found that dismissing-avoidant adults were less likely to protest the separation or attempt to regain the partner. Similarly, in another study, combining observations of couples separating at airports with a questionnaire, dismissing-avoidant adults protested the parting less and were more likely to turn away from their partners or hurry the separation. From the two studies, the researchers concluded that separation or threat of separation does not elicit attachment behavior in dismissing-avoidant adults as it does for other adults. Furthermore, they note that though the behavior is reminiscent of the behavior in Ainsworth's (1984) avoidant infants, the psychological structure is conceptually different. Avoidant adults have developed a memory structure that represents a deactivation of the attachment behavior system. Attachment, caregiving, and sexual behavior are all organized to minimize feelings of rejection and anxiety and to keep the attachment system from being activated. For example, dismissing adults do not let themselves become close to their partners or rely on them as a secure base. By doing this, they reduce the likelihood that attachment behavior will be strongly aroused if the relationship falls apart. Fraley and colleagues claim that evidence from other studies such as Mikulincer and Orbach's (1995) lends credibility to their conclusions. In their study, Mikulincer and Orbach asked participants to recall childhood memories specific to certain feelings, for example, happiness, anger, or sadness. They found that avoidant adults were slower to retrieve childhood memories of negative experiences, again suggesting a greater degree of defensive exclusion of attachment.

Cassidy and Kobak (1988) write that an inability to remember specific childhood events is comparable to the defensive mechanism of repression. Information that would arouse memories of rejection or mistreatment, and the feelings of anxiety and distress they would elicit, are actually shut off from processing. In addition to dismissing attachment and masking negative emotions, these individuals may form attitudes about relationships that restrict wanting or offering responsive care or closeness. They may also idealize their parents or themselves, or minimize the presence of stress or lack of social support in their lives. As we will see in the following illustration of Kelly, who was briefly mentioned in Chapter 1, defensively idealized representations can be an origin of the multiple, conflicting working models manifest in psychological disturbance. Kelly, was pressured by her mother to see her father as a "good" parent, which was in sharp contrast to her experience of him as frightening and unsafe. But as Cassidy and Kobak allege, and Ainsworth and Main agree, defensive exclusion and detachment can be adaptive in childhood, permitting some degree of proximity for protection while at the same time limiting attachment behaviors that could be met with rebuff and rejection.

> When Kelly began treatment, she told me she could barely remember anything about her childhood. She did remember that she always felt afraid, on guard, and cautious. Rare exceptions were occasional times of feeling safe during several visits to a therapist and from these distant memories came her decision to pursue therapy. Although avoidance and detachment may have served a client like Kelly well in childhood, the persistence of the attachment pattern into adulthood is a warning sign to a therapist.

Someone so fearful of investing in relationships might well be apprehensive about exploring interpersonal experiences in therapy (Bartholomew and Horowitz 1991). The therapist's first task, therefore, is to establish emotional contact and reduce the sense of threat that is associated with emotional expression. This can be accomplished in a safe therapeutic environment where the sensitivity and responsiveness of the clinician promote trust and the development of a secure base. Clinical work attempts to clarify how the belief that emotions were "dangerous" developed, and how adverse experiences led to the client's fear of attachment (Cassidy and Kobak 1988, Holmes 1997).

OVERCOMING FEAR OF ATTACHMENT

The story of Kelly (Sable 1983), a young adult single woman, illustrates the application of attachment theory to psychotherapy with an individual exhibiting an avoidant or detached style of personality. An intelligent, well-groomed, and stylishly dressed though quite overweight woman, Kelly appeared friendly, pleasant, and able to handle situations calmly and confidently. She lived alone and was attending night school for an advanced business degree, while teaching school for her livelihood.

KELLY

Kelly sought therapy because she had difficulty making or sustaining relationships. When someone tried to get close to her, she became anxious and afraid. Convinced that she was helpless to manage her side of a relationship, she would isolate herself and withdraw from the person interested in her. At these times, she described herself as "in a fog, talking through a gray mist." Kelly also had a variety of anxiety symptoms and fears, such as fear of the dark, fear of driving her car into "strange areas," and fear of going most places alone. She could not go shopping unaccompanied, and though she was particularly interested in the theater she stayed away because she was afraid of crowds. At times, Kelly retreated to her home, not answering the phone and going out only to work. The thought of devising a plan to advance her career, to diet, or to improve her social life overwhelmed her. She said of herself, "I feel like a tortoise, all shut off."

During her four years in therapy, Kelly's history

unfolded. She was the younger child of a disturbed and disorganized family. Both parents were alcoholic, and had frequent arguments and physical fights. They divorced when Kelly was 8, and she remained with her mother, who regularly reminded her that she was an irritating and difficult child. For example, when Kelly cried over leaving home for an upcoming vacation, her mother impatiently told her to stop acting like a baby. As an adult, she did not cry, claiming the only result was sore eyes.

From the time Kelly was 2 years old, her mother had hospitalizations for psychiatric problems that included suicide attempts. Kelly was never allowed to ask about her mother's periods of illness, and she came to believe that her own many childhood illnesses, temper tantrums, and annoying behavior were the cause. When she had misbehaved, Kelly was threatened that she would be sent to an orphanage. Her mother often threatened suicide and her maternal grandmother, who was Kelly's caregiver when her mother was unavailable, committed suicide when Kelly was 12. Kelly was then taken away from her mother, with no explanation, to live with her father, who had remarried. Kelly did not see her mother again for five years. Her stepmother, domineering and critical, repeated her mother's earlier prohibitions and warnings that she beware of men and sex, and implied that Kelly was peculiar, like her mother. Although her family continued to tell her that she had always been spoiled and self-centered, Kelly remembered a turbulent life of inconsistency, unpredictability, and unfair punishment. This made her want to be "invisible," to "slip by like a shadow," and left her frightened of closeness with others.

ATTACHMENT AND DETACHMENT

Generally, a woman presenting herself as Kelly is described here might be diagnosed as narcissistic, schizoid, or borderline, with the terms implying an immature self-centeredness, and/or some developmental deficit. In contrast, from a perspective of attachment theory, failed or flawed relationships with key affectional figures have given rise to certain personality disturbances, or attachment disorders, and these difficulties indicate insecurity, not immaturity. Kelly may have appeared preoccupied with herself and her problems, but this does not mean that she was necessarily fixated at an early developmental level or overinvested with self-love. Viewed in the framework of attachment theory, Kelly was diverting her attention away from hurtful memories and feelings. Because her mother had continually expressed her annoyance with her, telling her how difficult and demanding she was, Kelly came to see herself as such a person. Also, because both of her parents failed to respond to her desires for love and care, Kelly felt unwanted and believed she was undeserving of comfort and support from others. Kelly felt unloved and unlovable. The fact that she had no early stable attachment, together with threats of abandonment, overt confusing communication, and prohibitions against expressing feelings, caused Kelly to exclude many feelings and childhood memories and to be afraid to make personal bonds with others. These conditions combined to move her onto a developmental pathway leading to emotional detachment and avoidance. The deactivation of her attachment behavior resembled Winnicott's description of a "false self," but where Winnicott concentrated on the person's subjective experience, attachment theory emphasizes the influence of environmental interactions in the etiology of psychological distress (Karen 1994).

THE PROCESS OF PSYCHOTHERAPY

A therapist who uses concepts of attachment bases the approach to treatment on psychoanalytic and object relations principles with certain different points of emphasis. The support of the therapeutic bond, central to change, is perceived as providing an atmosphere in which to experience the security of an attachment relationship. As discussed previously, by being available with regular appointments, interested in and responsive to what is talked about, the therapist becomes a safe base from which to explore and understand one's attachment history. Experiences of separation and loss are particularly noted and discussed, including those that arise in treatment, for example when the therapist is absent due to illness or on vacation. Where the meanings of these events are misconstrued, they are examined in order to see if the client's responses derive from earlier separation experiences and are thus subject to change in the present.

With Kelly, the treatment relationship came to be a familiar and safe base only gradually and with time. In the beginning, her fear of attachment made her distant and tense. For many months she spoke softly, carefully, and without feeling. The therapy hours dragged by slowly for me; I held off, was unable to relax, and was aware that she watched my every move. In one interview, she noted, "I feel I am sucking in my personality." She was forcing me to do the same. Bowlby (1988a) notes that treatment for such deeply distrustful people involves a lengthy, low-keyed, and accepting patience. Not only was Kelly terrified of the closeness of a therapeutic bond, she was also reluctant to recall childhood memories. "I think I have always been afraid to remember," she said. She refused invitations to include family members in any sessions, commenting that she anticipated embarrassment if they were to attend and that she worried new information might spill forth from them. Because people were too confusing and difficult to figure out, Kelly had given up trying to understand them. Because they were too frightening, she sought refuge in reading fiction and watching horror movies. She saw in the latter a reflection of her own childhood.

One day Kelly called in a panic, upset by an incident at work. At the next session, she said that just knowing she could reach me if she wanted to had proven to be enough to relieve her stress. Until then she had feared I might not be there when she arrived or that I would find her demanding and consider her a burden. Her worries over the threat of separation or how she construed her relationship with her therapist were themes that repeatedly emerged. Whenever there was an interruption in treatment or an impending separation she expected the worst. But as she would not allow herself to experience separation anxiety or sadness, she would merely go blank, be unable to think clearly, and blot out her feelings.

Before my first vacation, Kelly appeared dazed and stiff. She sounded indifferent as she claimed to be resigned to always being alone. Upon my return, she reported that she had secluded herself at home while I was away, was plagued by suicidal thoughts, and was convinced I would not return. When I suggested that she might have felt this same despair at times of separation from her mother, she excluded any feelings or response. Subsequently, however, some painful memories began to emerge. Kelly recalled that she had not wanted her mother with her when, at 5 years old, she had her tonsils out. At that young age, she had already decided that she could not count on her mother to be available to comfort or protect her.

Kelly unconsciously longed for care and protection, and was angry that it had been denied her. She dared not expressed her anger, though, visualizing "dire consequences" if she did, or if she demanded anything for herself. The mere thought of showing her anger made her feel "wooden, with a whirl of thoughts and a knot in my stomach." Another vivid metaphor, which revealed this buried anger that she could neither acknowledge nor manage, was how Kelly felt like a pot on the stove, and had to exert great effort to keep the lid on so it would not "boil over."

It was some months later that Kelly asked me the question that marked the turning point in overcoming her reluctance to recall and review her life; she asked if I was trying to tell her that her problems came from what had happened to her in her family. The clear and full realization of this, she declared, made her feel less hopeless and less helpless because now, as an adult, she could do something about herself and therefore get better. (This was the question that Bowlby singled out when he read my manuscript about Kelly and detachment.)

As therapy proceeded, Kelly reported a "subtle thawing out." She seemed less afraid of attaching to her therapist. Now when she put up a wall, it indicated that she was detaching herself from some particular experience and we were able to discuss it. Furthermore, she began to link up current behavior and feelings of anxiety or depression to childhood experiences, such as her intense fear of being abandoned or sent away. When her parents fought, Kelly had worried they would both desert her, as each of them had continually threatened to leave. When she reached adulthood, she was apprehensive when away from home too long or when she ventured alone in strange areas. She recalled that as a child she had returned from school one day to find a "For Sale" sign on her house. Also, she had never been forewarned about the times her mother had been hospitalized or before she was sent to live with her grandmother.

When Kelly began to understand her ambivalent and anxious attachment to her family, she remembered a time when the family dog had suddenly disappeared, "put out," her mother had explained, because it had been too much trouble. This caused Kelly to worry that a similar fate might befall her, since an incident as minor as not hanging her towels correctly had brought an end to her piano lessons, a favorite activity. Kelly worked hard to be perfect at whatever she did, freezing in fear when she fell short. She also froze when she felt anger coming on. This freezing was reflected in the sessions when she felt responses grow "murky" and reported "hearing people through a filter." At these times, she acted reserved and unapproachable.

To escape her family, Kelly moved into her own apartment at 18. Although treated like an outsider at home, she nevertheless was homesick. Once away from home it puzzled her that she could still care for people who treated her so terribly. Later, these recollections brought emotional responses of tears and expressions of anger.

Gradually, Kelly's newfound self-confidence became apparent in her increasing ability to deal with others. She made new friends and obtained a responsible position in a large business firm. She attended the theater, even in unfamiliar areas, and began to diet. As therapy neared completion, Kelly was able to converse directly and with humor and to share her ideas and plans. She said that she realized everyone was not like her family, and that she was not the person they had pressured her to see herself as. She could assess and decide matters for herself, and she displayed enthusiasm for the experiences ahead.

REGAINING ACCESS TO ATTACHMENT FEELINGS

When separation is repeated or prolonged, and when it is compounded by factors such as threats of abandonment, unreliable caregiving, or parental rejection, defensive processes may lead an individual to develop a protective shell and to present a false self to the world. Attachment behavior becomes deactivated owing to the impact of real-life experiences that have caused painful feelings and troublesome behavior to proceed from angry protest, through despair, and lead finally to a detached personality. According to Bowlby, in response to separation and rejection, feelings move back and forth along a continuum of anxiety, depression, and anger, explaining the mixture of emotions often seen with patients. Kelly had bouts of depression and suicidal ideation, and was also plagued by agoraphobic fears and worries. This suggests that natural feelings, such as separation anxiety, which arise to keep attachment intact, had escalated. But Kelly had deactivated attachment and cut herself off from others. Her internal attachment organization, reflecting the hurt and anger of the past, prevented her from leaning on others or sharing emotional concerns. Her defensive exclusion, being quite extensive, left her vulnerable to symptoms of psychopathology when she was confronted with stress.

My sessions with Kelly suggest that fear of attachment can be overcome within a therapeutic relationship that provides a secure base and encourages the exploration of relations with others, both current and past, and with the therapist as well. Appropriate feedback and information provided by the therapist, such as clarifying the impact experiences can have on a small child, are part of the process (Peterfreund 1971).

Early experiences are especially significant because defensive exclusion and detachment often begin in childhood (Bowlby 1980, Sroufe and Waters 1997). How we apply this and other concepts, such as what issues we choose to focus on during therapy, is largely determined by our theoretical framework, values, and attitudes (Marmor 1974, Teitelbaum 1998). A therapist guided by attachment theory conceptualizes personality development and personality disorder in terms of real-life experiences, especially those of separation or loss, which are or were painful, frightening, or unhappy. These are not perceived as the product of fantasy, oedipal issues, or aggressive conflict, but rather as the reflection of actual situations within the family of origin or with those to whom the patient later had emotional ties. With Kelly, these attachment memories and her responses to them were retrieved and reviewed in an atmosphere that condoned the desire for close personal attachments as a natural part of human social behavior. This enabled her to express feelings, such as fear of being alone, without being made to feel that she was immature or overdependent.

A distinctive feature of attachment theory is the framework it provides for listening to clients' narratives and putting together a scenario of how their current difficulties originated and developed (Hamilton 1987, Karen 1990). The use of cognitive awareness builds a bridge between psychoanalytic and cognitive theory (Holmes 1993a, Karen 1990). Kelly's tumultuous, inconsistent, and alcoholic early family environment led her to forget most of her childhood memories and to develop a personality pattern of emotional detachment. In trying to help her retrace her history and regain access to her feelings, specific comments about the quality of her family life were made. For instance, Kelly related how emotionally abusive, reckless, and impulsive her father was. Yet her mother told her how lucky she was "to have such a good father." When I stated that it did not seem he would feel like a good and protective father to a child, she was able to begin to see how she had been pressured to misconstrue certain family behaviors. Using this cognitive awareness, Kelly could also begin to release excluded feelings and discover her "true self" (Winnicott 1965).

As one observes in the reunion scene in the Robertsons' film of *John* (1969), Kelly revealed the effects of cumulative trauma and distress in her avoidant and detached response to others. A dismissing style of attachment restrained her from relying on others, and it was only because of her episodes of dissociation and panic that she undertook therapy. But because bitter experiences had taught her to inhibit distress and not seek comfort when she was upset or frightened, she could not bring herself to automatically accept and rely on her therapist.

Applying attachment theory to work with someone who is emotionally detached like Kelly implies that it will take time to establish genuine trust and safety (Farber et al. 1995). At times, the current climate favoring short-term, cost-effective treatment does not seem to be conducive to providing a therapeutic experience that could counteract previous disappointments in attachment and restructure working models. The therapeutic process for someone who has learned to dampen expression of emotion requires sufficient time and space for the client to develop and actually experience secure attachment, learn to acknowledge and communicate feelings, and negotiate openly with others. Kelly could not have been rushed in this process. She needed treatment to last long enough for her to understand and overcome her fear of connection, and to feel more confident and worthy of finding secure affectional relationships. This assumption about attachment, that bonds form slowly over time and through on-going exposure and interaction, is also salient for understanding clinical work with individuals who have been given the diagnosis of borderline personality. It is these individuals, their dynamics and difficulties, that we shall now consider in the following chapter.

9

The Conflictual Attachment of Borderline Personality Disorder

Instead of exhibiting the cautious and dismissing attachment style of emotional detachment discussed in the preceding chapter, individuals who would meet the *Diagnostic and Statistical Manual of Mental Disorders* (*DSM-IV*) (American Psychiatric Association 1994) criteria for borderline personality disorder have an intensity and impulsivity to their emotions and behavior that is associated with an unstable self-image, fears of rejection and abandonment, and tumultuous relationships with others. The instability of their moods and inner representations is such that they shift from idealization to devaluation suddenly and dramatically, particularly in attachment relationships but also in career aspirations, sexual identity, or opinions about friends. In addition to having severe difficulties in interpersonal functioning, people with this condition may have symptoms that include self-destructive behavior, such as substance abuse or suicidal attempts and gestures; outbursts of anger, panic, or despair; and chronic feelings of loneliness, emptiness, or boredom. Along with sharp mood swings and impulsive actions such as binge eating and lack of self-control, those with this pattern have an absence of empathy and cognitive awareness of the impact they have on others, absences that can lead to grandiosity, distorted versions of reality, and even to "remarkable cruelty" (Fonagy et al. 1991, p. 205). In conversation, such persons' responses are vague, tangential, and overpersonalized; affect and word usage are often odd. In treatment, individuals in this diagnostic category, with their exaggerated symptomatology, negative affect, and demands for special consideration, such as immediate availability, can be wearing; therapists consider patients with this disorder among their most challenging and difficult to understand or treat (Callahan 1996, Dozier et al. 1999, Holmes 1993a, Johnson 1991, Nelsen 1995, Schore 1994, Stone 1992).

Although the *Diagnostic and Statistical Manual* outlines a borderline profile, there is still a lack of agreement that these individuals comprise a single, distinct diagnostic category (Fromm 1995, Holmes 1993a, Johnson 1991). Fromm, for example, asserts that borderline personality is not an entity, but a developmental area between neurosis and psychosis, suggesting a connection to serious disturbance. Moreover, the changing meanings of the term indicate its ambiguity. It has been suggested that many of Freud's famous neurotic patients would qualify as borderline (de Zulueta 1994, Finn and Sperling 1993), or that earlier diagnoses, such as hysterical or psychopathic, are now more precisely identified with the disorder (Minde and Frayn 1992). Borderline has become one of the common psychopathologies of our era.

During the past several decades, direct observation studies of young children and adults, as well as object relations theories such as those of Winnicott (1965), Kohut (1977), and Kernberg (1967), have deepened our understanding of the more serious mental disturbances (Hamilton 1989, Minde and Frayn 1992). As a result, there has been a gradual shift from viewing psychopathology in terms of oedipal conflict to an emphasis on the pathogenic effect of preoedipal experiences, in particular a lack of attunement between the infant and its primary caregiver, typically its mother (Minde and Frayn 1992, Muir 1995, Sugarman 1995). Likewise, Bowlby (1969a, 1973), in his formulations of attachment theory, recognized the significance of the mother–child bond in the development of future mental health and, using an ethological-evolutionary framework to describe its dynamics, explained psychopathology in terms of disruptions or adverse experiences with key attachment figures, both current and past.

This chapter applies Bowlby's attachment concepts to adults whose symptoms would meet the *DSM-IV* criteria for borderline personality disorder. Borderline pathology is conceptualized as a profound disturbance of attachment; adults with this pathology exhibit wide fluctuations between a desire for proximity and attachment to an emotional detachment, or even disengagement from others. The internal world of such persons lacks coherence both in thinking and affect regulation and their behavior is aggressive and ambivalent, yet there is also an egocentric view of these patterns and feelings (Bowlby 1973, Holmes 1993a, Melges and Swartz 1989, Schore 1994, Westen 1991). Psychotherapy provides the experience of a reliable and consistent relationship. The experience helps stabilize moods and offers an attempt to construct a narrative of influential life events, for instance, harsh caregiving or permanent losses, to affirm the impact of these events, and to clarify their meaning (Bowlby 1988a, Holmes 1993a, van der Kolk 1996). Three areas of particular emphasis with respect to borderline personality are the concept of trauma beginning in childhood, disturbances in affect regulation, and cognitive distortions. We will now discuss how each of these areas relates to the disorder and its treatment.

THE DEVELOPMENTAL PATHWAY
TO BORDERLINE DISTURBANCE

According to attachment theory, individuals construct inner working models of themselves, their interactions, and their expectations of others. This dynamic aggregate of attachment experiences, and the meanings attributed to them, begins to form in infancy and is the set of assumptions used to assess conditions of the moment, as well as to anticipate and plan for the future. When parents have been accessible, sensitive, and responsive to their child's attachment behaviors, working models will likely reflect security and confidence in the reliability of others, as well as a feeling that one is competent and worthy of care and comfort. With this foundation of a secure base in others, children move out into the world, exploring new experiences and relationships, yet also knowing they can return to find attachment figures available and supportive if they are needed (Bowlby 1988a, Holmes 1994, Karen 1994, Sable 1994a). Without a secure base, curiosity and exploration are inhibited, and the ability to tolerate separation is reduced. Working models may become rigid and difficult to update; access to information and feelings that are necessary for adaptive functioning may become cut off. When this happens, these defensive maneuvers are carried into subsequent relationships, affecting the individual's resilience in dealing with stressful situations such as separation or loss.

The concept of working models helps explain why attachment-related experiences persist. An adult who has internalized disturbed family-attachment patterns is more vulnerable to psychological breakdown when confronted with adversity. Those who grow up to exhibit a borderline personality have generally been subjected to more severe and/or prolonged discontinuities or mistreatment, such as child abuse and/or neglect, disconfirmation of the child's perceptions and feelings, or threats to abandon or withhold love. When repeated failures to find attachment figures comforting and caring occur, developmental pathways are diverted from healthy outcomes; instead, there is an incapacitating personality organization.

ATTACHMENT, DETACHMENT, AND BORDERLINE PERSONALITY DISORDER

From Bowlby's ethological perspective, borderline personality disorder can be conceived as a condition of insecure attachment, with extreme oscillations between attachment and detachment, between a yearning for secure affectional bonds and a dread and avoidance of such closeness. Working models show a lack of coherence, especially in relationships with others and in affect regulation (Bowlby 1973, Holmes 1993a, Melges and Swartz 1989, Schore 1994). Due to early traumatic childhood experiences, systems mediating attachment feelings and behavior have been deactivated and distorted, resulting in an inability to sustain relationships but also a heightened sensitivity to separation and loss. Melges and Swartz (1989) compare the fluctuating behavior in borderlines to that of prickly porcupines—there is need for another, but when anyone comes too close the individual's fear drives him away. These people are desperate for a secure base, but are afraid to allow themselves to become attached to anyone for fear of rejection and abandonment and the anxiety and anger to which that would lead (Bowlby 1979). It is the conflict between attachment and exploration, between maintaining distance while wanting connection, which accounts for the vacillating moods and behavior. Borderline individuals are preoccupied with regulating space (Melges and Swartz 1989) because they do not feel the "invisible elastic" (Bowlby 1969b, p. 45) of attachment from which to venture forth, either emotionally or physically. They cannot defend against separation anxiety, for example, by holding a sustaining image in working models when separated, or by soothing themselves (Adler and Buie 1979, Richman and Sokolove 1992, Schore 1994, West and Sheldon-Keller 1994).

Bowlby (1979, 1988a) attributes anxiety over separation to the influence of certain types of family experiences on the developing personality. Using data from the Robertsons' (Robertson and Robertson 1971) direct-observation studies of children separated from their parents, Bowlby identified the sequence of responses to separation: an initial protest phase proceeding to despair and depression and, if the separation persists or the conditions are acute, finally to a phase of emotional detachment.

An ethological approach considers fear of separation to be a universal response that arises in order to retain attachment and protection at times of threatened disruption. When moderate, these responses are functional. Anxiety connotes apprehension that an attachment figure will be inaccessible or rejecting, while anger is a response to frustration, a reproach to the endangerment of a bond, and acts as a deterrent against repetition of hurtful behavior by the attachment figure. Anger and anxiety tend, moreover, to aggravate each other. If caregiving is inconsistent or unreliable, these feelings may be heightened, yet distress is not terminated; instead, chronic fear and anxiety develop, combined with bitter anger and resentment (Bowlby 1973, 1984). Similarly, the "defensive numbing" (Bowlby 1979, p. 11) of detachment can persist beyond reunion and even into adulthood.

RESEARCH FINDINGS

In the histories of patients with borderline personality disorder, there is evidence of the experiences of abuse and trauma that Bowlby emphasized. For example, Links and colleagues (1988) found that inpatients diagnosed as borderline exhibited higher frequencies of lengthy separations, foster home placement, and physical and sexual abuse. Another inpatient study, done by Herman and colleagues (1989), found a higher incidence of physical and sexual abuse—as well as of the witnessing of domestic violence—in the histories of individuals diagnosed as suffering from borderline disorder than in the histories of subjects with no borderline diagnosis. The researchers concluded that it might be possible to relate qualitative differences of childhood trauma to diagnostic outcomes, with the most severe parental mistreatment being linked to conditions such as multiple personality, somewhat less severe treatment to borderline personality, and milder experiences of mistreatment to depression or anxiety disorders. This is consistent with Bowlby's opinion that parental mistreatment is a precursor of psychopathology, with more severe difficulties in adulthood reflecting more extensive childhood abuse experiences. Herman and colleagues caution, however, that a vulnerable temperament or the absence of protective factors, such as other caring relationships, may also be related to development; thus, it should not be assumed that trauma is the single cause of borderline disorder.

In a study using an attachment framework, Sperling and colleagues (1991) found more insecurity and hostile attachment in inpatient and day hospital patients diagnosed as borderline than in a comparison group of college students who were approximately the same age, sex, and socioeconomic background as the hospitalized sample. And in a later, larger study that yielded similar results, the researchers (Sack et al. 1996) found that the parents of patients diagnosed as borderline were described as more critical, abusive, and unresponsive than the parents of the college sample. Parents of the borderline patients were also described as less attentive, respectful, understanding, affectionate, and loving.

One of the measures used in the study was Hazan and Shaver's (1987) self-reporting attachment questionnaire, where the subject is asked to choose which of three statements most accurately describes his or her feelings in intimate relationships. Hazan and Shaver's demonstration of the continuity of attachment behavior has been one of the research procedures to find a relationship between early experience and later distress. Similarly, Main's (Main and Goldwyn 1984) Adult Attachment Interview (AAI) has found correlation between the attachment status of young children in the Strange Situation and their mothers' descriptions of their own relationships with their parents. As previously discussed, Main's semistructured interview assesses how adults organize their minds in relation to childhood experience. In particular, Fonagy and colleagues (1996) and Patrick and colleagues (1994) discovered that a high percentage of borderline individuals fell into the "preoccupied" category of insecure attachment. Adults with this state of mind tended to give incomplete, idealized and/or inconsistent descriptions of their past experiences.

In relating attachment research to borderline personality disorder, Fonagy and colleagues (1991, 1995, 1996) emphasize that early distressful experiences may inhibit mental processes such as the capacity to reflect on one's feelings and mental functions. When the AAI was given to a group of inpatients who met the *DSM III-R* criteria for borderline personality, three characteristics distinguished them from other personality disorder diagnoses: a higher prevalence of sexual abuse, lower ratings of self reflection, and less resolution of the abuse. This group also experienced their parents as less loving and more neglecting than nonborderline patients. Commenting on the results, the researchers suggest that the mistreated child learns that a parent will not be appropriately reflective and responsive; therefore, the child does not develop a feeling of security in relation to his own mental world. In the Strange Situation, the child who cannot rely on mother to alleviate distress appears undistressed (avoidant) or inconsolable (resistant) upon reunion with her. Similarly, an adult who is classified as dismissing, preoccupied, or disorganized on the AAI has developed habitual defensive strategies that are manifested by incoherence in the subject's personal narrative. Without coherence, the capacity to reflect about oneself in relation to others, or to resolve earlier losses or abuse, is impaired.

Fonagy's work (Fonagy et al. 1995) shows that traumatic attachment experiences can compromise effective functioning and produce the affective polarities and cognitive distortions that characterize the working models of borderline individuals. The speculation that borderline structure can be conceptualized as post-traumatic stress disorder (Herman et al. 1989, van der Kolk 1996) points to the overwhelming effects of childhood trauma in its etiology, because although the meaning given to real-life events is filtered through existing mental structures, this meaning is strongly shaped by the way a person was really treated.

In terms of neurobiological and cognitive development, Schore (1994) notes the importance of parental affect attunement and overall sensitivity to a child's needs. For example, in children the interval between the ages of 10 and 18 months is a time when critical maturation in a system of the prefrontal cortex of the brain occurs; this development is crucial for regulation of affect over the remainder of life. If a child's expressions of feeling, such as disappointment and anger, are met with sensitive responses and without retaliation, distress is modulated, expectations of responsiveness to attachment signals are enhanced, and the experience of negative affect is less apt to be appraised as threatening (Cassidy and Kobak 1988, Holmes 1996). By shielding their child from overstimulation or understimulation, and also by soothing discomfort, parents serve as a source of balance, evaluating the meaning as well as responding to the intensity of both distress and enjoyment. Holmes (1996) describes parents' attunement to their child as an "emotional alignment" that helps the child reconcile contradictions, such as those between pleasure and frustration. A secure child can control affects and impulses when necessary and identify and express feelings (Karen 1994, Sroufe 1996).

In contrast, inconsistent or misattuned caregiving can lead to deficits in affect regulation, such as an inability to delay action, control attacks of rage or overwhelming panic, or feel empathy for others (Allen 1995, Brown 1993, Schore 1994). In persons without internal representations of consistent, safe attachment figures, there is a tendency to rely on external sources of comfort, which can include activities such as self-cutting, violence, and substance abuse (Herman and van der Kolk, 1992, Stein et al. 1996). Fonagy (1999) suggests that projecting unassimilable parts of oneself onto external sources or others can help an individual retain some measure of coherence. Research has linked these kinds of acting-out behaviors to insecure attachment and also to early experiences of separation and loss. For example, childhood disruptions have been shown to be related to raised anxiety levels in adulthood (Holmes 1993a). Reite and Capitanio (1985) hypothesize that borderlines' sensitivity to separation and loss might reflect some type of hyperactivity of the brain structures underlying attachment behavioral systems. Supporting evidence that attachment experiences are associated with physiological regulation also comes from primate studies (Reite and Boccia 1994), which have shown that separation or abusive treatment can skew subjects' immune systems and their adult behavior, including how they eventually behave as parents.

With regard to cognitive distortions, such as egocentric thinking and paranoid projections, studies of adult borderlines show that these individuals have two opposite tendencies with regard to representing others: one that is too shallow and primitive, and another that represents others in overelaborate ways that are too complex for the limited data available (Westen 1991). Modell (1986) explains this as the borderline individual's inability to place what he notes in its proper context. Representations of relationships tend to be malevolent and poorly differentiated, with grossly illogical explanations for the causes of others' behavior, feelings, and thoughts. The related disposition to consider relationships and moral questions in self-centered and need-gratifying ways could explain the rationalization of cruelty (Westen 1991).

J. Weiss (1993) calls such misconstructions of experiences "pathogenic beliefs" (p. 74), and asserts that they are formed out of childhood trauma, compounded by the tendency of children to blame themselves for unfortunate things that happen to them. A common distortion among children who are sexually abused is to see themselves as the cause and to also feel a sense of shame. Developmental research has shown that incidents of child abuse and neglect, lengthy separation or losses before age 5, or psychiatric disturbance in the mother can interfere with cognitive functions such as coherence of early memories, object constancy, the ability to symbolize, and the capacity to differentiate one's own perspectives from others'. These factors may also provoke primitive defenses, such as denial, splitting, and projection (Beebe and Lachmann 1994, Brown 1993, Schore 1994, Silverman 1994, Westen 1991).

Research on cognitive processing has shown that traumatic incidents can disrupt both the encoding and storage of information, altering later retrieval of memories in both children and adults. Moreover, the emotional context surrounding an event, or an attachment figure's prohibitions against talking about it, may inhibit and limit the capacity to process incoming data (Herman et al. 1989, Siegel 1995). For example, the need to preserve attachment, at any cost, may lead individuals to divert attention away from the abusive elements of a situation or even to totally block them from consciousness (Freyd 1996). Fonagy and colleagues (1996) suggest that the refusal to consider the contents of another's thinking begins with mistreatment in childhood, and that it is a way for the child to avoid noting that a caregiver wished to harm the child. This defensive stance is then enacted in subsequent relationships. Not only are these persons unable to understand the mental states of others, they are less able to come to terms with abusive experiences, creating a vulnerability to emotional disturbance.

According to Fischer and colleagues (1997), therapists are misled if they believe that the defensive process involved in borderline pathology is a sign of developmental delay or immaturity. Instead, these persons should be seen not as retarded or delayed, but as "developmentally different" (p. 749). Although these individuals may appear erratic and primitive, they have actually constructed complex, sophisticated strategies of cognitive-affective regulation. Their "strange and distinctive patterns" (p. 749) of adaptation reflect the fact that they have taken a developmental pathway based on the need to sustain themselves in the face of stress and trauma. From Fischer and colleagues' study of hospitalized depressed adolescent girls between 10 and 18 years of age, the authors determined that traumatic experiences changed the organization of these young women's representations but not the level of their complexity. The authors explain that when children are mistreated they learn to live like chameleons, accommodating to the demands of the adults around them. They cannot allow expression of their true selves if they are to survive the physical and/or emotional assaults of a traumatizing environment. They also have to be able to adjust their behavior whenever their parents change from caring to rejecting and abusive. In due course, the working models of these persons come to be characterized by affective splitting and sudden, dramatic switches between positive and negative biases; for instance, they might suddenly reverse their view of another from wonderful to terrible. Fischer and colleagues emphasize that it is not the existence of splitting that is distinctive in borderline pathology, but rather the way the splitting switches frequently and rapidly across moods and situations. Also, although splitting is used to some degree by everyone, the impulsive and unpredictable switches of this disorder exceed the normative model of cognitive-affective organization presumed by therapists.

Fischer and colleagues (1997) suggest that a supportive environment such as therapy can help integrate positive and negative representations into a more coherent whole. A key ingredient in such therapy is to understand the patient's history from his own perspective in order to capture the complexity that goes into defensive strategies, such as dichotomizing people into all-good or all-bad. Another implication of the authors' research, which is compatible with the perspective of attachment, is the acknowledgment and validation of the psychic scars of painful experience; treatment cannot take away the fact of early impingement on a defenseless child, but it can help the client gain a new perspective on its meaning (Holmes 1997). Adults who come for psychotherapy may still be haunted by distant abuses in their current life, yet be unaware of the deep roots of their distress. A consistent and reliable therapeutic relationship can provide an alternative to past patterns of chaos and abuse, offering an opportunity to review and restructure working models.

IMPLICATIONS FOR PSYCHOTHERAPY

In applying concepts of attachment theory to borderline instability and ambivalence, there is emphasis on the need for the therapist to create a milieu that is sympathetic to clients' feelings of emptiness and despair and also validating of the pain of past experiences. One particularly salient aspect of the approach is the therapist's role in providing a secure affectional base, both in the therapeutic bond and in the physical setting of therapy. This involves creating an environment that promotes a "relationship of safety" (Pine 1990) for exploration of experiences and processing of negative affect, but that also sets limits and defines reality (Callahan 1996, Holmes 1993a, Johnson 1991, Sack et al. 1996). Sperling and Lyons (1994) note the importance of focusing on current functioning in the outside world, while Schore (1994) emphasizes the role of the therapist in being affectively attuned to the client. Attunement and responsiveness offer a holding environment (Winnicott 1965) that is especially important with the fluctuating rage, anxiety, and panic of borderlines. The therapist models a pattern of relating and modulation of emotions that clients gradually acquire and make their own in place of splitting off and projection (Brown 1993, Holmes 1993b, Schore 1994). Through internalizing the quality of the therapist's responses, the client begins to gain a more accepting view of herself, repair past disappointments, and modify defenses that were designed to deal with the terror and pain of separation (Holmes 1993b, 1996).

The implicit notion of attachment theory is that defensive processes are interpersonal, with two basic patterns, avoidance and anxious-ambivalence, particularly relevant to borderline adults (Gunderson 1996, Holmes 1993a). The pattern of anxious-ambivalent includes clinging and pleading for attention and can alternate unpredictably with a reluctance or fear of engaging in therapy. Because of insecure early attachments, borderline clients come to therapy hoping to find the idealized parent they never had but actually expecting rejection (Gold 1996). Summers (1988) portrays these polarized feelings of borderline transference as "walking a tightrope" (p. 348), with the client feeling suspended between the need for attachment and protection and a tremendous fear of separation and abandonment. This almost unbearable dilemma creates feelings of helplessness and tension and finally upsurges of anxiety and anger. Having to deal with such an intensity of emotions in addition to the strain of entitlement, lack of boundaries, and demands for special attention can try a therapist's patience (and equilibrium!) (Karen 1994, Sperling and Lyons 1994, Summers 1994).

Throughout, the therapist tries to stay steady and reliable, focused on establishing a trusting relationship while aware of the client's constant testing and sensitivity to the slightest hint of criticism or disregard (Gold 1996, Holmes 1993a). The therapist also knows that it will take time to overcome this tremendous fear of attachment, and that only as clients feel accepted and understood will they feel safe enough to begin to share unhappy feelings and memories. There is appreciation and affirmation of real experiences in helping these individuals put together a narrative of their life experiences. However, the extensive defensive exclusion and evasive communication in this dysfunction make it more difficult to get a sense of past experiences or of attachment figures. Since attachment experiences are imposed onto the therapist, transference can be used to understand and examine maladaptive working models, for example, the sudden disparagement or rage at any therapeutic response that implies that demands for attention or gratification are unreasonable (Fonagy et al. 1995). This was an issue in my work with Skye (Sable 1997a), a young adult single woman who often called early in the morning, insisting she needed to be seen within an hour and then becoming angry and depressed when told she couldn't be seen immediately. On the other hand, she was very quick to pull away from me if she felt misunderstood or pressured to reveal specific details or emotions about herself, resorting to elusive phrases such as "things are narrowing" or "it's a matter of energy levels."

SKYE

Skye sought therapy for physical exhaustion, isolation, and "lack of direction" in both work and social relationships following the breakup with a man she had hoped was going to marry her. She complained of numerous aches and pains, of being "sick and weird" in her body, "self-destructive," and "working against" herself. Although details about her family life were sketchy, we eventually put together a narrative of disappointing attachment relationships, and of parental figures who made her feel unlovable and unwanted. Both of her parents were unpredictable alcoholics who went on wild binges, and she had a sibling who was diagnosed with paranoid schizophrenia. Her mother, a compulsive house-cleaner, was unavailable to her children, and this did not improve after her father was killed in an automobile accident when Skye was 13. In addition, Skye reported a terrifying gang rape when she was in her early twenties, an encounter with a man who came at her with a knife soon after, and, while in therapy, several instances of hearing or seeing prowlers outside her apartment at night. Whether all of these events actually occurred as she claimed, it appeared that Skye did not feel safe within herself or in her world and used metaphors to let her therapist know the torment of her affectional relationships.

Sometimes she began a session with attacking, piercing questions, such as "How do I know you are who you say you are?" or "How do I know that this is really your office?" which suggest a working model of paranoid thinking and fear of relying on others. She could not sustain a positive image of her therapist between sessions. From a perspective of attachment, this incapacity for object constancy and failure to move beyond concrete thinking to symbolization reflects early caregiving failures both in providing adequate proximity and attunement (Fonagy et al. 1995). Young children require the physical presence of caregivers until they have a working model of confidence in the ready accessibility and responsiveness of attachment figures. Skye lacked an internal sense of security, and without it she could not tolerate the routine separations of adult life without panic and/ or fury. She quickly felt abandoned, yet was terribly afraid of getting close to anyone.

Gunderson (1996) applies concepts of attachment theory to improving borderline inconstancy and intolerance of aloneness by assuring clients of availability during crises, but by accompanying extra appointments with repeated exploration of the needs and reactions to intersession contact. Furthermore, when appeals for increased availability are made through coercive behaviors, such as Skye's early-morning insistence on her pressing distress, it may be pointed out that these kinds of maladaptive appeals mostly alienate those with whom connection is being sought. This can also help clients begin to see events and feelings from another's perspective, a crucial step in overcoming egocentric thinking and in forming relationships that are neither too involved nor too distant.

It took nearly ten years of sporadic treatment for Skye to gradually become less afraid of attachment and also of the anger that alienated her from others. With the stability and acceptance of treatment, Skye started to express herself more directly, settled down to a steadier job, and began to date. She was able to talk about the loss of her father and grieve for him and also to admit anger, for example, toward her mother, without becoming evasive and frightened by the power of her excluded feelings. She no longer had to say she was "locked in my head" when threatened by closeness or trying to inhibit anger.

Part of the therapeutic process is to inform patients that attachment behavior is a natural part of life, that it is apt to be evoked at times of stress, and that there can be grave consequences when parents discount or ridicule these basic inclinations. It is emphasized, however, that exploring the way parents behaved is not done for the purpose of assigning blame but in order to understand current problems (Bowlby 1973). Including family members in sessions, to discuss concerns such as the intensity of interactions and how to anticipate and deal with early signs of stress, can help diminish oscillating behavior. Melges and Swartz (1989) note that a particularly typical borderline-client entanglement that perpetuates oscillations occurs with the mother. For Skye, occasional joint appointments with her mother helped ease the volatile fluctuations of their past relationship.

One question in the ongoing debate about treating borderline disturbance is whether the therapist should be bold and confronting, setting limits and interpreting negative transference in the way advised by Kernberg (1984), or be accepting and empathetic as recommended by Kohut (1977). Holmes (1997) suggests that both techniques have a place in treatment. Restating the techniques in attachment terms, he writes that when acceptance and connection are the concern, affirmation and empathy are called for; when self-reliance and autonomy are compromised, a firmer stance and an acknowledgment of hostility and aggression are needed. With Skye, for instance, I tried to be sensitive to her misery and panic of abandonment but also to be careful to maintain therapeutic boundaries and not allow her demands or diffuse affect to overwhelm either of us.

An attachment framework provides a perspective for understanding the history and behavior of individuals with borderline personality disorder (Farber et al. 1995). Within this framework, the therapist adjusts her style to the client's need for emotional distance, while working toward more adaptive attachment patterns (Dolan et al. 1993). By proving to be a "trusted companion" (Bowlby 1988a, p. 138) who will not punish or abandon, the therapist helps the client sustain attachment and come to terms with experiences and feelings of separation and loss. And, because attachment endures, inner representations of the therapeutic situation will remain with the client and be used as a model for forming affectional relationships and solving subsequent difficulties (Farber et al. 1995).

THE BORDERLINE CONFLICT
OF ATTACHMENT AND DETACHMENT

Formulating an assessment of patients' distress is considered essential to gaining the knowledge necessary for effective intervention (Firth 1994). Despite the current controversy over whether one diagnostic entity can encompass such a variety of symptoms, Holmes (1993a) claims the term "borderline" is indispensable to describing a severity of psychological distress characterized by impoverished, disturbed relationships and inflexible and maladaptive personality traits. Research findings that have documented a connection between early mistreatment and borderline personality, and others that have found borderline symptoms congruent with post-traumatic stress disorder, all support Bowlby's contention that working models reflect an accumulation of real-life experiences, and the meaning assigned to them. These studies have also expanded our theoretical understanding of the impact of stressful experiences, such as trauma, loss, or threat of abandonment on those with a susceptibility to psychological distress. The use of the narrative dimension in treatment helps clients gain a clearer picture of their lives and attachment experiences (Holmes 1993a).

In many ways, the approach to borderline disorder proposed in this chapter is consistent with, and builds on, the groundbreaking work of Klein (1946), Mahler (1972), Masterson (1981), and Kernberg (1975), which revolves around issues of separation and abandonment, the struggle between space and distance, and the internalization of interpersonal experiences. An attachment perspective differs in its addition of ideas substantiated by attachment-based research, particularly on trauma, affect regulation, and cognitive functioning. A major innovation is Bowlby's (1969a) use of concepts from the field of ethology as an alternative to drive theory. This changes the way we listen to and frame our clients' stories. It is possible that the borderline quandary has more to do with difficulty in attaching rather than separating, a circumstance that would give even greater priority to the therapeutic bond and its value in demonstrating what is involved in a satisfactory, give-and-take relationship. Bowlby asserted that attachment behavior is lifelong, but he also made the point that attachment forms over time, with ongoing interaction and familiarity. When we validate clients' experiences as "reasonable approximations" (Bowlby 1988a, p. 149) of how they were really treated, we convey sympathy and respect for their versions of their attachment experiences and an understanding of why they are so fearful of genuine connection.

Winnicott (1965) and Ainsworth (1967) have noted two overall parenting patterns that foster secure bonds; the first occurs when parents respond appropriately to their child's calls for love and attention, and the second when the parents themselves regularly initiate social interaction with their children. Borderline pathology may represent extreme distortions of these two types of caregiving, as when parents are anxious and intrusive or, conversely, distant and dismissing of their child's emotional and physical needs. The child's conflict over the need for attachment is further exacerbated by the fact that the one who should be sought for protection and security is the individual who is simultaneously causing fears of abandonment and domination (Melges and Swartz 1989). Also, the traumas that set the foundation for borderline dysfunction may not be limited to those occurring very early in life. Westen and colleagues (1990) found, in a study of female adolescents diagnosed as borderline, that the high incidence of sexual abuse they linked to borderline outcome occurred during latency years. The researchers concluded that abuse instigated at this time could produce disturbances that would have a permanent effect on personality organization.

Bowlby (1985) has noted that parental patterns may have repercussions in later years and are usually repeated;

instances of physical and/or emotional abuse, the discounting of children's appraisals of what they have seen or heard, and outright rejection and ridicule could be constant and unrelenting. When this is the case, the extraordinary is ultimately experienced as the ordinary.

Kelly, who was discussed in Chapter 8, reported that she liked to watch horror movies because they reminded her of her abusive and unstable family. From a perspective of attachment, the "bad objects" of her inner working models held pervasive images and expectations of hurtfulness, inconsistency, and fear. In a similar way, Skye thought women at work were "witches" and "monsters" who could not be trusted, which suggests that in some way they reminded her of her family. There were also obvious transference references in these frightening images of women. Both Skye and Kelly tended to process current transactions in terms of a traumatic affectional history, which had a pervasive influence on their current relationships.

These illustrations suggest that personality disorders can be understood as disturbances in the organization of attachment behavior that occur along a continuum of secure versus insecure. Borderline functioning would fall toward the extreme of the insecure, presenting more disorganization, rigid defenses, and traumatic histories. Additional benefits of using attachment principles in therapy are improved understanding, treatment techniques, and guidelines for prevention. The latter would include noting the harmful effects of physical or emotional abuse among family members and directing efforts toward educating parents about hurtful behaviors such as unleashed anger or threats to abandon the child or to withhold love. Bowlby (1979) is known for calling attention to disruptive events, such as bereavement, that can be systematically measured, but he makes it clear that parental behavior, such as that of a depressed mother whose mood makes her withdrawn and indifferent, can also engender insecure attachment.

An argument for prevention of such behavior comes from findings that indicate that early mistreatment can cause lasting changes in affect regulation and cognitive development. Unless parents can be helped to change, or the child has another source of love and support, mistreatment increases the risk of later psychopathology and can undermine the child's ability to reflect on, or resolve, the abusive experience. Because patients themselves have difficulty recognizing how badly they were treated, experiences such as recurrent physical or emotional abuse may go undetected. Therapists can explain how the need for attachment leads individuals to bond to those with whom they interact and become familiar, regardless of how badly they may be threatened or treated, and that children do what they have to do in order to survive a tormenting environment. Also, because they lack the cognitive sophistication to think through what is happening to them, children are prone to misinterpret and misrepresent the meaning of these communications and to underestimate their damage (Karen 1994). Parents' perspectives are "contagious," especially to young children, and when the child is continually exposed to illogical constructions, there is a risk that she will lose objectivity and the capacity for logical thinking. Fonagy (1999) explains that when children are exposed to either confusing communication or hostile caregiving, they are forced into internalizing aspects of their parents that they are incapable of integrating into a coherent self image; this is how communication can be "crazy-making."

Since the publication of Bowlby's original formulations, there has been increasing emphasis on the total accumulation of family experience, as well as on the way a complex of variables interact to influence the organization of attachment behavior. There is need for further research to delineate the different manifestations of insecurity (for example, on the AAI), to specify the stressful life events that set a developmental pathway of insecure attachment in motion (Minde and Frayn 1992). Additional research is also needed to determine how concepts of borderline pathology might differ from those concerning the relationship between childhood abuse and neglect and post-traumatic stress disorder. Of course, and as with any emotional disorder, not all physically abused children become borderline, and conversely, not every borderline has been physically abused (Allen 1995). Bowlby's (1973) belief that psychological distress is the "product of bitter experience" (p. 210) has expanded our awareness and conceptualization of damaging situations, including physical and/or emotional abuse, that may be relevant to borderline personality disorder. Attachment theory gives us a perspective that can improve our ability to understand and help individuals whose affectional experiences have been so extremely painful and disabling.

10

Emotionally Abusive Attachments

From its inception, attachment theory has been known for recognizing the key role affectional relationships play in providing security and well-being throughout the life cycle. It is generally assumed that most adults care about having close attachments and maintaining them over time. Yet we know from our high divorce rate and the number of individuals seeking help for troubled relationships and family dysfunction that many people find it difficult to establish and sustain the kind of secure bonds they desire. Physical battering and other forms of violence are among the conditions that can seriously undermine the security of a bond, and during the past several decades increasing public and professional attention has been given to the high incidence of physical and sexual abuse in our society. There are now a variety of community-based services, such as shelters for battered women and crisis hotlines to assist with needs for protection and exploration of options (Goodman et al. 1993, Jacobson 1989, Karen 1994, Loring 1994, Meloy 1992, Mills 1996, Muenzenmaier et al. 1993, Robinson 1992). Clinicians now know to look for violence among family members, especially when the symptoms of disturbance are intense or the information presented has suspicious details or omissions in terms of what we know could be indications of physical mistreatment. Separate and distinct from physically violent behavior, however, are a range of verbal and emotional assaults that are extremely distressing and damaging to individuals of any age and that can be specifically conceived as emotional abuse.

Emotional abuse is defined as a consistent pattern of threatening, humiliating, and degrading behavior, representing an attempt to demean and control another person. It is characterized by repeated name-calling, continuous criticism, and undermining insults and/or manipulative behavior, such as punishing actions or withholding affection. Other features include false accusations, outright rejection, extreme jealousy, imposed isolation from others, possessiveness, and lying or breaking promises. Provocative acts, such as smashing furniture or dishes or driving fast and recklessly, are intended to frighten and intimidate, as are threats of harm or violence to another or someone close to the individual, or threats of abandonment. Threat may be communicated through body language, verbal content, or tone of voice (American Psychiatric Association 1994, Goodman et al. 1993, Loring 1994, Mills 1996, Moeller and Bachman 1993).

The possible manifestations of emotional abuse are so varied that Tolman (1992) described a continuum, extending from momentary withdrawal, lack of interest, or an angry comment to pervasive "severe psychological torture" (p. 292) resembling the brainwashing and mistreatment of prisoners of war. A further distinction is made by Loring (1994) between overt and covert psychological abuse. Overt abuse includes openly hostile and belittling actions, such as sulking, threats to abandon, mistreatment of children or pets in front of the adult victim, or coercion in daily schedules or activities. Covert abuse is more subtle and consists of negative feedback and labeling in ways that convey that the whole person is worthless, "bad," unimportant, or more difficult than comparable others, such as siblings. Other covert tactics include ignoring and discounting needs, feelings, or opinions.

Although much of our clinical work entails sorting out clients' painful feelings and memories, there is scant literature on the concept of emotional abuse as a separate phenomenon. Emotional mistreatment has been found to be related to psychological disturbances in both children and adults, which include depression and suicide, accidents, desperation, and confusion (Adam et al. 1995, Alexander 1993, Crittenden et al. 1994, Hart et al. 1996, Loring and Myers 1994), delinquency (Davis 1996), divorce (Kincaid and Caldwell 1995), and women's health problems (Moeller and Bachman 1993). However, there is no *DSM-IV* category for this diagnosis, in contrast to that for "relational problems" of physical and sexual abuse or neglect. When emotional abuse is considered, it is usually seen as an adjunct to physical abuse; however, although psychological maltreatment does sometimes escalate to violence and even suicide or murder, it often does not. Since young children do not have the cognitive ability to assess the extent of such dangers, they may believe that harm or death is imminent, and are, therefore, particularly vulnerable to post-traumatic stress reactions.

It is difficult to isolate and define emotional maltreatment because symptoms vary from person to person and are not as clear-cut as physical evidence (Adam et al. 1995, Davis 1996, Hart et al. 1996, Loring 1994, Moeller and Bachman 1993). Herman (1992) attributes a lack of comprehension of emotional abuse to the inadequate attention to chronicity in diagnostic thinking, and specifically to the fact that the therapeutic community does not recognize and understand the symptoms of repeated trauma,

such as the terror of living in an ongoing abusive situation. Thus, clinicians may focus on underlying pathology,
failing to connect symptoms to the real experience of
trauma. The devastating and harmful effects of certain interpersonal experiences, possibly in the past but also in
the present, may be overlooked.

According to Bowlby (1988a), this shortcoming is due
to Freud and traditional theory, which tended to disregard
the "reality" of life events and to see them as less significant in treatment than fantasy or the person's internal
world and unconscious defenses. As we have seen throughout this book, Bowlby perceived personality development
and psychological distress in terms of personal experiences with attachment figures, both current and past, and
asserted that treatment must explore these actual events
and the perceptions and the meanings ascribed to them.
He had connected adverse family experiences to the etiology of psychopathology as early as 1944, when he discovered that maternal deprivation and separation could
distort personality development. He argued (1973) that
a close, continuous relationship with a sensitive and reliable mother-figure was essential to an infant's future mental health, and that a mother who threatens to abandon or
withhold love from her child, or one who is depressed, indifferent, or unresponsive "probably has an immeasurably
greater pathogenic effect than is yet recognized" (p. 23).

With the goal of enhancing this recognition, this chapter applies attachment theory to the understanding
and treatment of adults who have had, or presently have,
emotionally abusive attachments. Communication and
behavior between abused adults and their abusers reflect
insecure attachment, with abused persons struggling to
preserve some degree of connection, and in doing so distorting the experience of abuse. The abusers, too, fear loss,

and try to control this by threats of abandonment and denigration. This dysfunctional pattern of attachment behavior places abused individuals at risk of developing psychopathology, particularly at times of stress, such as separation, loss, or when threatened with separation or abandonment (Loring 1994, Rohner and Rohner 1980).

Treatment provides the conditions necessary for an exploration of internal representations of oneself and one's attachment figures, in order to reappraise and restructure them to be more in line with the understanding acquired and a new model of what a secure relationship can be (Bowlby 1988b, Karen 1994). There is opportunity to practice more open and satisfactory relating and communicating with others. Clients learn they do not have to pay the price of abuse for connection. With a clear identification of emotional abuse, the client feels less frightened and "crazy" (Loring 1994).

Because of space constraints, this discussion is limited to aspects of emotional abuse that affect the abused individual and does not extend to the features of the abuser, or social inequalities, such as racism or sexism. However, the importance of identifying the "mental injury" (Lourie and Stefano 1978) of emotional abuse, and validating the client's experience, is equally relevant with societal mistreatments, and may also add to our knowledge of what leads abusers to abuse their closest relationships.

ATTACHMENT, ATTUNEMENT, AND WORKING MODELS

From an attachment perspective, an individual's working models reflect the internalization and organization of affectional experiences, beginning in infancy with the primary caregiver, and continuing into the present. According to Schore (1997), the mother's psychobiological attunement to her infant's internal emotional states is the mechanism that mediates the formation of the attachment bond. Her ability to maintain optimal levels of positive emotions in her child and to help regulate its negative affect states comes to be registered in the child's unconscious, influencing the development of psychic systems that will determine how information is processed for the rest of its life. Schore asserts that this first relationship with the mother affects the individual's capacity to enter into later emotional relationships because of the way these early experiences are imprinted into the emotion-processing right brain. When the mother is attuned to her infant, and modulates its emotional states, she facilitates the development of secure and consistent working models. For example, when a mother comforts her baby and helps it negotiate a stressful state, she transforms negative into positive emotion. This "interactive repair" (Tronick 1989) teaches the child that negative emotions can be endured and conquered. If, however, there is inconsistent, disconfirming, or misattuned parenting, the ability to regulate affects—from shame, rage and excitement to elation, disgust, panic, and fear—may take a form of either under- or overregulation.

D. Siegel (1999) explains that when children are exposed to trauma at a young age the release of stress hormones leads to destruction of neurons in areas of the brain (neocortex and limbic system) responsible for emotional regulation. An underproduction of synapses has a toxic effect on the developing brain; the consequent loss of the ability to regulate responses places the child at risk of psychological disturbance when stressful conditions call for adaption and flexibility. In essence, Schore (1997) writes, defensive processes represent strategies of affect regulation that avoid, minimize, or convert emotions that are too difficult to tolerate. The defensive exclusion of thoughts and feelings related to attachment leads to multiple, incompatible working models that interfere with adaptive functioning and the capacity to sustain satisfactory relationships (Adam et al. 1995, Bowlby 1973, 1988b, Bretherton 1988, Schore 1997, Siegel 1995). In the constructions of an emotionally abused individual, for example, although there may be experiences of ridicule, scapegoating, or contradictory explanations of an event, defensive processes have altered the individual's perceptions and memories, impairing affect regulation, coherence of details about the events of one's life, and relationships with others.

ATTACHMENT BEHAVIOR AND EMOTIONAL ABUSE

Utilizing a framework of attachment allows one to perceive psychological distress and defensive processes in terms of interpersonal experiences, both current and past. Symptoms such as anxiety and despair stem from the internalization of adverse attachment experiences, especially those that undermine feelings of self-reliance and security. Because the causes of disturbance are closely related to defensive distortions of attachment behavior, syndromes are more a matter of the degree of severity, or age and circumstances of traumatic incidents than exactly comparable to traditional diagnostic categories (Bowlby 1991, Herman et al. 1989, Holmes 1993a). In this vein, Bowlby (1984) conceives family violence as a form of disordered attachment behavior elicited to preserve bonds;

however, instead of strengthening relationships, it weakens them. The specific types of relationships that are apt to provoke this pattern of dysfunctional attachment are those with a sexual partner, parents, or children. Similarly, emotional abuse may be considered an exaggeration and distortion of potentially adaptive attachment behavior when it is characterized by psychological assaults that diminish security and heighten fear of separation and abandonment. Generally, attachment behavior is directed toward a person who can be relied on to respond with comfort and care at times of illness, fatigue, or alarm. A paradox of emotional abuse is that the person who would be sought for protection is the source of the anxiety and threat of separation. This sets up a vicious circle in which the more abuse a person receives, the more the person makes desperate attempts for connection with the abuser, giving the abuser more license to again mistreat (Holmes 1995). As with those who have suffered acts of violence, the abused person experiences a feeling of shock and disbelief after each episode.

An ethological perspective highlights the way their strong need for attachment leads individuals to bond to those with whom they interact and become familiar, regardless of how badly they may be threatened or treated. In fact, when a person is frightened by threat of separation or loss the attachment behavior system is activated, and there is an increased tendency to seek proximity for protection from the perceived threat to security (Bowlby 1973, James 1989, van der Kolk 1996). The distress of unmet attachment need is further compounded by the abuser's egocentric attitudes toward the abused person, which include discounting feelings and perceptions, denying accountability, and projecting blame for the problems onto the abused (Loring 1994).

Psychological injury is either denied or justified to such an extent that abused persons become distraught and confused about their own perceptions and feelings, and they are apt to take on the confusing messages and cruel statements of the abuser. Attempts for support become urgent and, feeling isolated and alone but unaware of the blatant cruelty, abused persons may appear to cling and demand attention (Rohner and Rohner 1980). They may try to connect to the abuser through validation and empathy, and when met with scorn, they try even harder; they hang onto any crumbs of warmth they may be given, and when these are inevitably withdrawn, they keep trying to get them back (Loring 1994).

Bowlby (1973) calls the feeling of desperation and insecurity over the stability of bonds an "anxious attachment." Adults who have developed an anxiously attached pattern of relating to others are apprehensive and afraid that attachment figures will not be available or responsive if called upon, and hence resort to defensive strategies to maintain contact at all costs. If these adults were emotionally abused as children, old fears and clinging behavior are more readily triggered (Loring 1994).

A major contribution of Bowlby's work was the emphasis he placed on the significance of real traumatic events, most notably disruptions—such as separations from and losses of main affectional relationships—in the etiology of insecure attachment and the susceptibility to develop psychological disturbance. Basing his conclusions on observational studies of children's and animals' reactions to separation from a figure to whom they were attached (Bowlby 1973, Heinicke and Westheimer 1966), Bowlby held that fear of separation was a universal response to retain attachment and protection at times of threatened disruption. This offers an explanation for the way certain pathogenic attachment experiences, such as intrusive caregiving or disclaiming what was said or heard in a family episode, can intensify or minimize reactions and cause an individual to develop an insecure style of relating to others. In considering attachment-related circumstances and emotional abuse, anxiety and anger may be elicited to protect a bond that was felt to be in jeopardy. Repeated threats of abandonment or contempt in reaction to pleas for care can further intensify these basic feelings. In this scenario, distress is not terminated by the responsiveness and affirmation of an attachment figure, nor is negative affect regulated and reduced. Instead, the uncertainty of support and the sense that others are hostile and not to be trusted engender anxious and possessive behavior, as well as bitterness and anger (Bowlby 1973, 1984).

RESEARCH FINDINGS

There is now convincing empirical evidence that exposure to chronic demeaning and coercive behaviors or attitudes in attachment relationships is related to the development of insecure or anxious attachment (Belsky et al. 1995, Bowlby 1973, Cicchetti and Toth 1995, Hamilton 1985). Ainsworth's Strange Situation procedure demonstrated that insecure attachment could arise from everyday interactions and not only specific traumatic situations (Main 1995). Longitudinal research has begun to document that the patterns of secure and insecure attachment that Ainsworth identified remain stable, at least until age 10, suggesting their influence on later personality functioning (Sroufe 1996).

Earlier chapters have discussed the extension of Ainsworth's Strange Situation protocol to adults' perceptions of their current romantic and parenting relationships. For example, Hazan and Shaver's (1990) single-item self-report measure, where respondents are asked to choose which of three statements most accurately describes their feelings in intimate relationships, found a correlation between Ainsworth's infant attachment categories and the quality of young adults' romantic relationships. Insecure adults, for instance, recollected fewer supportive attachment experiences, suggesting a continuity of expectations from earlier events into current working models of affectional bonds. Another modification of Ainsworth's measure, the Adult Attachment Interview, developed by Main and colleagues (Main and Goldwyn 1984) to assess adults' current state of mind regarding early attachment, found a correlation between the attachment status of young children in the Strange Situation and their mothers' descriptions of past relationships with their own parents. Additionally, in a study of suicidal adolescents by Adam and colleagues (1995), the semistructured interview revealed that episodes of significant separation, loss, or physical abuse were associated with the insecure classifications labeled as dismissive, preoccupied, or unresolved. The researchers concluded that attachment-related trauma was correlated with later psychiatric distress, and that surrounding circumstances, such as threat of abandonment or contradictory explanations, were apt to compound trauma and how it was understood, making the effects cumulative. Adam and colleagues (1995) claim that whether an experience is one of separation or loss, or physical or sexual abuse, it represents a fundamentally unacceptable and, for a child, incomprehensible violation of the attachment behavior system with its inherent expectation of protection and safety. Furthermore, they suggest that attachment experiences be classified along a continuum of organization-disorganization, based on responses to attachment-related trauma. At one extreme of the continuum would be secure attachment, with self-confidence and resilience in the face of stressful situations. At the other extreme, insecurity and susceptibility to disorganization would be associated with more stressful, traumatic histories, such as emotional abuse.

Although it was not conducted within an attachment framework, Loring and Myers's (1994) clinical interview study of 102 married women and their husbands was able to differentiate emotional abuse from physical abuse. The study, which also included a control group of nonabused women, found that every woman who was currently in an emotionally abusive marriage had been subjected to emotional abuse as a child, compared to 65 percent of the physically abused and none of the nonabused. There were other findings unique to emotional abuse, such as the almost continuous pattern of covert and overt verbal abuse rather than the cyclic one of physical abuse found by Walker (1984). Another difference was a tendency for emotionally abused women to be neither aware of nor to report that they were being emotionally abused. Whereas more than half of the physically abused women reported that they were also emotionally abused, less than one-third of the emotionally abused women saw themselves in that way. In spite of numerous threats and criticisms, even during the interview, the women did not realize or understand the impact the contemptuous communication was having. Moreover, even when they complained about their spouses' intrusiveness and criticism, their complaints were weakened by the abusers' denial and projection of blame. The women thus blamed themselves for their mistreatment, and focused on their longings for "respect" and "affirmation." They described more profound sadness and loneliness than the other groups, as well as constant fears of abandonment and feelings of being "unconnected" and "desperate."

The researchers concluded that there are individuals who are emotionally, but not physically, abused and that psychological assault itself is just as devastating as physical battering. This conclusion is supported by Moeller and Bachman's (1993) eight page, mail-back questionnaire on long-term health consequences of women subjected to physical, sexual, and/or emotional abuse during childhood. Moeller and Bachman found that either physical or emotional abuse led to a greater number of physical and psychological problems, and more frequent visits to physicians or hospitalizations. Of special interest to clinicians was their finding that 62 percent of emotionally abused women sought psychotherapy compared to only 13 percent of the physically and/or sexually abused women.

Briefly, several other avenues of research shed light on the link between early mistreatment and later insecure attachment. Elliot and King (1960) found that underfeeding puppies caused them to attach more rapidly than puppies that were overfed, indicating anxious attachment in the underfed puppies. Hooven and colleagues (Hooven et al. 1995) found that derogatory and belittling comments made to preschool children caused negative attitudes about emotional regulation and expression three years later. Magai (1999) found that parents who used coercive disciplinary practices engendered insecure attachment behavior in their children. Finally, Alexander (1993), using a self-report, attachment-based questionnaire, found a higher incidence of insecure attachment and a number of personality disorders in women who had been victims of incest in childhood.

IMPLICATIONS FOR TREATMENT

Taken together, these research studies suggest that certain childhood experiences can derail personality to a developmental pathway of insecure attachment. Furthermore, the more severe and/or prolonged the pathogenic events, the greater the propensity for developing psychological disturbance, especially when the individual is later confronted with precipitating stress, such as separation, loss, or psychic trauma. It is important for clinicians to know that emotional abuse may not be easy to detect because symptoms are varied and disguised and clients are not aware of the context of their complaints (Loring 1994). The therapist acts as a trusted companion who encourages exploration of current and past attachment experiences and the responses to them. With clarification and affirmation that intensely distressing experiences, such as verbal cruelty, did occur, or are occurring, clients can reconsider their meaning and reconstruct working models so that they feel "less under the spell of forgotten miseries and better able to recognize companions in the present for what they are" (Bowlby 1988b, p. 137).

In describing the role of the therapist as a trusted companion who enlists clients in an exploratory journey through their attachment experiences, Bowlby (1988b) places particular emphasis on the creation of a secure base for sharing thoughts and memories and for restructuring working models. Clients who are currently in an emotionally abusive relationship need an alternative attachment to enable them to give up the destructive one. By being consistent and reliable, reducing fear at times of heightened stress, and showing interest in trying to understand and help, the therapist provides a supportive presence that helps abused persons feel valued and comforted, less alone, and more integrated. For the first time, they may feel someone is on their side (Loring 1994). Both the physical setting of sessions, with its structure and consistency, and the sympathetic responsiveness of the therapist contribute to a sense of safety, as well as a sense of comfort and confidence that there will be relief from pain and confusion (Farber et al. 1995, J. Siegel 1999). It also helps to recite incidents of abuse, but clients need the time to feel attached and safe enough to acknowledge such intolerable behaviors. If the client feels frightened by the new experience of closeness, the therapist can explain that these feelings are an aspect intrinsic to forming secure attachment, something they have been denied in previous relationships.

Because emotionally abused persons rarely perceive themselves as maltreated, they usually seek therapy for symptoms that range from intrusive thoughts and suicidal ideation to anxiety, despair, and loneliness, or feelings of desperation and unreality. They may complain of a troubled relationship, but will be apt to blame themselves and not comprehend how the relationship is the source of their suffering (Loring 1994). Therefore, it may take time and careful listening on the part of the therapist for evidence of emotional abuse to surface. Loring lists several factors that assist diagnosis, such as questioning the nature of attachment relationships, feelings of self-blame, hopelessness and loneliness, and detecting specific mechanisms of abuse and what evokes them. When the client is ready, it is essential that a condition of emotional abuse be identified and labeled. Not only does this give words to the client's experience, but it conceptualizes the abusive process and the impact it has had.

Treatment for emotional abuse clarifies the components of psychological mistreatment to the abuser when this is possible, and also validates clients' feelings and perceptions about their experiences. For example, it helps to eliminate confusion when intrusive thoughts and flashbacks are identified as reactions to abuse. Together, the therapist and client try to understand how these "terrible kind[s] of attachment" (Loring 1994, p. 34) originated and developed and, if they are current, why the person is unable to resolve the present relationship. Even when indignant about their mistreatment, clients may dwell on events, pondering what they did wrong and considering what they might do to make things right. As these clients often think they can improve their situation, the therapist must encourage a realistic appraisal of the abuser's motivation and potential to change. If improvement seems unlikely, the therapist must be emphatic; the abuse is not the client's fault, and there is nothing the client can do which would alter the abuser's behavior. This tactic is more directive than the usual therapeutic technique and is used in conjunction with a clear identification of emotional abuse and validation of clients' feelings and distress. Validation of emotional trauma is a precondition for reestablishing feelings of self-worth and hope and for giving up the struggle to rationalize abusive behavior. Affirmation helps the client cope with feelings such as fear of "coming apart" or beliefs that psychological abuse was fair or deserved. Identifying what triggers abuse, combined with confirming its pain, is reassuring to individuals whose feelings have been discounted and who have lost confidence in their perceptions and attitudes (Loring 1994).

Attachment-oriented therapists want to learn details of what has actually happened, not only in the past, but what still may be going on in the present, and to understand how all of these experiences are woven into working models (Bowlby 1973, 1988b, Farber et al. 1995, Sable 1994b). Research (Bower 1987) on cognitive processing has shown that traumatic experiences such as emotional abuse can be prone to distortions of memory when there is a need to preserve attachment.

We saw this with Kelly, whose terror of losing her mother caused her to shut away and forget her mother's threats of suicide for over twenty years. Although Kelly's parents did not physically mistreat her, they were so abusive emotionally that, by the time she sought treatment as a young adult, she was anxious and afraid of being close to anyone. Kelly had defensively excluded most of her childhood memories, as well as her desires for attachment and comfort. This interpersonal view of defensive strategies to maintain affectional bonds also explains the loyalty of abused persons to their abusers; there exists an underlying need for attachment and connection regardless of how one is being treated. As Fairbairn (1943) noted, a bad object is felt to be better than having no object at all. For a long time, Kelly wondered how she could continue to care about people who had been so unreliable, abusive, and unconcerned about her. Thus, psychological trauma, such as threat of abandonment or betrayal by a person who should signify trust, affects how information about attachment is processed and how it will appear in the narratives clients tell about themselves. In addition, a historical narrative can be clouded by events in the present. Kelly was subjected to severe punishment, threats of abandonment, and actual separations as a child, and these emotionally abusive parents were still in her adult life. Though they were older and less explosive, she was continually confronted with their disturbed behavior and unwillingness to change. Over the years of therapy, Kelly did come to accept that they would never be the kind of parents she yearned for, and she was able to eventually reach an acceptable degree of untroubled interaction with her father that allowed her to have periodic contact with him. Finding that her mother remained critical and belittling, Kelly disengaged herself almost completely from her.

Besides tracing their history of early emotional abuse, as was the case with Kelly, clients may also be confronted with mistreatment in current relationships.

KATE

Such a history is illustrated by Kate (Sable 1998a), who returned to treatment after an angry breakup with Brian, with whom she had lived for a year. She was anxious and distraught, and appeared more upset than at any time the therapist had seen her in their previous three years of work together. She cried and grieved over the loss of the relationship, although she described Brian as critical, belittling, and controlling; for instance, he told her she was incompetent in her career and needed to acquire better skills. Kate kept wondering why she was so terribly "beaten down" and "obsessed." At a particularly distressed moment, I asked her whether she thought that Brian had been emotionally abusive to her. Upon hearing that phrase, Kate grew quiet and thoughtful and then appeared relieved. She seemed to now have a way to grasp and make sense of what she had been feeling and the degree of anxiety and despair that she had reported. Kate began to reassess their relationship, and, with a perspective of how insulting and demeaning Brian had been toward her, was more prepared to complete grieving and accept her loss. We were able to connect up her choice of that kind of relationship with certain childhood experiences and expectations, such as her submissiveness to a demanding and controlling father, and to finally resolve some of her difficulties in forming a lasting adult attachment. It may have been possible that she provoked Brian to treat her as her father had; however, since this had not occurred in her other earlier relationships, it seemed likely that this was an emotionally abusive relationship over which she had no control and for which she was not to blame.

This conclusion is supported by a study (Feeney 1998, 1999) of seventy-two dating couples that found that a securely attached person who is involved in a negative relationship can lose confidence and become upset and insecure. Feeney determined that the impact of a negative experience depended on how long the relationship lasted and how significant it was felt to be. Feeney also stated that helping the abused person understand the effects of the experience could change working models. With Kate, I had the advantage of already having a therapeutic relationship with her; we had previously worked on understanding her family history and dynamics. Helping her come to terms with a traumatic experience involved elucidating the fact of emotional abuse, reviewing and giving her cognitive awareness of the implications of her family's influence on her subsequent relationships, and affirming the severity of both Brian's and her father's mistreatment. As I had before, I conveyed that desires for attachment are a natural part of life and that compromise solutions, such as excluding the pain of mistreatment, are often the only means available to maintain attachment. This helps clarify the confusion and self-loathing that may be experienced when the individual desires proximity to abusing persons.

THE TRAUMA OF EMOTIONAL ABUSE

Adults seeking psychotherapy may still be dealing with troubling residues from their families of origin as well as current interpersonal problems (Karen 1994). Bowlby's approach calls for careful scrutiny of clients' perceived and actual experiences and for therapists to be informed about the wide array of situations that influence personality development. I propose that the concept of emotional abuse enhances our ability to recognize the impact of certain severe events on individuals as well as to confirm responses to them. With this portrayal of clients' experiences, therapists acknowledge the depth and extent of psychological mistreatment to which clients have been, or are presently being, subjected. An ethological orientation explains the intensity of attachment behaviors that abusive treatment elicits as well as the way these behaviors reflect inherent tendencies to protest maltreatment and regain protection and feelings of safety. The overwhelming terror and distress of psychological abuse has been compared to post-traumatic stress disorder, which follows "exposure to an extreme traumatic stressor" (American Psychiatric Association 1994), and is characterized by comparable problems, such as difficulty concentrating or sleeping, or experiencing recurring memories and images (Browne 1993, Loring 1994, van der Kolk 1987).

Emotional abuse can lower the threshold of attachment behavior because, like PTSD, it tends to occur in an environment that should connote safety. Just as we pull our hand away from a hot stove, we instinctively react if emotional well-being is threatened. There is something that doesn't feel right, that seems to be off-track and intolerable. When we identify emotional abuse, we are making a strong statement that there is a quality of experience that has gone beyond what is acceptable or reasonable. The label explains what is happening and why abused persons feel the way they do. Emotional cruelty exceeds what can be tolerated, justified, or excused. It steps over a line, putting the abused person at the whims of a tormentor, who intersperses cruelty with apologies and promises to change.

Affirming the abusive process can be empowering for clients. Some may have been aware of abuse but thought they deserved it or that all families behaved that way. Bringing the abuse to light will allow them to now feel understood and no longer alone, and will reduce feelings of guilt and self-blame. With the support of a therapeutic bond and consideration of attachment patterns that emerge in transference, clients come to know what a positive relationship feels like, realize they do not deserve to be abused, and can now modify previous misconceptions. If presently in an abusive situation that shows no promise of mending, they may be able to resolve their feelings about the relationship.

It has been noted in Chapter 1 (and see Farber et al. 1995, Hamilton 1987, Holmes 1993a) that treatment using attachment theory is not yet fully articulated and that its value may be more one of emphasis and a way to frame our clients' experiences. Despite its relevance to the treatment of emotional abuse, there is still a lack of knowledge about the theory's application with maltreated populations, since most of the research has been of normative samples (Cicchetti and Toth 1995). Also, research has tended to give priority to specific incidents, such as physical abuse or parental loss, rather than to the groups of influential variables that interact to shape developmental pathways (Adam et al. 1995). Further studies can help define and designate acts constituting emotional abuse, which may even be increasing due to society's prohibitions against physical and sexual abuse (Davis 1996). Research can offer guidelines for treatment, such as optimal ways of dealing with transference or cognitive processing of traumatic memories. For example, the issue of trusting the therapist is crucial to someone who has been subjected to mistreatment by parental figures (Siegel 1995).

Finally, more specific findings on the variations in attachment patterns and how they relate to later pathology can be used to educate parents and professionals, as well as to plan prevention. For example, Fonagy's (Fonagy et al. 1991) finding that traumatized children do not develop a theory of mind that allows them to understand the feelings of others has implications for understanding and treating the self-centered thinking of abusers. Children whose feelings and attitudes about their experiences are disconfirmed or obliterated not only defensively disbelieve the intentions of an abuser in order to survive verbal cruelty, but may themselves grow up to be abusers. Better understanding and treatment of psychological mistreatment can also decrease the risk of its escalating to physical abuse. Meloy (1992) makes the sobering point that most interpersonal violence is directed toward those with whom the perpetrator has a close affectional bond. Thus, it seems we are compelled to face certain fundamental facts about attachment and bonding and what we can do to promote the security of affectional relationships. For instance, there is accumulating evidence that an adult partner can buffer stress and be reparative of earlier losses (Brown 1982, Holmes 1993a, Wallerstein 1995).

The concept of emotional abuse has been overlooked in our theoretical development for too long. Recently, I was discussing a troubled family with a colleague who was treating the parents. In response to the observation that certain attitudes and behavior sounded emotionally abusive and needed to be addressed, the therapist exclaimed, "But they're the parents." This comment exemplifies the way physical abuse and neglect was once dismissed as a private family affair, because it occurred in a protected space into which others did not intrude. Emotional abuse can be perilous to mental health and security of attachment. Persistent mistreatment from an attachment figure is insidious and destructive, and seriously undermines self-reliance and perceptions about oneself and others. By identifying and affirming responses to this pattern of dysfunctional behavior, and clarifying the context in which it developed, clients can be helped to move away from abusive affectional ties and toward the capacity for healthier relationships.

11

Pets and Attachment

In the United States today, over half of all households include a dog or cat. Our canine population exceeds 52 million and the feline population is even larger. One has only to sit in the waiting room of a veterinary clinic, talk to a bereaved pet owner, or observe people interacting with their animals to see how profound a connection is felt toward a pet. Many perceive their companion animals as members of the family (Cain 1985), give them human names, and indulge them with cavalcades of products and services such as health foods, extravagant attire, mobile doggie grooming, designated doggie parks, and day care. Pictures of pets are everywhere in the media and advertising, which suggests that they will appeal to and catch a viewer's attention. There is now a national official "take your dog to work day" in June, and some major league ballparks have also sponsored similar occasions. A church in New York allows dogs to accompany members of its congregation to Sunday morning services. Sport utility vehicles are being sold that have a built-in apparatus to restrain and protect a dog.

Although the bond between people and animals dates back to prehistoric times (Netting et al. 1987), the current preoccupation with family pets indicates an unprecedented cultural phenomenon. From rather ordinary and simple creatures who were fed and occasionally walked or played with, companion animals have assumed an exalted position that includes open emotional expression toward them. Previously, children, and to some degree older people, could harbor affectionate feelings for their pets without appearing foolish (Knapp 1998). But in the film *As Good as It Gets* (1997), a small dog penetrates one character's social isolation and inspires him to begin to overcome some of his compulsive behavior. Pets are also prominent in television shows and films such as *Mad About You* and *You've Got Mail* (1993), where, unlike the character portrayed by Jack Nicholson, their young adult owners do not lack for human connection.

Research has begun to support what most pet owners already know: having a family pet enhances and enriches the quality of life. Although Keddie (1977) wrote that it is difficult to assess this benefit in scientific terms, there is now evidence that animal companionship alleviates loneliness and even keeps us healthier (Cusak 1988, Kale 1992, Muschel 1984). Pets have proven effective in reducing anxiety (Barker and Dawson 1998, Cole and Gawlinski 2000, Sussman 1985) and blood pressure (Katcher 1982), and in promoting survival in coronary artery illness (Cole 1999). In a follow-up study of ninety-three patients who returned home after heart attacks, only 6 percent of those with pets died, compared to 44 percent without a pet (Friedman et al. 1980). These results occurred independent of the existence of other social relationships, leading the researchers to conclude that pets influenced people in ways different from, and in addition to, human relationships. Similarly, in a large telephone interview study of Medicare enrollees, Siegel (1990) found that elderly pet owners reported less psychological distress and fewer physician visits over a one-year period than respondents who did not own pets. She also noted that 58 percent of the sample did not live alone; therefore, pets were not necessarily their only relationship; in another study (Garrity et al. 1989) of individuals 65 years or older, pet ownership was inversely related to depression.

Animal-assisted therapy has proven successful with children (Levinson 1965), medical patients suffering depression (McCulloch 1981), institutionalized mentally ill patients (Corson and Corson 1965, Siegel 1962), and elderly persons living alone or in nursing homes (Brickel 1984, Bustad and Hines 1982, Cusack 1988, Mugford and McComisky 1975). An animal-assisted therapy program (Muschel 1984) for cancer patients and those close to them concluded that pets might help individuals in ways people may not be able to. Though based on a relatively small sample, a follow-up questionnaire revealed that twelve out of fifteen patients felt that animals lessened their fears, despair, loneliness, and isolation, thereby increasing their adaptation to a difficult situation. The researcher attributed the effectiveness of contact with the animals to the pet's quiet, accepting, and nurturing manner. Pets neither intruded upon nor avoided dying patients.

Another animal-assisted therapy program (Cole and Gawlinski 1995, 2000) in the cardiac care unit of a hospital, found that a twenty-minute visit from a dog made patients happier, calmer, and less lonely. When the patients were asked what could be improved in the program, the most common response was to have the dogs visit more often, and most replied that the visits would be a positive factor in future decisions about their returning to that hospital. Finally, in a laboratory and home study (Allen et al. 1991) of forty-five female dog owners with a mean age of 38, it was demonstrated that the presence of a pet reduced stress (physiological measures included pulse rate, blood pressure, and skin conductance) in a threatening circumstance (mental arithmetic tests), whereas the presence of a friend did not. The researchers speculated that pets are associated with positive feelings, such as making people laugh, and are always happy to see their owners. These qualities induce a positive feeling state that may not be evoked as dependably by friends, and that reduces the stress of a threatening situation.

Pets offer people friendship and unconditional love; they offer and receive affection and are readily available. The presence of pets increases feelings of happiness, bolsters self-confidence and self worth, and reduces feelings of loneliness and isolation on a daily basis and during stressful times or transitions such as spousal bereavement (Gerwolls 1990, McCulloch 1981, Rynearson 1978, Sable 1991c, Stewart 1983, Zasloff 1996). Konrad Lorenz (1952) equated a need for the companionship of his dog to a bond with nature and Heiman (1965) saw pets as helping to maintain psychological equilibrium. Knapp (1998) wrote that pets give their owners something that people cannot. She said that her dog gave her an uncomplicated connection that made her less afraid and taught her about love. Knapp quotes a dog owner in Los Angeles: "Love is love. I don't care if it comes from humans or from animals: it's the same feeling" (p. 14).

What makes pets such a compelling emotional force in our lives? Why is it that our affection for our dog or cat doesn't fade, and often lasts longer than many adult romantic relationships? Some speculate that pets take the place of children or are substitutes for partners in a mobile society that is less committed to permanent relationships. But what does it mean when nearly one-third of the participants, in a study of 122 families with dogs (Barker and Barker 1988), said they felt closer to the pet than anyone else in the family? Granted pets, and especially dogs, are credited with giving uncompromising love and devotion and accepting us just as we are, but is there not possibly some deeper meaning to the intense bonds we form with these companion animals, one that is connected to the roots of our emotions and relationships? Using Bowlby's framework of attachment, this chapter explores the way family pets, in particular dogs and cats, provide certain components of attachment that may account for our strong ties to them. Furthermore, affectional bonds with pets are examined in the context of Weiss's (1974, 1978, 1982b) concept of the social provisions of relationships. Clinical implications, as well as issues of prevention, social policy, and future research, are also discussed.

ATTACHMENT AND CAREGIVING BEHAVIORAL SYSTEMS

From an ethological perspective of attachment, humans possess a lifelong psychobiological need for proximity to familiar figures, especially at times of stress (Holmes 1996, Schore 1994). This need for closeness is regulated by an attachment behavioral system that is designed to bring one discriminated figure together with another. Unless there is maltreatment or a mismatch of temperament or relatedness, increased exposure is associated with greater affection. Infants require a continuous watching over that the caregiving system assures as adults respond to cues of distress, vulnerability, and also, their child's babyish features (Hazan and Shaver 1994). According to evolutionary theory, natural selection favors the development of traits that facilitate parental care. The infantlike features (such as round heads, large, round eyes, and short extremities relative to body size) of puppies and kittens signal vulnerability and the need for care, and attract human adults in the same way human infants

do. Moreover, dogs and cats retain babylike characteristics when they mature; in a sense they are like children
who do not grow up (Bogin 1990). They are cute, and
their cuteness rivets us and draws us to them, facilitating their survival with food and shelter as well as the
proximity and familiarity that promote the establishment
of attachment.

Research has shown, moreover, that in some circumstances mere proximity brings comfort, even if the attachment figure cannot do anything. This could explain the
relief experienced in a familiar pet's company, particularly
under trying circumstances. Also, once it is formed, attachment is exclusive and persistent and is not easily relinquished or redirected to others (Marris 1982, Weiss
1982a). However, the capacity to make an affectional bond
generalizes to others. This characteristic explains how a
securely attached child is reassured by a friendly and familiar teacher if upset while at school. This feature, which
recognizes that exposure facilitates attachment, could also
explain why individuals who are not exposed to pets are
less interested in them, or have difficulty understanding
a pet owner's attachment.

In addition to the effects of proximity and familiarity, attachment is promoted by responsiveness. For example, socially responsive children are liked better by
their peers (Rubin 1980) and adults are more attracted to
those who find them appealing (Aron et al. 1989). Who is
more responsive than a devoted dog that just wants to be
close by and is always attuned to its owner's moods? Companion animals have a boundless capacity for accommodating to the rhythm of their owners' routines, always
available, waiting quietly and patiently until they are sum-
moned. As Knapp (1998) puts it, "dogs strike deep chords

in us" (p. 25). "[They have a] healing power [in] what they bring out in us, with what their presence allows us to feel and experience" (p. 209).

SOCIAL PROVISIONS OF RELATIONSHIPS

According to attachment theory, adult bonds are conceived as a continuation of the earlier mother–child attachment behavior system, modified by age and experience, and later directed toward others such as a spouse or other committed relationship. In his definition of adult attachment, Weiss (1991) noted that it is a personal relationship that contributes to the maintenance of an inner sense of well-being and feelings of security. Further, Weiss (1982a, 1991) has specified some criteria of adult attachment that distinguish it from childhood attachment and also from other relational bonds. Just as children do, adults seek contact and security from attachment figures at times of stress; attaining proximity or assurance of accessibility reduces fear and anxiety. Even for adults, any threat to the accessibility of attachment figures evokes protest, distress, and other measures to ward off separation or loss.

Weiss (1974) considered attachment one of a variety of "social provisions"—relationships that adults require for well-being, some other provisions being social affiliation, opportunity for nurturance, and the possibility of obtaining help and guidance. These social provisions can only be met through relationships and we need different provisions from different sources, depending on the situation. Attachment relationships have the potential to meet the provisions in the other categories because they imply the assurance of proximity.

PETS AND ATTACHMENT

Research evidence now indicates that there are elements of attachment in a variety of close adult relationships, including adult committed partnerships and therapy relationships. Scharlach (1991) and Ainsworth (1989) identified types of attachment between adults and their parents, and Ainsworth (1989) suggested that certain friends and other companions provide components of attachment. I propose that family pets, in particular dogs and cats, also have the potential to provide an emotional bond of attachment that promotes a sense of well-being and security for adults of any age. In terms of Weiss's (1974) social provisions of relationships, pets can provide opportunities for attachment and the nurturance of others while broadly offering extended social networks and social interaction. For instance, a person out walking a dog or playing with her animal at a doggie park is likely to invite conversation. Pets can uniquely fill a combination of emotional needs, sometimes substituting for an absence of attachment in a way that makes people feel they are not alone, and at other times expanding the range of relationships and social contacts that add to the pleasures of life and give a feeling of comfort and companionship at times of difficulty. Furthermore, pets offer an opportunity for commitment and taking responsibility for a life beyond one's own. Finally, the loss of a pet may precipitate not only grief and mourning, but also intensified anxiety, depression, and anger, the same characteristics that mark responses to loss of human attachment (Keddie 1977, Rynearson 1978, Stewart 1983).

Gerwolls (1990) presented evidence that dogs and people formed bonds many thousands of years ago, and suggested the protective value of early doglike wolves and thus the adaptive nature of this relationship for actual survival. Although we do not generally rely on our pets to physically protect us, Melson (1989) posited that the bond with a pet becomes part of inner working models of attachment and family relationships. Evidence that pets are seen as family members who provide affection and attachment came from a telephone interview study of 612 adults conducted by Albert and Bulcroft (1988) in order to examine the psychological and emotional roles of pets in an urban area. A factor analysis of twelve items related to loving relationships among humans revealed nine items that were identified as pet attachment:

1. I feel closer to (pet's name) than to many of my friends.
2. I like (pet's name) because he/she accepts me no matter what I do.
3. (Pet's name) makes me feel loved.
4. (Pet's name) gives me something to talk about with others.
5. I feel closer to (pet's name) than to other family members.
6. (Pet's name) keeps me from being lonely.
7. I like (pet's name) because he/she is more loyal than other people in my life.
8. (Pet's name) gives me something to take care of.
9. There are times when (pet's name) is my closest companion. [p. 547]

The responses revealed that pets were considered important family members, with dogs the favorite, followed by cats. The authors suggested that this preference may have been based on the greater affection demonstrated by dogs toward their owners, and that the way dogs and owners interact may have resulted in a higher level of attachment.

Albert and Bulcroft also found that changes in pet ownership at different times of the life cycle affected feelings of attachment. They concluded that pet attachment was particularly important among divorced, never-married, and widowed people, childless couples, newly-weds, and empty-nesters. Because pets both give and receive affection, they can be emotional substitutes and contribute to maintaining morale when people are alone or going through difficult periods of transition. Muschel (1984) explained that transitions sometimes make people feel like outcasts of society. This was apparent in the bereavement study (Sable 1989), mentioned in Chapter 7, in which I interviewed women who had been widowed one to three years and explored variables related to adjustment following the loss of their spouse. In contrast to comments such as "I feel they patronize me" and "I'm a dropout of society," they used to describe how they perceived the support of their friends, women referred to their pets in a positive, affectionate way. Women who had pets, in particular dogs, and then cats, also reported significantly less loneliness to a specific question about feeling lonely. The following statements appeared at various points in the interview and not always in response to the actual question inquiring if they owned a pet. The warmth and caring of the comments attest to the fondness the women felt for their pets and also show how pets are felt to allay loneliness.

> "[I] hug my dog every day. Hug for you [husband] as well as myself. [It is] good to have an animal."

"I love dogs. They're very comforting. They're my good friends. Maybe they are man's best friend."

"I adore her. She's the first thing I hug every morning and again at night. I've transferred a lot of my . . . feelings toward her."

When asked if she had had other recent losses, one woman cited the loss of her husband's dog. She went on to describe how she felt when she had to euthanize the pet. "[It was] awful. The last tie to him." Of her current dog she said: "[You] need a place to put your love."

A young woman responded that her two dogs were extremely helpful in dealing with her loss and difficulty with anxiety. "[When I had] panic at night, my dogs [were the] only things that helped. I sat on the floor with them. [They're] just being there."

In response to a question about whether the person lived alone, one woman said, "Yes, but I have two dogs." Another woman also answered that she lived with her dog, going on to explain: "If it weren't for the dog, I wouldn't have gotten up at first. That poor dog. After I started to cry, he'd get up and comfort me. I don't know how he knew." This quotation illustrates the provision of caregiving as well as the sense of meaning she derived from her dog.

Albert and Bulcroft (1988) observed that in the modern urban world companion animals make no economic sense and furnish no financial profit, yet owners spend vast amounts of time and money on them. Pets behave in ways that foster a sense of being needed and are dependent on their owners for physical care, which may explain the tendency of pet owners to call them "baby" or "child." A veterinary oncologist (Cardona, personal communication) reported that pets' attachment behavior intensifies and that they show increased proximity to their owners when pets develop cancer. The owners' response of caregiving reflects a distinct behavioral system that Melson (1989) identified as a dimension of attachment. She noted a range of caregiving behaviors such as providing pets with proximity to reduce stress, cleaning up after them, and holding and sleeping near them. Although her study was limited to an investigation of the relationship between pets and children, Melson outlined four dimensions of human–pet attachment that equate with several elements of attachment and caregiving: time spent with and activities directed toward the pet, interest in and affect toward the pet, knowledge about the pet and its care, and behavioral responsiveness to the pet and its needs.

One unique aspect of pets is their constant proximity. A complaint of bereaved spouses, for example, is that social support tends to be mobilized at the time of loss but is then quickly withdrawn (Glick et al. 1974, Sable 1991a). Parkes and Weiss (1983) noted that for social support to be effective it must continue throughout the period of mourning. Pets may help fill this gap and reduce the feeling of aloneness that comes with the loss of a close, loved person, especially for elderly people or those living far away from relatives.

Siegel (1990) measured affectional attachment in elderly pet owners with a question about how important the pet was to the respondent. Owners of dogs showed the most attachment and referred to their pets more frequently, especially to mention that their pets gave them love and security. Noting that only certain bonds are effective buffers against stressful life elements, Siegel claimed that dogs, more than other types of pets, provided their owners with companionship and attachment.

Evidence that caregiving benefits the physical health of the elderly comes from a large, one-year longitudinal telephone interview study (Raina et al. 1999) of individuals aged 65 and older. The researchers found that individuals who owned either cats or dogs enjoyed better physical health than those who didn't. Noting that even though cats do not require (and thus do not provide) activities such as exercise, the way dogs do, the study suggests that the caregiving of a cat or a dog results in a sense of purpose and responsibility that fosters vitality.

Attachment theory highlights the lifelong requirement for close affectional bonds with others. Because the substitute attachment of a pet provides closeness, touching, and a chance to feel worthwhile and needed (Albert and Bulcroft 1988, Keddie 1977, Muschel 1984), it may have special value for elderly people, who are apt to experience disruptions in relationships with familiar people, places, and things, as well as declining health, physical incapacity, and limited financial resources. The loss of a pet may also compound distress. For instance, one woman in my bereavement study (Sable 1991a), in response to an inquiry about other recent losses, replied that she was forced to give her pet away. Her mention of this event indicates that losing her pet added stress to an already difficult time. This bond can be protected by advocating for policies that ensure that pets be allowed in housing facilities, whether nursing homes, retirement communities, or individual apartments. Pet-restriction policies are becoming a more pronounced social problem as the population ages (Monahan et al. 1992); the increasing number of elderly people in our population makes it imperative to discover and utilize effective attachment substitutes (Bock and Webber 1972).

CLINICAL IMPLICATIONS

If pets are seen as family members and attachment figures, they hold implications for therapeutic treatment, prevention, and social policies. In treatment, clients should be encouraged to discuss pets; for example, they should be asked about them as attachment figures when taking an inventory of family relationships (Rynearson 1978). Showing interest in the animal allows for discussion of issues such as euthanasia or loss of a pet that may arise during sessions or may actually be a precipitating reason for seeking help. Unless it is clearly permitted, clients may be reluctant or embarrassed to reveal their devotion to their pets. Or, clients might worry that they are overreacting if they feel pain and anguish at the loss of a pet and may suppress feelings that need to be examined and expressed (Rynearson 1978). Moreover, dealing with these feelings may lead to a deeper understanding about themselves and other relationships. Cowles (1985) found, in a small bereavement study of adults who had lost a pet, that the loss reminded many adults of earlier losses. Discovering unresolved grief or other feelings connected to an animal may be an entry into other feelings and attachments (Rynearson 1978). This can offer an opportunity to clarify that attachment forms over time, and that protest and distress at disruption is a natural response when bonds are in jeopardy or lost. Thus, pets can be a vehicle to facilitate awareness of clients' emotional attachments as well as their attachment behavior itself.

Pets are also useful in clinical practice for discovering patterns of personality organization and relationship to others that may be observable in the pet relationship. Rynearson (1978) identified anxious attachment and insistent caregiving in the treatment of pet owners with pathological reactions to the loss of their pets when these reactions were related to an early history of insecure attachment. These two attachment categories would be comparable to a distortion of two of Weiss's (1974) social provisions: attachment and the opportunity to nurture others. Still another useful aspect of pets in treatment involves the tendency of pet owners to attribute their feelings to their pets. When asking someone how his pet feels, the therapist may open the door to exploring the client's feelings (Muschel 1984). Likewise, in family sessions clients may exhibit attachment behavior toward a pet that can be a way to examine difficulties among family members (Rynearson 1978).

Although he rarely wrote about pets, Freud was known to have one of his beloved chows sitting quietly near the couch in therapy sessions (Gay 1988). I have found it informative when clients have brought their dogs to sessions, and also when I have observed them interacting with one of my dogs. For example, a young adult woman let her puppy jump around the room and interrupt our session. She relied on me to note he might be thirsty or need to go out. As I pointed her behavior out to her, she began to admit her fear of parenting, and how she didn't feel prepared for children. Not only did this lead to explanation and understanding of the roots of her feelings of inadequacy, she became competent in caring for the pet, which gave her confidence to think about having a child.

LOSS OF A PET

Losing a pet can be traumatic. Yet animals' shorter life cycles make it inescapable that the average pet will die before its owner. The loss of a companion animal represents the loss of an attachment as well as the particular provisions associated with the relationship. There is evidence that the process of grief and mourning that follows the loss of a pet resembles the response to the loss of a close person. Although there are some differences in intensity and the length of time grief lasts, nevertheless there are sadness and despair, anxiety, and anger—the same responses that occur when a human relationship of attachment is lost. Bereaved pet owners describe problems sleeping and eating and attempts to search out and recover the pet (Cowles 1985, Stewart 1983). Gerwolls (1990), for example, in a questionnaire study of adults who had lost a companion animal, found similarities between grief over a pet's death and the death of a child. Several of her findings, moreover, indicate conditions of attachment. The mean age of the pet was eight years, which suggests that the owner had the animal long enough for a bond to form. Also, those who felt a greater attachment to the pet were initially worse off after its death, which she attributed to the strength of the tie to the animal.

Gerwolls further found that the presence of other household pets did not diminish grief, especially when the lost pet was the favorite. This suggests that each pet is perceived on its own; one bond cannot readily substitute for another. These findings led Gerwolls to conclude that the owner should resolve grief over the death of a companion animal before obtaining another pet. Society does not usually give much attention or support to bereaved pet owners, so there is often a lack of awareness of the intense grief a person may be feeling. Owners may feel ridiculed if they are sad and do not quickly resume normal activity (Cowles 1985, Gerwolls 1990, Stewart 1983). This insensitivity may interfere with normal grieving, either inhibiting or prolonging it, and may put the individual at risk for future disturbance, both physical and psychological. Keddie (1977) found that when clients sought therapy following the loss of their pets and were helped to share their grief, they quickly responded to the support and began to adjust to their loss within one week to three months.

Most veterinarians are aware of how deeply people feel about their pets and how intense the grief and mourning is when pets die. It is probable that the development of pet loss support groups, generally under the auspices of veterinarians, reflects an awareness of this and is a type of prevention against a maladaptive adjustment. Clinicians could be involved in these areas, both to educate the public about the place of pets in our lives, and to inform veterinarians about referring human clients who may need psychological help, perhaps in order to resolve questions about euthanasia, or to deal with pet loss (Netting et al. 1987). Clinicians can affirm the emotional importance of a companion animal and promote societal sympathy and support for bereaved owners, for example by recommending that friends and family spend time with those grieving, call, or send flowers or the pet-loss cards now available.

ATTACHMENT NEEDS OF PETS

Attachment theory has implications from the pet's point of view as well. Like human infants, animals need attachment for protection and survival (Fischer-Mamblona 2000, Rynearson 1978) and, therefore, are affected by separation and loss. For example, Scott (1987) repeatedly observed depression in dogs whose owners left them in boarding kennels. He also described how a Shetland sheep dog, adopted at the age of six months, never wagged its tail. Scott surmised that the puppy was not removed from its mother at the optimum time, around eight weeks, and that the effects of the delayed separation from its familiar environment had continued indefinitely.

There are touching reports of dogs who mourn their lost owners. One of the most famous in the literature is the Akita Hachi-Ko in Tokyo, who kept returning to the train station, waiting for his dead owner, for ten years (Garber 1996). Solnit (1990), in a review of Bowlby's (1988a) book, *A Secure Base*, noted that human studies should be used to enable better understanding and care for animals. For example, just as children need their parents with them in the hospital, pets need their owners with them as well; veterinary practices should try, whenever possible, to keep a pet with its owner during medical procedures. Perhaps in the future pets will also be allowed to visit their owners in hospitals. This would undoubtedly benefit both the pet and its human companion and help speed recovery. A colleague of mine told me how she stood outside a hospital with the dog of a friend dying of cancer while the patient looked down longingly from five flights above. This was the last time the woman ever saw her pet. Finally, abusing or neglecting a pet, or randomly surrendering the pet, is not only heartless and cruel but undermines the foundation of human attachment.

ATTACHED TO OUR PETS

Attachment-based research and theory have shown that emotional well-being is largely affected by personal relationships not only in childhood but throughout life. People need a combination of relationships, from close affectional attachments to broader social contacts (Levitt 1991, Weiss 1991). There is now reason to include pets among significant attachment figures, not only in treating disturbed populations but also for promoting physical and mental health (Cowles 1985, Rynearson 1978). The closeness of pet contact may help maintain physiological regulation, especially for someone who has had a recent loss or elderly people who are alone. Amini and colleagues (1996) posit that pets are one of a group of attachment figures who can reestablish homeostatic regulation, preventing the development of more severe affective dysfunction. Poignant reports of reaching withdrawn people, or reviving seriously ill patients by exposing them to a pet indicate that something remarkable is happening in these brief encounters.

As we are learning about the benefits of pets, our devotion to them makes more sense. Our pets—especially dogs and cats—provide certain components of attachment that enhance our emotional and social well-being. Companion animals afford opportunities for nurturance and commitment and can be a pathway to relationships with others. They can help repair past wounds and restore self-esteem and a feeling of being lovable. The study of women and their dogs by Allen and colleagues (1991) suggests that merely looking at pets may tap into attachment feelings and reduce stress, as the women's dogs were kept in sight, but not touched, during the study procedure. The fact that there is some effect from simply seeing them could also explain the usefulness pets appear to have in advertising.

Holmes (1996) and Kobak (1999) note that we still have a lot to learn about attachment relations in adulthood; others, such as O'Hare (1991), agree with attachment theorists on the need for practitioners to add research findings to their techniques of practice. One direction research could take would be to explore components of attachment in the relationship between pets and people. Despite findings that suggest companion animals contribute to both physical and emotional health, and although there are now mental health practitioners working in veterinary hospitals (see Cohen 1985), much of our evidence remains anecdotal. The psychological literature has given little attention to the psychological role of pets, and in particular to research or theoretical explanation of the dynamics of this relationship (Albert and Bulcroft 1988, Keddie 1977, Melson 1989, Rynearson 1978, Sable 1995, Siegel 1990). Melson (1989) suggested attachment theory as a framework for more precise measurement of the human–animal bond, and Katcher (1982) recommended that questions on pets be included in studies on psychological and social factors in health and illness.

The bond with a pet generates feelings of happiness and security and reduces feelings of loss and loneliness. As the landscape of family life continues to change, pets will be increasingly important as attachment figures for providing the comfort of proximity and giving purpose to life. Psychotherapists need to recognize and respect the advantages of pets in clinical practice and to work toward social policy that does the same. This would include necessary support services, such as assisting the elderly with walking a dog or taking it to the veterinarian, services that would enable them to keep their companion animal.

PAWS (Pets Are Wonderful Support) is an example of an organization dedicated to keeping owners and their pets together. The organization raises funds to help AIDS patients maintain their pets and furnishes financial assistance for pet food or substitute care if the owner is hospitalized. There are also proven mental health benefits in such projects; a study of men living with AIDS found that those who owned pets were less likely to suffer from depression than those not owning pets (*Daily Bruin*, UCLA, May 13, 1999).

By providing solace and a steady presence, pets remind us that we are not alone. Companion animals have a place in our intrinsic desire for close and caring affectional bonds with others. Roger Caras (1995), a past president of the ASPCA, could have said the same thing about any of our family pets when he wrote: "Dogs are not our whole life, but they make our lives whole" (p. 143).

12

Experiencing
Secure Attachment
through Therapy

John Bowlby started us thinking in a new way about our closest affectional relationships. Searching for a more complete explanation of the effects of real experiences—especially separation or loss—on personality development, he discovered the field of ethology. Combining an ethological-evolutionary perspective with his training in psychoanalytic object relations, and adding concepts from cognitive science and control theory, Bowlby advanced a point of view about human social behavior that updated Freud's theories of motivation and emphasized an infant's instinctive tendency to seek affectional relationships. In what has come to be called attachment theory, Bowlby argued that emotional engagement with a readily accessible and responsive caregiver is the necessary precursor to healthy development and that a lack of reliable connection is directly related to psychological distress. Although this perspective was part of the broad trend toward viewing individuals in terms of their relationships with others, Bowlby was also a research scientist who called for theory to be based on systematic investigation. It was at this juncture that Ainsworth brought innovative techniques and research findings to a number of attachment concepts, furnishing corroborative evidence for Bowlby's evolving propositions. Using the Strange Situation procedure, Ainsworth demonstrated that the quality of relationships, as well as their individual differences, could be measured. She also provided the impetus that has led to the vast and rapidly expanding body of attachment-based research, which includes increasingly sophisticated studies of adult attachment such as Kahn and Antonucci's (1980) social convoy diagram, Hazan and Shaver's (1987) "love quiz," and Main's (Main and Goldwyn 1984) Adult Attachment Interview.

The theory of attachment is now truly a "life-span developmental theory" (Crowell et al. 1999, p. 434), with empirical evidence that there is a biologically based behavioral system of attachment that promotes the formation of lasting bonds for both children and adults. Main (1999) even suggests that Bowlby may actually have underestimated the ultimate importance of attachment interactions. Bowlby conceived that attachment assured a protective base, but Schore (2000), in the foreword to the republication of Bowlby's volume *Attachment*, alleges that attachment also provides for regulation of positive affect. Schore (1994, 1997) explains that the mother of an infant not only minimizes her baby's negative affect but also maximizes its positive affect states. Furthermore, these early affective interactions are crucial to brain development and the capacity for affect regulation throughout life. D. Siegel (1999) agrees with Schore that emotional relationships are important for the developing brain and also for organizing ongoing experience. Amini and colleagues (1996) explain that the nervous system of social mammals requires external input from other figures in order to maintain internal homeostasis. Because the input is achieved through social contact and bio-behavioral synchrony with attachment relations, it is possible that the attachment system is "the central organizing system in the brain of higher social animals (p. 223)." When early experience is inadequate, for instance if there is a lack of stimulation or emotional contact, the neural structures critical to long-term stability do not develop the capacity for optimal internal self-regulation. Rosenblum and colleagues (1994), in a study of nonhuman primates, found that altering the infant's environment, either by disturbing its relations with its mother and/or subjecting it to other stressors, predisposed the infant to later anxiety and affective disorders and also to poorer social functioning. While acknowledging that primate studies may not replicate data on humans, the researchers posited that their findings are consistent with the opinion that early events can alter the neurodevelopment of systems related to the expression of adult anxiety disorders. According to D. Siegel (1999), traumatic experiences, especially continuous ones, can change the human brain structures involved in memory, narrative, emotion, and states of mind, resulting in difficulties consolidating experience, and increasing the risk of insecurity and psychopathology.

ADULT ATTACHMENT AND PSYCHOPATHOLOGY OF WORKING MODELS

Current attachment theory and research suggest that the attachment system initiated in infancy remains active in adults. This accounts for an inclination to attain and maintain proximity and contact with attachment figures in times of stress or danger, to experience feelings of increased comfort and security in their presence, and to feel anxiety, fear, and grief if these figures are unavailable or permanently lost (Crowell et al. 1999, Weiss 1982a, 1991). There are certain aspects of adult attachment, however, that distinguish it from parent–child bonding and that complicate its conceptualization or measurement (Crowell et al. 1999). Some adult attachment relationships, such as pair bonds, are reciprocal, or in D. Siegel's (1999) phrase, symmetrical; others, such as parent–child or client–therapist ties, are asymmetrical. In the former, there is a give and take between the dyad that is not expected in the latter. Also, although the biological function to provide protection and security remains the same, adults have a complex network of memories, thoughts, and feelings that enable them to think through the details and consequences of a particular situation. Their inner working models of attachment, built over years of experience, make it possible to weather adversity and handle temporary setbacks with less overwhelming distress than those of a child.

These working models are perceived to be cognitive maps for making sense of the world. Adults can use their internal representations of attachment to regulate emotions, assess the intentions and behavior of others, and to imagine possible outcomes of their own actions. Although somewhat automatic, relatively stable, and self-perpetuating, the constructs are dynamic, not static, and therefore can be revised as conditions in the environment change. When models are kept up-to-date by accommodating to developmental and environmental changes, people are able to reflect on their attachment feelings and experiences, communicate their thoughts and needs, and decide on the goals and strategies for obtaining them. Furthermore, because working models are a composite or assemblage of real experiences that begin early in life, their flexibility and adaptability depends on the history of attachment relationships. Young children need steady caregivers to ensure their protection and actual survival, and they also need enough love to promote feelings of self-worth and well-being. If affectional figures have proven to be emotionally available and supportive of exploratory activities, a person feels valued and competent in pursuing a variety of goals, secure in the expectation of help and comfort as needed (Bretherton and Munholland 1999, Feeney 1999). However, if a person does not have "good-enough" attachment experiences, defensive processes can lead to conflicting and constricted working models that interfere with the integration of experiences into a coherent construct of oneself and others. Although defensive exclusion and distortion may be adaptive in the short run, protecting a person from unbearable fear and anxiety, adaptive functioning is eventually undermined, as working models that are not open and flexible are no longer able to assimilate new information objectively, and, therefore, are not kept up to date (Bretherton and Munholland 1999).

Patients in therapy often show the inconsistencies of their representations by "blind spots" concerning the effects of certain experiences or communications with attachment figures. For a Bowlbyan, the client's exploration of these past events with the trusted support, sympathy, and encouragement of the therapist is at the core of coming to understand how working models have been generated and maintained. Bowlby believed that feelings of anxiety, anger, and sadness arise naturally, as part of our innate equipment to preserve vital connections of attachment. However, certain circumstances, particularly threats to the accessibility of attachment figures, can exacerbate these emotions, resulting in clinical symptoms that motivate individuals to seek psychotherapy. As Kobak (1999) puts it, behind a client's presenting symptoms and defensive distortions lie frightening threats to the availability of attachment figures.

THE REPARATIVE RELATIONSHIP
OF THERAPY

Shortly before his death, Bowlby said that he had developed his theoretical ideas because he was a clinician and wanted theory to fit clinical experience (Hunter 1991). The explosion of attachment-based research is now contributing evidence that the theory does indeed provide a context for understanding emotional difficulties, as well as guidelines for treatment (Grotstein 1990, Holmes 1997, Slade 1999). From a perspective of attachment, psychotherapy is a unique kind of attachment relationship, one that encompasses the past (transference), but is mostly focused on providing the opportunity to experience secure attachment in the present. Aron (1996) wrote that attachment theory emphasizes the "interpersonal space between self and other" (p. 33). Within this space an interaction takes place between two individuals, therapist and patient, and as this "new experience rooted in a new relationship" (p. 214) is internalized, it becomes an integral part of the patient's emotional life. Insight and interpretation are used, but sparingly, mostly as a means to deepen emotional contact between the two participants, convey understanding, and further exploration. Above all, experiencing secure attachment with the therapist offers a reparative relationship that is emotionally healing and can compensate to some extent for earlier painful experiences.

Attachment theory contends that only by establishing a secure base with the therapist is it possible to investigate and re-experience various unfortunate and unhappy aspects of one's life, some of which would be too difficult to think about and reconsider without the empathy, support, and occasional guidance of a trusted companion (Bowlby 1988a, Farber et al. 1995, Hamilton 1987, Karen

1994). Through therapy, an individual can approach the thoughts and feelings that have been defensively locked away and begin to see them in a new light. Within the safe setting of the therapist's office, and facilitated by the constancy, accessibility, and responsiveness of the therapist, a bond of secure attachment gradually forms. Though patients presume the therapist will be helpful, and may even see the therapist as "stronger and wiser," it often takes time for an authentic attachment to develop (Farber et al. 1995). As it does, it will influence existing attitudes and feelings, tipping the balance away from confusion and self-doubt and toward feelings of competence and self-reliance; the patient comes to see the glass as half full, not half empty. The working model of the therapeutic relationship eventually exerts dominance over hurtful experiences and models of the past, countering the patient's image of himself as unlovable and unworthy of secure affectional ties.

Since individuals are in distress when they seek professional help, therapists are in a natural position to fulfill the role of an attachment figure (Kobak and Shaver 1987). The therapist offers an emotional availability, a comforting presence, and regulation of affect, all of which increase the opportunity for attachment to develop (Mallinckrodt et al. 1995). Although these features of treatment, together with the therapist's interest in trying to understand and help, resemble those of a caregiver, Farber and colleagues (1995) do not see the therapeutic bond as an exact replica of childhood attachment relationships. Just as adult attachment is a modification of the attachment behavioral system, there are significant differences in a therapeutic arrangement. Besides the obvious restrictions of scheduled appointments, prescribed boundaries, and definite rules about physical touching, the therapist is more objective and less emotionally involved. This does not mean that therapists are blank screens and that they do not enter into the moment or experience counter-transference, only that they assume a format of confidentiality within a therapeutic process that has its own advantages. For example, patients can try out new ways of negotiating interchanges, which they can then apply in the real world. The sense of safety in therapy permits expression of feelings, such as anger, that the person may have had trouble expressing before. By experiencing the therapist's ability to deal with and survive the anger, the patient feels freer to acknowledge and express feelings and opinions in other relationships. Moreover, Holmes (1997) suggests that some of the constraints of therapy, such as regularly scheduled sessions punctuated by interruptions and endings, provide an opportunity to understand and deal with the inevitable partings of life, because the therapeutic process is a "microcosm of attachment and separation" (p. 246). As attachment with the therapist is established, it serves as a base from which to explore both the inner world and the outer environment, offering a haven of refuge at times of fear and anxiety, and a source of information for understanding the underlying meanings of troubling symptoms. In terms of separation, events such as the therapist's vacation will elicit a range of feelings that are specific to attachment relationships; the therapist is missed during treatment interruptions, and if something upsetting occurs clients are reluctant to utilize substitute "on-call" therapists. Though negative affect may be exhibited following separations, appreciation of reunion is often expressed as well. And, commensurate with the nature of affectional bonds, attachment generally endures, even after therapy is terminated. The image of the therapist and setting may continue to be evoked for problem solving or soothing discomfort as these were learned in treatment (Amini et al. 1996, Farber et al. 1995).

Amini and colleagues (1996) describe the attachment relationship of therapy as a physiologic process capable of maintaining homeostasis as well as revising ingrained patterns of relating. As the affective experience with the therapist is gradually internalized, it becomes encoded in memory, producing lasting changes in the neural structures that influence attachment behavior. The increasing evidence that secure adult bonds can counteract earlier hurtful experiences suggests that a secure therapeutic experience can modify individuals' working models, especially as transference manifestations are added to understanding. Whereas Freud ascribed maladaptive patterns of relatedness to intrapsychic conflict and the repetition compulsion, Amini and colleagues perceive them in terms of the psychobiological processes of attachment and implicit memory. They propose that an individual's memory system operates by extracting prototypes and rules from familiar attachment experiences and then unconsciously imposing them onto later situations. Like Schore (1994), Amini and colleagues conceptualize psychotherapy as an affectional relationship whose purpose is to regulate affect and also to revise the inaccurate implicit memories related to existing attachment patterns.

Holmes (1999b) describes lingering remnants of the past as "ghosts in the consulting room" (p. 115). Therapy enables patients to get in touch with their ghosts and then dismiss them, particularly through the development of a coherent narrative. This involves understanding how present thoughts and feelings are dictated by attachment experiences, and also the expression of emotions, such as anger and disappointment, at the parental mistreatments and/or inadequacies that are connected to unhappy memories. As Holmes (1999b) and Bowlby (1977) both noted, we cannot erase the past, but we can ameliorate its consequences and interrupt the intergenerational transmission of dysfunctional attachment patterns. Through a new and less constricted narrative, parents can be seen as products of their own bitter experiences and, whether or not they are forgiven, can finally be accepted for who they are. Patients come to realize that their fate is not sealed by unfortunate or unhappy family experiences, and that they can realign their relationships to the ghosts of the past so that they are no longer haunted by them in the present.

NARRATIVES OF ATTACHMENT

Although Bowlby's three volumes, *Attachment and Loss* (1969a, 1973, 1980) contain innumerable clinical implications, his most in-depth discussion of treatment was first outlined in a 1977 paper and then revised for the book *A Secure Base* (1988a). In these works, Bowlby described the overall task of a therapist who is applying attachment theory as the provision of conditions in which patients can safely explore their working models of themselves and their attachment figures with a view to reconsidering and restructuring them to be more in line with current knowledge and circumstances. Therapists promote the sense of safety for exploration by becoming a secure base where patients can put together a scenario of how events unfolded and how they were woven into inner representations. At first, Bowlby stated that the principle of the therapist acting as a trusted companion in the joint exploration of attachment experiences was a new point of emphasis, but in the 1988 revision, he described the role as similar to Winnicott's concept of "holding" and Bion's "containing." The main difference between attachment theory and other object relations theories, Bowlby now stated, was its view that a client's misunderstandings and misconstructions were not the result of irrational and unconscious fantasies, but acquired from real experiences, both current and past, and including what parents may have said that was different from what was observed. The therapist, therefore, asks patients to travel mentally through time, to retrieve memories of childhood trauma and thwarted attachment, and to consider them in the context of their present-day lives.

From my experience as a therapist, I have found that patients mostly talk about their immediate difficulties and interpersonal relationships, especially those that they perceive have led them to seek treatment. Individuals come to a psychotherapist because they are troubled and confused and want relief from their discomfort and uncertainty. In guiding them into and through what it means to be in therapy, they are helped to tell a story of their lives, sorting through experiences and memories and shaping them into a more affirming version of events. Basically, a narrative is formed by the clinician listening to the client's material, reframing it, and reflecting it back to the client in a way that clarifies and expands understanding, and then checking its effect by the client's response (Holmes 1999a).

The person of the therapist provides a "quiet background presence" which Holmes (1999a) compares to Winnicott's (1965) concept of the child playing alone in the presence of the mother. The atmosphere frees the client's thoughts to wander without distraction or demand. Of course, the therapist is also involved in the process. While remaining affectively attuned to clients' moods and needs, the therapist encourages the client to explore details of current affectional bonds and to examine whether expectations and unconscious biases have been brought to these close relationships, creating difficulty. The therapist also encourages the client to consider how significant experiences from the past are being reenacted with the therapist (transference).

Even though therapists try to be sympathetic and supportive, patients may not perceive them as such, and will impose the way they have experienced past relationships onto what is happening between the two of them. In these instances, the clinician's task is to consider whether current feelings, perceptions, and expectations could be a product of events and situations encountered during childhood and adolescence (or even still occurring), or may be due to misleading messages, especially from parents (also possibly still occurring). Where attachment figures have discounted or ridiculed a client's feelings and perceptions as a child, the therapist sanctions the client to experience and express emotions that parents discouraged or prohibited and to consider actions that parents criticized or did not allow (Bowlby 1988a).

In pursuing painful memories of the past, therapists are confronted with two aspects of the client's experience: an internal world of thoughts, feelings, and memories, and an external environment that became part of that inner world and now influences the way current situations are perceived and responded to (Bacal and Newman 1990, Bowlby 1988a,b, Casement 1991). Bowlby (1988a) stresses that because the internal world is so strongly determined by real-life experiences, an essential part of treatment is to uncover and thoroughly review what these have been.

We have learned from counseling the bereaved and abused, and from dealing with those who seek help following disasters and traumas, that the majority of therapeutic clients want to talk about certain aspects of these real incidents when they are ready, and need to go over specific details in order to understand how events evolved and are coloring present-day feelings and perceptions. With a detailed exploration of memories and thoughts of the past, there is an opportunity to sort out what is real from what is fantasy and to consider various hypotheses with regard to why clients have come to feel and behave as they do (Bowlby 1988a, Hunter 1991). Generally, Bowlby (1988a) believed clients' accounts should be accepted as "reasonable approximations to the truth" (page 149). To question the credibility of a story, or to imply that a memory is imagination, fantasy, or magical thinking may make clients feel as misunderstood and discounted as they have in other relationships. It is better to be cautious and believe what clients report, even if the actualities are later discovered to be quite different. An emphasis on fantasy may be misleading, diverting attention away from traumatic memories of the way parents behaved or what they repeatedly said (Bowlby 1988a, Hunter 1991). Bowlby (1985) writes that "what is so facilely dubbed as fantasy [should] be recognized as the reflection of grim reality and that a therapeutic task is to identify the real-life experiences lying close behind the deceptive camouflage [of symptoms]" p. 197).

When there are contradictions or inconsistencies in a narrative, it is likely that certain attachment attitudes and feelings, especially those that would elicit painful or frightening emotions and recollections, have been defensively excluded from awareness. I particularly look for separation or loss, lack of attunement or disconfirmation

of feelings, or abusive experiences with attachment figures when details do not seem to make sense or hang together (Holmes 1999a). In some situations, such as with
Skye (Chapter 9) and Garrett (Chapter 4), the access to
feelings and memories was so inhibited that I never got a
real sense of their attachment figures. Dozier and Kobak
(1992) contend that this kind of obscure communication
would have originated in the earliest years when the child
learned to limit retrieval of information, and to defensively exclude feelings such as fear and anger when parents would not tolerate their expression. Since models
are increasingly complex, as well as persistent, by the time
these individuals reach therapy, their dynamics are often
unclear and difficult to untangle. Sparse and incoherent
narratives such as those of Skye and Garrett suggest that
they had deactivated and distorted attachment thoughts
and feelings and were replaying these styles of relating
with me. As is true with any of our clients, their particular attachment styles were associated with how they felt
about themselves, how they related to others, including
the therapist, and how they discussed their lives. According to Bowlby (1977), the internalization and organization of attachment experiences leads to the development
of these patterns of personality, which come to govern a
person's expectations and behavior. Bowlby's original classifications—secure attachment, anxious attachment,
compulsive (insistent) self-reliance, compulsive (insistent)
caregiving, and emotional detachment—have been modified and expanded by infant and adult research, but
his basic view that attachment behavior is either over-
activated or deactivated in the insecure patterns remains
the underlying premise for understanding attachment-
related problems in terms of different attachment styles.

ATTACHMENT STYLE

The process of psychotherapy is somewhat like solving an intriguing mystery. Clients come with troubling symptoms, puzzling and disjointed stories, and the therapist tries to help crystallize them into a "coherent explanation" (Holmes 1993a) that links their expressions of anxiety and anger to disturbances in affectional relationships (Kobak 1999). As Holmes (1996) notes, therapy involves the language of emotions. Both Main's (1991) work on the structure and form of narrative style and Fonagy's (Fonagy et al. 1997) on reflective function have shown that the way individuals talk about themselves and their feelings, and the way they relate to others, can help the therapist imagine and construct a story of the patient's early life and affective experience. Main identified specific patterns of representation in adults—secure/autonomous, insecure/dismissing, and insecure/preoccupied—and later added two more insecure categories, disorganized (unre solved), and cannot classify. These patterns were determined by the way childhood events were remembered and organized, not by the events themselves. In fact, some adults rated secure/autonomous had had quite distressing childhoods, but could discuss them consistently and without distortion or contradiction. These individuals are known as having "earned security," in contrast to others in the secure group. Fonagy and his colleagues (1995) extended Main's work by suggesting that coherence is a manifestation of the capacity to reflect upon one's internal emotional experience—what the researchers called reflective self-function—and they connected these psychological processes to the security of childhood experiences. Holmes (1999a) divides Fonagy's concept of a securely attached adult's "theory of mind" (Fonagy et al. 1995) into three components: the ability to distinguish one's feelings and experiences from others, the ability to tell a story of one's feelings, and the ability to restructure narratives so they are kept up to date. In contrast, adults who lacked affective interaction with parents or who were subjected to traumatizing events may not be able to reflect on their feelings or see that others have their own point of view. From an attachment perspective, these individuals' limited access to attachment thoughts and feelings can be understood as an insecure style of attachment behavior in which attachment behavior is either heightened and intensified, or deactivated, to a degree that interferes with the ability to tell a consistent and coherent narrative of affectional experiences.

Eagle (1997) and Slade (1999) write that understanding a client's narrative style can inform clinical diagnosis, as well as therapeutic technique. A client's pattern of attachment behavior offers a perspective on how her inner world is organized, how emotion is regulated and relationships managed. D. Siegel (1999) adds that such patterns are also associated with access to autobiographical memory, self-reflection, and narrative coherence. Bowlby (1977) distinguished between the overactivation and deactivation of attachment behavior in the two categories called anxious attachment and insistent (compulsive) self-reliance, respectively. Although the more commonly used term for the latter is now "dismissing" or "avoidant," it is actually characterized by an assertion of independence, a discounting of the need to feel cared for by others, including the therapist. These individuals seem emotionally vacant and may be more reluctant to pursue or remain in therapy (Dozier and Tyrrell 1998). Owing to early rejection, abuse, or consistent unavailability of attachment figures, avoidant persons try to insulate themselves against further disappointment, anger, or loss. The pattern, like the other atypical categories, is not synonymous with psychopathology, but research has shown that a condition of insecure attachment is associated with a higher incidence of mental disorder (D. Siegel 1999). Clinically, the overregulation and avoidance of attachment thoughts and feelings could be manifest in depression, psychosomatic illness (Bowlby 1977), eating disorders (Cole et al. 1996), and obsessional, schizoid, or narcissistic personality disorders (Slade 1999).

Anxious-ambivalent attachment is a pattern diametrically opposite to that of the dismissing attitude. Main (1991) labeled the hyperactivating strategies of this pattern "preoccupied," denoting chronic anxiety and an undercurrent of uncertainty regarding the reliability and responsiveness of affectional bonds. The lowered threshold for eliciting attachment behavior is manifest by a sensitivity to separation, shaky self-reliance, and fear of exploring too far away from whatever sense of secure base does exist. Childhood is remembered as chaotic and inconsistent, often with anger and role reversals in which parents pulled for care from their offspring. The continuing apprehension about the intentions and availability of attachment figures can make the person appear clinging, coercive, or emotionally needy. In addition to depression and anxiety disorders, individuals diagnosed as borderline might also fall into this category (Cole et al. 1996, Patrick et al. 1994, Slade 1999).

Although the direction of developmental pathways varies with these two patterns, both indicate that a "flight from feeling" (Karen 1994, p. 401) was used to sustain connection to unreliable, abusing, or rejecting caregivers. Similarly, the patterns of insistent caregiving and emotional detachment represent defensive attachment strategies, but agreement on the specifics of their organization is not as uniform as for the other two classifications. Slade (1999), for example, conceives anxious attachment and avoidance at opposing ends of a continuum, with secure attachment in the middle. However, she acknowledges uncertainty about Main's other categories, noting that the unresolved/disorganized pattern appears to be an extreme form of the preoccupied pattern. Generally, the emotional withdrawal of detachment and the conflicting attachment behavior in borderline personality disorder seem distinguished by a greater degree of exclusion and disorganization of attachment feelings and memories. And, although there are different treatment techniques—as for instance trying to help avoidant individuals get in touch with their feelings while encouraging anxiously attached individuals to quell the intensity of their attachment emotions (Eagle 1997)—a major feature of each category is an underlying yearning for secure attachment, with disappointment and sorrow where this has been denied.

It is important to realize that there are variations within categories, and that classifications alone cannot be expected to define the complexity of human experience (Slade 1999). As Fonagy (1999) notes, attachment categories are observed clusters of behavior and should not be reified as theoretical entities. Nor should a coherent narrative style be seen as the goal of treatment. As Eagle (1997) points out, a plausible explanation of life experience may lead to more accurate reflection and better understanding, but it does not necessarily define attachment status. According to Bowlby (1973), secure attachment refers to confidence that attachment figures will "be there" and be appropriately responsive if called upon, and also that the person feels worthy of receiving support and affection. Generally, these two features of mental constructs develop in a complementary fashion; that is, when parents are accessible and affirming, the child feels deserving of being cared for. In adult relationships, secure attachment allows for both self-reliance and connectedness (West and Sheldon-Keller 1994). Development is not perceived as having progressed from dependence to independence, but as having achieved a balance between confidence in oneself and others, and between attachment and exploration, which continues throughout life. A person of any age needs to feel that he has a safe and secure base from which to operate. For this reason, Bowlby (1973) wrote that the concept of dependency is pejorative and misleading; we should not be as "independent" as the sterotypical use of the term implies. Genuine self-reliance is reflected in the capacity to rely on others when occasions demand it and to also know on whom it is appropriate to rely. Secure adults have a high regard for their relationships and feel they can talk to others about their problems; in turn they offer these same attachment provisions to their affectional figures.

Therapists help clients map out their attachment experiences so they can then ideally make more authentic relationships in the "real world" (Harris 1997). It is through the process of experiencing an attachment relationship with the therapist, together with composing a historical narrative, that a person may be able to change working models to feel more confident and deserving of reliable relationships.

When my client, Auri, who had come to therapy over a harassing work situation, stated to me, "I don't deserve this," and subsequently quit her job, she exhibited a new confidence and sense of worthiness. Her ability to take protective action did not result solely from the revised story therapy enabled her to tell, but from the way she came to feel about herself as she reached new understanding about her experiences. This brief example also demonstrates that situations in the external environment, as well as the inner world of thoughts and feelings, determine a person's attachment style and proneness to pathology. From the perspective of attachment, affectional relationships exist in and are affected by a larger social world (Marris 1982, 1991). For instance, Auri's harassment at work had a pronounced effect on her mental state and on her inclination to seek psychotherapy. Harris (1997) claims that therapy will founder if there is too great a focus on internal features at the expense of the outer context, because clients may still be dealing with difficult situations that will continue to undermine functioning until they are understood and dealt with. Attachment theory has been at the forefront of developing a psychodynamic perspective that helps us appreciate that what happens in this broader cultural context also has a crucial effect on our internal world and the security we derive from attachment throughout the life cycle.

ATTACHMENT NOW AND FOR THE FUTURE

Bowlby found a missing link in analytic theory when he discovered the impact of real-life experiences and parenting behavior on the development of personality (Karen 1990). He said he chose to focus on the effects of parent–child separations because these events were unmistakable, and could be documented and systematically studied for either short-term or long-term effects (Bowlby 1973, Hunter 1991, van Dijken 1998). From that beginning, attachment research has branched out and shown that there are myriad hurtful situations or crises that may compromise healthy development, and also that there is an interplay between events as well as the meanings attributed to them. Bowlby (1977, 1988a) thought it was important for clinicians to be aware of the specific experiences, for example, the disclaiming of a child's perceptions, that could detour development, and to also recognize that each person's experiences, even in the same family, are unlike anyone else's.

Many factors contribute to the quality of our lives. Besides family experiences, these include temperament, physical appearance, socioeconomic status, characteristics of the environment (such as its safety), and cultural norms about relationships (Berlin and Cassidy 1999). Attachment theory, however, is concerned with one particular aspect of experience: the protection and security that key relationship figures provide at times of threat or danger. These attachment figures are considered unique and irreplaceable, essential to well-being throughout life. If something happens that threatens the security of these bonds, the system of attachment activates fear and anxiety, and although an adult is more capable of assessing and dealing with stressful situations such as a temporary separation, the potential for separation anxiety continues in adult years. In other words, we do not become immune to separation and loss; the more a person is subjected to ruptures of attachment, the greater the proneness to anxiety, anger, depression, or detachment. For example, Bowlby broke the sequence of responses to separation into the three phases of protest, despair, and detachment. However, after repeated separations, protest may be blunted, and despair may occur sooner and become more severe (Kraemer 1992). This might explain the tendency of certain clients such as Elizabeth (Chapter 7), to quickly become angry and depressed, when, for instance, therapy sessions are interrupted. Her experience of early loss, never fully explained until adulthood, and compounded by family secrets about her father's death and her mother's suddenly distancing herself from her daughter, prevented Elizabeth from healthy grieving and adjustment at the time of her childhood bereavement. The representations of these early events, and the pattern of relating to others that they engendered, emerged both in transference and in Elizabeth's narrative of attachment.

The concept of narrative is not one associated solely with attachment theory. Byng-Hall (1999) sees all talking therapies as narratives and Phillips (1999) claims Freud's approach could be considered a narrative one because of his concern to make sense of the details of a patient's life and symptoms. What is unique to attachment theory is the framework it provides for listening to clients' stories and constructing a scenario of how they have fallen prey to their current difficulties. Cognitive awareness is connected to the unconscious and to emotions, uniting the inner world of attitudes and imagination with an outer world of actual experiences with others. Reconstruction involves looking at the kinds of pressures parents may have exerted on their child to misconstrue experiences, either by what they specifically said or how they behaved, as well as trying to uncover the attachment patterns that parents modeled in their own relationships. Added to this is an ethological perspective, and although standardized observations of children and adults have mostly replaced the early reliance on animal studies, Bowlby's premise that attachment behavior is instinctive remains at the core of the theory.

Harris (1997) writes that people often seek treatment because their instinctive needs to feel safe and protected are not being met. The therapist both validates these basic feelings and helps clients understand the inherent nature of their attachment behavior. This includes explaining how symptoms, such as fear of being alone or fear of the unfamiliar, are an elaboration of natural clues that have been heightened by uneasy circumstances. Fear of isolation or being in unfamiliar territory, as well as fear of the dark, heights, and loud noises, are innate responses to an increased risk or danger, and serve the evolutionary purpose of protection and survival. When affectional bonds are fractured, we instinctively respond with various behaviors intended to preserve attachment. In my work with patients troubled by phobic symptoms, for example, I have found that this explanation is informative and relieving. It seems to give words to feelings these patients cannot get hold of, offering a perspective on troubling and seemingly irrational fears. Similarly, I have used the ethological orientation to explain the fear of approaching surgery, or the intensified anxiety following a disaster.

Attachment-based psychotherapy addresses and affirms that a wide range of emotions, from joy and sadness to anxiety and anger, reflect what is happening within affectional relationships. Through therapy, feelings are clarified, experiences are chronicled, and working models updated and revised. Through the alternative attachment provided by the therapist, clients learn to reflect on their feelings, and to retell their life stories without having to resort to maladaptive defenses (Holmes 1994). No longer enthralled by the past, they are ready to live more fully in the present, better able to cope with stress and trauma, and also more capable of a broader spectrum of emotional expression.

THE SIGNIFICANCE OF ATTACHMENT

John Bowlby has left us a grand legacy. Over the course of his lengthy and distinguished career he changed our ideas about the nature of attachment experiences, advanced our awareness of what children need for emotional security, and gave us a new view of how our inner world is developed and organized. His concept of working models to explain internal representations accounts for the continuity observed in patterns of relating, as well as for the possibility of change (Feeney 1999). Bowlby showed us how research could inform theory and practice, and his shift in perspective to an interpersonal psychopathology is biologically based and empirically supported. Reconceptualizing emotional disturbance from an ethological framework of attachment emphasizes the relational nature of personality development, both healthy and pathological, and provides a context for clinical practice. Affective responses of anxiety and anger signal the danger of actual or threatened physical separation or emotional adversity, and are inherent, adaptive efforts to sustain attachment. However, they may become dysfunctional, either intensified to excessive and persistent anxiety and distress, or excluded and/or redirected to other persons or situations.

Bowlby (1973, 1991) perceived emotional disturbance as a distortion of the attachment behavioral system. Those who succumb to anxiety or depression have omitted, suppressed, or falsified certain painful aspects of their lives, shutting them away from consciousness. But the effects of these events live on to haunt them, surfacing in symptoms of psychological disorder when something happens that reminds them of these experiences, whether they are aware of them or not.

Attachment-based research has identified a variety of interpersonal experiences that can be damaging to the growing child. These experiences can generate anxiety and anger to a point where they eventually dominate the adult personality to a dysfunctional degree. Parental threats to abandon or withhold love, hostile punishments, and illogical constructions of reality, as well as separation or loss, can affect the organization of attachment behavior and undermine development (Holmes 1995, Karen 1994, Lieberman 1997).

Concepts of attachment provide a backdrop against which the histories of adult clients can be untangled and sorted through. Careful scrutiny of experiences can reveal destructive behaviors, such as emotional cruelty or physical abuse, that de Zulueta (1994) calls "attachment gone wrong" (p. 64). Besides having the potential to identify conditions like physical or emotional abuse, an attachment framework shows promise for defining and depicting a range of problems. For example, I propose that the excessive anxiety of post-traumatic stress disorder represents an intensification of attachment behavior, where proximity to a safe base takes priority over exploration at times of trauma or danger. Likewise, the anxiety of agoraphobia represents such terror of exploration away from base that the person may become afraid to leave home (Bowlby 1973, Liotti 1991, Sable 1994a). In evaluating individuals whose symptomatology would meet the *DSM-IV* criteria for borderline personality disorder, one finds a marked degree of insecure attachment, with extreme vacillations between wanting and dreading engagement, as well as disturbances in affect regulation and cognitive functioning (Sable 1997a, Schore 1994).

Another contribution of attachment theory is the bridge it makes between objective research and individual experience (Grossman 1995). Because Bowlby felt that real experiences had been underplayed in traditional theory and in treatment, he emphasized the necessity of systematically studying the influence of real-life events in the etiology of psychopathology (Hunter 1991). Even though research and clinical application to adults is now coming into its own, there is still much to learn about adult attachment, in particular how it functions and how it is linked to early childhood and the development of pathology (Berlin and Cassidy 1999, Grossman et al. 1999, Insel 1997, Patrick et al. 1994, Sperling and Lyons 1994, Weiss 1994a). We need more data on current relationships (Kobak 1999), clinical work (Berlin and Cassidy 1999), and the intricacies of working models (Bretherton and Munholland 1999). It is not yet clear how the many different measures of adult attachment relate to each other (Crowell et al. 1999), and whether they are tapping into similar underlying dynamics (Bretherton and Munholland 1999). Berlin and Cassidy (1999) see a similar lack of precision in distinctions between social support and intimate relationships.

The basic concept that attachment is a precondition for adult coherence has implications for prevention and social policy (Grossman 1995, Karen 1994). For example, there is evidence that secure affectional bonds are related to the capacity to benefit from social support networks (Antonucci 1994, Florian et al. 1995, Patrick et al. 1994). Another implication for the concept's use in prevention is its potential to clarify disruptions, such as death or divorce as well as the dilemma of working mothers and day care, serious issues that go to the heart of clinical work and societal values. Leach (1994) and Marris (1991) are writers from diverse fields who are confronting what they assert is our current cultural disregard of what children need to grow up to feel secure and confident, be able to make lasting adult bonds, and eventually be responsible, caring parents. We cannot shy away from facing certain fundamental facts about bonding and attachment as well as their ensuing economic realities and necessities. Bowlby's biopsychosocial perspective is a systems approach that calls on us to give infants continuous and reliable love and care, while at the same time recognizing that "poverty, malnutrition, inadequate schooling, and various forms of prejudice and discrimination in the wider culture can leave scars on personality development fully as deep as those left by poor parenting or a broken home" (Marmor 1988, p. 488). A society fully appreciative of the power of attachment would support families and communities, for example, with affirmation to stay-at-home mothers (or fathers) (Fox 1996) or for adequate leave options and quality day care for those who work. Although this is an extremely complex and difficult issue, there is a lot at stake. When risk factors such as inconsistent care, exhausted parents, or unsympathetic employers accumulate, and especially if they are not balanced by compensations, the chance of insecure attachment and psychopathology rises (Belsky 1999b, Karen 1994).

At the other end of the life cycle, we must address the attachment needs of our aging population. According to concepts of attachment, many of the conditions that come with aging, such as the loss of familiar people and places, and declining health and income, are those that intensify attachment behavior and lead a person to seek proximity and assistance from trusted figures. Marris (1991) asserts that these kinds of changes can put elderly adults in particular jeopardy, not only because of the persistent nature of attachment, but also because of their tendency to view their lives retrospectively. For example, the loss of a close attachment figure such as a spouse may make them feel their life is over, affecting the nature of their remaining years. Marris claims this may prevent these persons from making sense of their loss or restoring a sense of meaning to life. Supportive friends and family do help alleviate loneliness, and thus are very important, even though it should not be presumed that they can replace an exclusive affectional bond. However, beneficial arrangements could assure elderly persons of consistent personnel, such as nurses, when they are in hospitals or institutions. Just as it would have lessened John's distress in the Robertsons' 1969 film documenting separation, repeated access to a familiar person can reduce the fear and anxiety of unfamiliarity and aloneness for aging people (Main 1999).

Besides the people surrounding the elderly, pets, especially dogs and cats, provide an element of proximity and attachment that can help in dealing with the changes and losses of later years. However, many elderly people live in environments where pets are not permitted. Advocating changes in housing restrictions can remove this barrier, easing loneliness and contributing to the maintenance of connection and well-being. Pets should also be permitted to visit their owners in hospitals, where their presence can be comforting and soothing and would most likely promote healing.

Another issue pertinent to our aging population is the beneficial effect elderly persons can have, for example as grandparents. The combination of extended life spans, which afford older adults spare time, and the increasing numbers of working mothers warrants investigation of what special comfort and security elderly adults might provide. Derdeyn (1985) writes that grandparents offer benefits not derived from any other relationship, though from a clinician's perspective the bond also has potential to cause distress and depression. Raphael (1989) notes that although grandparents become attached to grandchildren, they generally have little influence over certain conditions of involvement with them, for example, in cases of divorce, or if their children decide to move away. A grandparent may seek help for depression, unaware and/or embarrassed to admit concern over a grandchild, especially since this is a bond so glamorized in our society. A recent Supreme Court decision to review the issue of grandparents' rights, though defeated, suggests that theory could be having an influence on cultural attitudes and social change— concerns always central to Bowlby's work and his advocacy for conditions that would promote healthy personality development.

In terms of intimate attachments, the Adult Attachment Interview (Main and Goldwyn 1984) has shown that some adults, despite depressing childhoods, can present their histories coherently and be classified as securely attached. Wallerstein (1995) also found couples who reported difficult childhoods and yet were able to make satisfactory marriages. There is evidence that a securely attached adult appears to have a better chance of sustaining fulfilling affectional ties, but we do not yet know what enables some adults to resolve early trauma and make satisfactory marriages while others do not. Although we perceive therapy as one route to achieving understanding and coherence, how do we account for those adults who have not had treatment and would be rated secure? Attachment theory has shown that childhood experience influences adult working models, but there is still an important piece of the puzzle to put into place.

It is probable that we have not yet given enough attention to the influence of current experiences, either in theory or practice. Hazan and Shaver's (1987) finding that individuals are less affected by childhood as they are increasingly removed from it (i.e., as they age), together with the idea that working models are flexible and open to revision, suggests that ongoing experiences do have a significant impact on feelings of security. One way to expand the understanding of how adults achieve secure attachment would be to further extend Schore's (2000) premise concerning affect regulation and attachment to adult relationships. Schore explains that the infant actively seeks interaction with its mother, and their developing bond depends both on the mother's sensitivity to her baby's cues and on the nature of their interaction. A central component of the attachment dynamic between adults in pair-bond relationships might likewise depend on affective responsiveness and communication between the dyad. Their security may depend primarily on subtle affective attunement or synchronicity, that is, the ability of each participant to respond to the other with reassurance and support. As Amini and colleagues (1996) noted, an attachment relationship can reestablish homeostatic regulation, and this might explain how therapists, pets, and other affectional figures are beneficial at times of distress, suggesting the relevance of reliable figures for maintaining or regaining a psychobiological equilibrium that is associated with interaction with others. Perhaps a greater understanding of the dynamics of attachment—for example the need to share feelings and experience, to feel heard and affirmed by attachment figures, and to feel assured of their reliability—could help couples better meet each other's affectional needs and find renewed satisfaction in their relationships. Our high divorce rate, which causes many children to be raised in single-parent homes, suggests the pressing nature of the problem. Attachment research has shown that men and women are not really from Mars and Venus, and that while there may be differences in how they express their affectional needs, both sexes have a basic desire for connectedness. Both sexes also need to feel safe emotionally as well as physically in their relationships. The concept of affective regulation or dysregulation adds a dimension to understanding the defensive reactions that adults might employ in their committed love relationships, which could subvert security (George et al. 1999) and which, if treated, could also improve these relationships.

Finally, further investigations of experience in the functioning of the brain, such as Schore's, will continue to elucidate this groundbreaking area of study, and benefit treatment techniques. For example, Schore (2000) writes that recent neurobiological data both support and expand Bowlby's concept of control systems, by showing that pathology is associated with dysregulation and inefficient orbitofrontal function. Schore alleges that future psychoneurobiological studies will further describe differences in brain organization, such as between securely and insecurely attached individuals, and will also be able to reveal the psychobiological mechanisms that mediate resilience or vulnerability to later psychopathology.

BOWLBY AND THE PHENOMENON OF ATTACHMENT

In the epilogue to the final volume of his trilogy, *Loss*, Bowlby wrote that he had concentrated his work on problems of etiology and psychopathology because effective treatment and prevention were dependent on understanding the causes and conditions underlying psychiatric disorder. This conviction led him to recast traditional theory, and his endeavors have given us a perspective on human social behavior that complements prevailing theory and therapy (Schneider 1991) while also expanding the general framework for defining mental health and psychopathology. The theory of attachment has opened a window into understanding how adults feel and behave in their relationships with others; it recognizes and emphasizes that much of the happiness and security we find in our daily lives comes from the condition of our affectional bonds, whether they are available and responsive at times of stress or illness, and whether their love and support feels deserved. It is likely that attachment theory will continue to be refined and modified and it may or may not preserve its present stature. For now, the theory has highlighted that attachment behavior, separation anxiety, loneliness, and grief are biologically based, natural responses that arise to safeguard our intrinsic need for connection. The phenomenon of attachment is lifelong, and adults have a small cluster of key relationships that they feel are fundamental to the meaning of their lives and to their well-being. Symptoms of psychopathology evolve out of these personal interactions, both past and current, and reflect the mixed feelings and messages of conflicting working models. The framework of attachment provides a context for restructuring our clients' life stories, and a language that brings our theoretical understanding and clinical practice closer to their actual lived experiences. With it, we can communicate simply and directly, without jargon. In addition to giving words and clarity to some of our deepest emotions, Bowlby takes us forward by taking us back to the basics of human nature—to our innate desire for secure attachment and to the anguish and yearning we feel at separation and loss. It was Bowlby's vision to portray the profound effects of attachment, separation, and loss experiences in the roots of our emotional lives, and it is our good fortune to have concepts of attachment as we try to help our clients overcome misfortune and form more secure affectional bonds with others.

References

Adam, K. S. (1994). Suicidal behavior and attachment: a developmental model. In *Attachment in Adults: Clinical and Developmental Perspectives*, ed. M. B. Sperling and W. H. Berman, pp. 275–298. New York: Guilford.

Adam, K. S., Keller, A. E. S., and West, M. (1995). Attachment organization and vulnerability to loss, separation and abuse in disturbed adolescents. In *Attachment Theory: Social, Developmental, and Clinical Perspectives*, ed. S. Goldberg, R. Muir, and J. Kerr, pp. 309–341. Hillsdale, NJ: Analytic Press.

Adler, G., and Buie, D. H. (1979). Aloneness and borderline psychopathology: the possible relevance of child development issues. *British Journal of Psycho-Analysis* 60:83–96.

Ainsworth, M. D. S. (1967). *Infancy in Uganda: Infant Care and the Growth of Attachment*. Baltimore: Johns Hopkins University Press.

———. (1982). Attachment: retrospect and prospect. In *The Place of Attachment in Human Behavior*, ed. C. M. Parkes and J. Stevenson-Hinde, pp. 3–30. New York: Basic Books.

———. (1984). Attachment. In *Personality and the Behavior Disorders*, vol. 1, 2nd ed., ed. N. S. Endler and J. McV. Hunt, pp. 559–602. New York: Wiley.

———. (1989). Attachments beyond infancy. *American Psychologist* 44:709–716.

Ainsworth, M. D. S., and Bell, S. M. (1970). Attachment,

exploration, and separation: illustrated by the behavior of one-year-olds in a strange situation. *Child Development* 41:49–67.

Ainsworth, M. D. S., Blehar, M. C., Waters, E., and Wall, S. (1978). *Patterns of Attachment: Assessed in the Strange Situation and at Home*. Hillsdale, NJ: Lawrence Erlbaum.

Albert, A., and Bulcroft, K. (1988). Pets, families and the life course. *Journal of Marriage and the Family* 50:543–552.

Alexander, P. C. (1993). The differential effects of abuse characteristics and attachment in the prediction of long term effects of sexual abuse. *Journal of Interpersonal Violence* 8:346–362.

Alfin, P. L. (1987). Agoraphobia: a study of family of origin characteristics and relationship patterns. *Smith Studies in Social Work*, pp. 134–154. Northampton, MA: Smith College School for Social Work.

Allen, J. (1995). Explaining borderline personality disorder. *Treatment Today*: Fall, 37–39.

Allen, K. M., Blascovich, J., Tomaka, J., and Kelsey, R. M. (1991). Presence of human friends and pet dogs as moderators of autonomic responses to stress in women. *Journal of Personality and Social Psychology* 61:582–589.

American Psychiatric Association (1980). *Diagnostic and Statistical Manual of Mental Disorders*, 3rd ed. Washington, DC: American Psychiatric Association.

———. (1994). *Diagnostic and Statistical Manual of Mental Disorders*, 4th ed. Washington, DC: American Psychiatric Association.

Amini, F., Lewis, T., Lannon, R., et al. (1996). Affect, attachment, memory: contributions toward psychobiologic integration. *Psychiatry: Interpersonal and Biological Processes* 59:213–239.

Antonucci, T. C. (1986). Social support networks: a hierarchical mapping technique. *Generations* 10:10–12.

———. (1994). Attachment in adulthood and aging. In *Attachment in Adults: Clinical and Developmental Perspectives*, ed. M. B. Sperling and W. H. Berman, pp. 256–272. New York: Guilford.

Antonucci, T. C., and Akiyama, H. (1987). Social networks in adult life and a preliminary examination of the convoy model. *Journal of Gerontology* 42:519–527.

Antonucci, T. C., and Levitt, M. J. (1984). Early prediction of attachment security: a multivariate approach. *Infant Behavior and Development* 7:1–18.

Aron, A. P., Dutton, D. G., Aron, E. N., and Iverson, A. (1989). Experiences of falling in love. *Journal of Social and Personal Relationships* 6:243–257.

Aron, L. (1996). *A Meeting of Minds*. Hillsdale, NJ: Analytic Press.

Arrindell, W. (1980). Dimensional structure and psychopathology correlates of the Fear Survey Schedule in a phobic population: a factorial definition of agoraphobia. *Research and Therapy* 18:229–242.

Atkinson, L. (1997). Attachment and psychopathology: from laboratory to clinic. In *Attachment and Psychopathology*, ed. L. Atkinson and K. J. Zucker, pp. 3–16. New York: Guilford.

Bacal, H. A., and Newman, K. M. (1990). *Theories of Object Relations: Bridges to Self Psychology*. New York: Columbia University Press.

Bacciagaluppi, M. (1985). Inversion of parent–child relationships: a contribution to attachment theory. *British Journal of Medical Psychology* 58:369–373.

Balint, M. (1965). *Primary Love and Psycho-Analytic Technique*. New York: Liveright.

Ballenger, J. C. (1989). Toward an integrated model of panic disorder. *American Journal of Orthopsychiatry* 59:284–293.

Baker, J. E., Sedney, M. A., and Gross, E. (1992). Psychological tasks for bereaved children. *American Journal of Orthopsychiatry* 62:105–116.

Barker, S. B., and Barker, R. T. (1988). The human-canine bond: Closer than family ties? *Journal of Mental Health Counseling* 10:46–56.

Barker, S. B., and Dawson, K. S. (1998). The effects of animal-assisted therapy on anxiety ratings of hospitalized psychiatric patients. *Psychiatric Services* 49:797–801.

Barlow, D. H. (1988). *Anxiety and Its Disorders*. New York: Guilford.

Barlow, D. H., Mavissakalian, M., and Hay, L. (1981). Couples treatment of agoraphobia: changes in marital satisfaction. *Behavioral Research and Therapy* 19:245–255.

Barrett, H. (1997). How young children cope with separation: toward a new conceptualization. *British Journal of Medical Psychology* 70:339–358.

Bartholomew, K. (1990). Avoidance of intimacy: an attachment perspective. *Journal of Social and Personal Relationships* 7:147–178.

Bartholomew, K., and Horowitz, L. M. (1991). Attachment styles among young adults: a test of a four-category model. *Journal of Personality and Social Psychology* 61:226–244.

Baum, A., Solomon, S. D., and Ursano, R. J. (1993). Emergency/disaster studies: practical, conceptual, and methodological issues. In *International Handbook of Trau-*

matic Stress Syndromes, ed. J. P. Wilson and B. Raphael, pp. 125–133. New York: Plenum.

Beebe, B., and Lachmann, F. M. (1994). Representation and internalization in infancy: three principles of salience. *Psychoanalytic Psychology* 11:127–165.

Belsky, J. (1999a). Modern evolutionary theory and patterns of attachment. In *Handbook of Attachment*, ed. J. Cassidy and P. R. Shaver, pp. 141–161. New York: Guilford.

———. (1999b). Interactional and contextual determinants of attachment security. In *Handbook of Attachment*, ed. J. Cassidy and P.R. Shaver, pp. 249–264. New York: Guilford.

Belsky, J., Rosenberger, K., and Crnic, K. (1995). The origins of attachment security: classical and contextual determinants. In *Attachment Theory: Social, Developmental, and Clinical Perspectives*, ed. S. Goldberg, R. Muir, and J. Kerr, pp. 153–183. Hillsdale, NJ: Analytic Press.

Bennun, I. (1986). A composite formulation of agoraphobia. *American Journal of Psychotherapy* 40:177–189.

Berlin, L. J., and Cassidy, J. (1999). Relations among relationships: contributions from attachment theory and research. In *Handbook of Attachment*, ed. J. Cassidy, and P. R. Shaver, pp. 688–712. New York: Guilford.

Berman, W. H. (1988). The relationship of ex-spouse attachment to adjustment following divorce. *Journal of Family Psychology* 1:312–328.

Berman, W. H., and Sperling, M. B. (1994). The structure and function of adult attachment. In *Attachment in Adults: Clinical and Developmental Perspectives*, ed. B. Sperling and W. H. Berman, pp. 1–28. New York: Guilford.

Bion, W. R. (1970). *Attention and Interpretation*. New York: Basic Books.

Bock, E., and Webber, I. L. (1972). Suicide among the elderly: isolating widowhood and mitigating alternatives. *Journal of Marriage and the Family* February, 24–31.

Bogin, B. (1990). The evolution of human childhood. *Bio-Science* 40:16–25.

Boman, B. (1986). Early experiential environment, maternal bonding, and the susceptibility to post-traumatic stress disorder. *Military Medicine* 151:528–531.

Bower, G. H. (1987). Commentary on mood and memory. *Behavioral Research and Therapy* 25:443–456.

Bowlby, J. (1942). *Personality and Mental Illness*. New York: Emerson.

———. (1944). Forty four juvenile thieves: their characters and home life. *International Journal of Psycho-Analysis* 25:19–53, 107–128.

———. (1949). The study and reduction of group tensions in the family. *Human Relations* 2:123–128.

———. (1951). *Maternal Care and Mental Health*, Monograph Series No. 2. World Health Organization.

———. (1958). The nature of the child's tie to his mother. *International Journal of Psycho-Analysis* 39:350–373.

———. (1960a). Separation anxiety. *International Journal of Psycho-Analysis* 41:89–113.

———. (1960b). Grief and mourning in infancy and early childhood. *Psychoanalytic Study of the Child* 15:9–52. New York: International Universities Press.

———. (1961). Processes of mourning. *International Journal of Psycho-Analysis* 42:317–340.

———. (1969a). *Attachment and Loss*, vol. 1, *Attachment*. New York: Basic Books.

———. (1969b). Affectional bonds: their nature and origin. In *Progress in Mental Health*, ed. H. Freeman, pp. 38–52. London: Churchill.

———. (1973). *Attachment and Loss*, vol. 2, *Separation, Anxiety and Anger*. New York: Basic Books.

———. (1975). Attachment theory, separation anxiety, and mourning. In *American Handbook of Psychiatry*, ed. D. A. Hamburg and H. K. Brodie, pp. 292–309. New York: Basic Books.

———. (1977). The making and breaking of affection bonds. *British Journal of Psychiatry* 130:201–210, 421–431.

———. (1979). Psychoanalysis as art and science. *International Review of Psycho-Analysis* 6:3–14.

———. (1980). *Attachment and Loss*, vol. 3, *Loss: Sadness and Depression*. New York: Basic Books.

———. (1982). Attachment and loss: retrospect and prospect. *American Journal of Orthopsychiatry* 52:664–678.

———. (1984). Violence in the family as a disorder of the attachment and caregiving systems. *American Journal of Psychoanalysis* 44:9–27.

———. (1985). The role of childhood experience in cognitive disturbance. In *Cognition and Psychotherapy*, ed. M. Mahoney and A. Freeman, pp. 181–200. New York: Plenum.

———. (1987). Defensive processes in the light of attachment theory. In *Attachment and the Therapeutic Process*, ed. J. L. Sacksteder, D. P. Schwartz, and Y. Akabane, pp. 63–79. Madison, CT: International Universities Press.

———. (1988a). *A Secure Base*. New York: Basic Books

———. (1988b). Developmental psychiatry comes of age. *American Journal of Psychiatry* 145:1–10.

———. (1991). *Charles Darwin*. New York: Norton.

Bowlby, J., Robertson, J., and Rosenbluth, D. (1952). A

two-year-old goes to hospital. *Psychoanalytic Study of the Child* 7:82–94. New York: International Universities Press.

Brennan, K. A., Clark, C. L., and Shaver, P. R. (1998). Self-report measurement of adult attachment. In *Attachment Theory and Close Relationships*, ed. J. A. Simpson and W. S. Rholes, pp. 46–76. New York: Guilford.

Bretherton, I. (1985). Attachment theory: retrospect and prospect. In *Growing Points of Attachment Theory and Research*, ed. I. Bretherton and E. Waters, 50:3–35, Monograph of the Society for Research in Child Development, Serial Number 209.

————. (1988). Open communication and internal working models: their role in the development of attachment relationships. In *Socioemotional Development*, ed. R. Thompson, pp. 57–113. Lincoln, NB: University of Nebraska Press.

————. (1995). The origins of attachment theory: John Bowlby and Mary Ainsworth. In *Attachment Theory: Social, Developmental, and Clinical Perspectives*, ed. S. Goldberg, R. Muir, and J. Kerr, pp. 45–84. Hillsdale, NJ: Analytic Press.

————. (1997). Bowlby's legacy to developmental psychology. *Child Psychiatry and Human Development* 28:33–43.

Bretherton, I., and Munholland, K. A. (1999). Internal working models in attachment relationships: a construct revisited. In *Handbook of Attachment*, ed. J. Cassidy and P. R. Shaver, pp. 89–111. New York: Guilford.

Bretherton, I., Ridgeway, D., and Cassidy, J. (1990). Assessing internal models in the attachment relationship: an attachment story completion task for 3-year-olds. In *Attachment during the Preschool Years*, ed.

M. T. Greenberg, D. Cicchetti, and E. M. Cummings, pp. 272–308. Chicago: University of Chicago Press.

Brickel, C. M. (1984). Depression in the nursing home: a pilot study using pet-facilitated psychotherapy. In *The Pet Connection*, ed. R. K. Anderson, B. Hart, and L. A. Hart, pp. 407–415. Minneapolis: University of Minnesota Press.

Brown, D. (1993). Affective development, psychopathology, and adaption. In *Human Feelings*, ed. S. L. Ablon, D. Brown, E. J. Khantzian, and J. E. Mack, pp. 5–66. Hillsdale, NJ: Analytic Press.

Brown, G. W. (1982). Early loss and depression. In *The Place of Attachment in Human Social Behavior*, ed. C. W. Parkes and J. Stevenson-Hinde, pp. 232–268. New York: Basic Books.

Brown, G., and Harris, T. (1978). *The Social Origins of Depression*. London: Tavistock.

Browne, A. (1993). Violence against women by male partners. *American Psychologist* 48:1077–1087.

Buglass, D., Clarke, J., Henderson, A. S., et al. (1977). A study of agoraphobic housewives. *Psychological Medicine* 7:73–86.

Bunch, J. (1972). Recent bereavement in relation to suicide. *Journal of Psychosomatic Research* 16:361–366.

Bustad, L. K., and Hines, L. M. (1982). Placement of animals with the elderly: benefits and strategies. *California Veterinarian* 36:37–44.

Byng-Hall, S. (1999). Creating a coherent story in family therapy. In *Healing Stories*, ed. G. Roberts and J. Holmes, pp. 131–151. New York: Oxford University Press.

Cain, A. O. (1985). Pets as family members. In *Pets and the Family*, ed. M. B. Sussman, pp. 5–10. New York: Haworth.

Callahan, J. (1996). A specific therapeutic approach to suicide risk in borderline clients. *Clinical Social Work Journal* 24:443–459.

Caras, R. (1995). By definition. In *Dog People*, ed. M. J. Rosen, pp. 142–143. New York: Artison.

Carey, R. G. (1977). The widowed: a year later. *Journal of Counseling Psychology* 24:125–131.

Carnelley, K. B., and Janoff-Bulman, R. (1992). Optimism about love relationships: general vs. specific lessons from one's personal experiences. *Journal of Social and Personal Relationships* 9:5–20.

Carr, A. C., and Schoenberg, B. (1970). Object-loss and somatic symptom formation. In *Loss and Grief, Psychological Management in Medical Practice*, ed. B. Schoenberg, pp. 36–48. New York: Columbia University Press.

Casement, P. J. (1991). *Learning from the Patient*. New York: Guilford.

———. (1994). Lecture, Los Angeles, CA, January.

Cassidy, J., and Kobak, R. R. (1988). Avoidance and its relation to other defensive processes. In *Clinical Implications of Attachment*, ed. J. Belsky and T. Nezworski, pp. 300–323. Hillsdale, NJ: Lawrence Erlbaum.

Chassler, L. (1997). Understanding anorexia nervosa and bulimia nervosa from an attachment perspective. *Clinical Social Work Journal* 25:407–423.

Cicchetti, D., and Toth, S. L. (1995). Child maltreatment and attachment organization: implications for intervention. In *Attachment Theory: Social, Developmental, and Clinical Perspectives*, ed. S. Goldberg, R. Muir, and J. Kerr, pp. 279–308. Hillsdale, NJ: Analytic Press.

Clarke, J. C., and Wardman, W. (1985). *Agoraphobia*. New York: Pergamon.

Cobb, J. P., Mathews, A. M., Childs-Clarke, A., and Blowers, C. M. (1984). The spouse as co-therapist in the treatment of agoraphobia. *British Journal of Psychiatry* 144:282–287.

Cohen, S. P. (1985). The role of social work in a veterinary hospital setting. *Veterinary Clinics of North America: Small Animal Practice* 15:355–361.

Cole, K. M. (1999). Animal-assisted therapy. In *Nursing Interventions: Effective Nursing Treatments*, 3rd ed., ed. G. M. Bulechek and J. C. McCloskey, pp. 508–519. Philadelphia: Saunders.

Cole, K. M., Detke, H., and Kobak, R. (1996). Attachment processes in eating disorder and depression. *Journal of Consulting and Clinical Psychology* 64:282–290.

Cole, K. M., and Gawlinski, A. (1995). Animal-assisted therapy in the intensive care unit: a staff nurse's dream comes true. *Nursing Clinics of North America* 30:529–537.

———. (2000). Animal-assisted therapy: the human–animal bond. *American Association of Critical-Care Nurses Clinical Issues* 11:139–149.

Collins, N. L., and Read, S. J. (1990). Cognitive representations of attachment: the content and function of working models. In *Advances in Personal Relationships*, ed. D. Perlman and K. Bartholomew, pp. 53–90. London: Jessica Kingsley.

Conway, P. (1988). Losses and grief in old age. *Social Casework* 69:541–549.

Corson, S. A., and Corson, E. O. (1980). Pet animals as nonverbal communication mediators in psychotherapy in institutional settings. In *Ethology and Nonverbal Communications in Mental Health*, ed. S. A. Corson and E. O. Corson, pp. 83–110. Elmsford, NY: Pergamon.

Cowles, K. U. (1985). The death of a pet: human responses to the breaking of the bond. In *Pets and the Family*, ed. M. B. Sussman, pp. 135–148. New York: Haworth.

Crittenden, P. M. (1992). Quality of attachment in the preschool years. *Development and Psychopathology* 4:209–241.

Crittenden, P. M., Claussen, A. H., and Sugarman, D. B. (1994). Physical and psychological maltreatment in middle childhood and adolescence. *Development and Psychopathology* 6:145–164.

Crowell, J. A., Fraley, R. C., and Shaver, P. R. (1999). Measurement of individual differences in adolescent and adult attachment. In *Handbook of Attachment*, ed. J. Cassidy and P. R. Shaver, pp. 434–465. New York: Guilford.

Crowell, J. A., and Waters, E. (1994). Bowlby's theory grown up: the role of attachment in adult love relationships. *Psychological Inquiry* 5:31–34.

Cusak, O. (1988). *Pets and Mental Health*. New York: Haworth.

Davidson, G. P. (1981). Sudden death: bereavement sequelae and interventions. *New Zealand Medical Journal* 94:265–267.

Davidson, J. (1993). Issues in the diagnosis of posttraumatic disorder. In *Annual Review of Psychiatry* 12, ed. J. M. Oldham, M. B. Riba, and A. Tasman, pp. 141–155. Washington, DC: American Psychiatric Press.

Davis, P. W. (1996). Threats of corporal punishment as verbal aggression: a naturalistic study. *Child Abuse and Neglect* 20:289–304.

Davison, G. C., and Neale, J. M. (1990). *Abnormal Psychology*. New York: Wiley.

Derdeyn, A. P. (1985). Grandparent visitation rights: Rendering family dissension more pronounced? *American Journal of Orthopsychiatry* 55:277–287.

Derogatis, L. R., Lipman, R. S., Rickels, R., et al. (1974). The Hopkins Symptom Checklist (HSCL): a self-report symptom inventory. *Behavioral Science* 19:1–15.

Derogatis, L. R., and Spencer, P. M. (1982). *The Brief Symptom Inventory (BSI): Administration, Scoring and Procedures.* Baltimore: Clinical Psychometric Research.

de Zulueta, F. (1994). *From Pain to Violence.* Northvale, NJ: Jason Aronson.

Dolan, R. T., Arnkoff, D. B., and Glass, C. R. (1993). Client attachment style and the psychotherapist's interpersonal stance. *Psychotherapy* 30:408–412.

Dozier, M., and Kobak, R. R. (1992). Psychophysiology in attachment interviews: converging evidence for deactivating strategies. *Child Development* 63:1473–1480.

Dozier, M., Stovall, K. C., and Albus, K. E. (1999). Attachment and psychopathology in adulthood. In *Handbook of Attachment*, ed. J. Cassidy, and P. R. Shaver, pp. 497–519. New York: Guilford.

Dozier, M., and Tyrrell, C. (1998). The role of attachment in therapeutic relationships. In *Attachment Theory and Close Relationships*, ed. J. A. Simpson and W. S. Rholes, pp. 221–248. New York: Guilford.

Dumont, M. P. (1991). Agedanken experiment, part II: anxiety as a social disease. *Readings* 6:16–19.

Durkin, M. S., Khan, N., Davidson, L. L., et al. (1993). The effects of a natural disaster on child behavior: evidence for posttraumatic stress. *American Journal of Public Health* 83:1549–1553.

Eagle, M. (1997). Attachment and psychoanalysis. *British Journal of Medical Psychology* 70:217–229.

Elliot, O., and King, J. A. (1960). Effect of early food deprivation on later consummatory behavior in puppies. *Psychological Reports* 6:391–400.

Erikson, E. H. (1950). *Childhood and Society*. New York: Norton.

Eth, S., and Pynoos, R. S. (1985). *Post-traumatic Stress Disorder in Children*. Washington, DC: American Psychiatric Press.

Fairbairn, W. R. D. (1940). Schizoid factors in the personality. In *Psychoanalytic Studies of the Personality*, pp. 3–27. London: Tavistock, 1952.

———. (1943). The repression and return of bad objects (with special reference to the 'war neuroses'). *British Journal of Medical Psychology* 19:327–341.

———. (1952). *Psychoanalytic Studies of the Personality*. London: Tavistock.

———. (1963). Synopsis of an object-relations theory of the personality. *International Journal of Psycho-Analysis* 44:224–225.

Farber, B. A., Lippert, R. A., and Nevas, D. B. (1995). The therapist as attachment figure. *Psychotherapy* 32:204–212.

Feeney, J. A. (1998). Adult attachment and relationship-centered anxiety: responses to physical and emotional distancing. In *Attachment Theory and Close Relationships*, ed. J. A. Simpson and W. S. Rholes, pp. 189–218. New York: Guilford.

———. (1999). Adult romantic attachment and couple relationships. In *Handbook of Attachment*, ed. J. Cassidy and P. R. Shaver, pp. 355–377. New York: Guilford.

Feeney, J., and Noller, P. (1996). *Adult Attachment*. Thousand Oaks, CA: Sage.

Finn, M. G., and Sperling, M. B. (1993). Therapists' representations of psychotherapy: special patients. *Contemporary Psychoanalysis* 29:343–351.

Firth, M. T. (1994). Assessment in mental health: present problems as past history. *Journal of Social Work Practice* 8:3–17.

Fischer, K. W., Ayoub, C., Singh, I., et al. (1997). Psychopathology as adaptive development along distinctive pathways. *Development and Psychopathology* 9:749–779.

Fischer-Mamblona, H. (2000). On the evolution of attachment-disordered behavior. *Attachment and Human Development* 2:8–21.

Fish, B. (1996). Clinical implications of attachment narratives. *Clinical Social Work Journal* 24:239–253.

Fisher, H. E. (1992). *Anatomy of Love*. New York: Norton.

Florian, V., Mikulincer, M., and Bucholtz, I. (1995). Effects of adult attachment style on the perception and search for social support. *Journal of Psychology* 129:665–676.

Fodor, I. G. (1974). The phobic syndrome in women: implications for treatment. In *Women in Therapy*, ed. V. Franks and V. Burtle, pp. 132–168. New York: Brunner/Mazel.

Fonagy, P. (1999). Psychoanalytic theory from the viewpoint of attachment theory and research. In *Handbook of Attachment*, ed. J. Cassidy and P. R. Shaver, pp. 595–624. New York: Guilford.

Fonagy, P., Leigh, T., Steele, M., et al. (1996). The relation of attachment status, psychiatric classification, and response to psychotherapy. *Journal of Consulting and Clinical Psychology* 64:22–31.

Fonagy, P., Steele, M., Steele, H., et al. (1991). The capacity for understanding mental states: the reflective self in parent and child and its significance for security of attachment. *Infant Mental Health Journal* 12:201–218.

———. (1995). Attachment, the reflective self and borderline states: the predictive specificity of the adult attachment interview and pathological emotional development. In *Attachment Theory: Social, Developmental, and Clinical Perspectives*, ed. S. Goldberg, R. Muir, and J. Kerr, pp. 233–278. Hillsdale, NJ: Analytic Press.

Fonagy, P., Target, M., Steele, M., and Steele, H. (1997). The development of violence and crime as it relates to security of attachment. In *Children in a Violent Society*, ed. J. D. Osofsky, pp. 150–177. New York: Guilford.

Fox, I. (1996). *Being There: The Benefits of a Stay-at-Home Parent*. Hauppauge, NY: Barron's.

Fox, N. A., and Card, J. A. (1999). Psychophysiological measures in the study of attachment. In *Handbook of Attachment*, ed. J. Cassidy, and P. R. Shaver, pp. 226–245. New York: Guilford.

Fraley, R. C., Davis, K. E., and Shaver, P. R. (1998). Dismissing-avoidance and the defensive organization of emotion, cognition, and behavior. In *Attachment Theory and Close Relationships*, ed. J. A. Simpson and W. S. Rholes, pp. 249–279. New York: Guilford.

Fraley, R. C., and Shaver, P. R. (1999). Loss and bereavement: attachment theory and recent controversies concerning "grief work" and the nature of detachment. In *Handbook of Attachment*, ed. J. Cassidy, and P. R. Shaver, pp. 735–759. New York: Guilford.

Fraley, R. C., and Waller, N. G. (1998). Adult attachment patterns: a test of the typological model. In *Attachment and Close Relationships*, ed. J. A. Simpson and W. S. Rholes, pp. 77–114. New York: Guilford.

Frances, A., and Dunn, P. (1975). The attachment autonomy conflict in agoraphobia. *International Journal of Psycho-Analysis* 56:435–439.

Freud, S. (1917). Mourning and melancholia. *Standard Edition* 14:237–258.

———. (1919). Lines of advance in psychoanalytic therapy. *Standard Edition* 17:139–168.

———. (1920). Beyond the pleasure principle. *Standard Edition* 18:1–64.

———. (1926). Inhibitions, symptoms and anxiety. *Standard Edition* 20:75–175.

———. (1933). New introductory lectures on psychoanalysis. *Standard Edition* 22:3–182.

Freyd, J. F. (1996). *Betrayal Trauma*. Cambridge: Harvard University Press.

Friedman, E., Katcher, A., and Meislich, G. (1980). Animal companions and one year survival rate of patients after discharge from a coronary care unit. *Public Health Reports* 95:307–312.

Fromm, M. G. (1995). What does borderline mean? *Psychoanalytic Psychology* 12:233–245.

Frustaci, J. (1988). A survey of agoraphobics in self-help groups. *Smith Studies in Social Work*, pp. 193–211. Northampton, MA: Smith College School for Social Work.

Gabbard, G. (1992). Psychodynamic psychiatry in the "decade of the brain." *American Journal of Psychiatry* 149:991–998.

Garber, M. (1996). Dog days. *New Yorker*, July 16, pp. 72–78.

Garrity, T. F., Stallones, L., Marx, M. B., and Johnson, T. P. (1989). Pet ownership and attachment as supportive factors in the health of the elderly. *Anthrozoos* 3:35–44.

Gay, P. (1988). *Freud: A Life for Our Time*. New York: Norton.

George, C., West, M., and Pettem, O. (1999). The adult attachment projective: disorganization of adult attachment at the level of representation. In *Attachment Disorganization*, ed. J. Solomon and C. George, pp. 318–346. New York: Guilford.

Gelfond, M. (1991). Reconceptualizing agoraphobia: a case study of epistemological bias in clinical research. *Feminism and Psychology* 1:247–262.

Gerwolls, M. K. (1990). *Effects of confiding, emotional expression and additional pet ownership on adult adjustment to the death of a companion animal*. Unpublished thesis, the University of Toledo School of Psychology.

Gilligan, C. (1982). *In a Different Voice*. Cambridge: Harvard University Press.

Glick, I. O., Weiss, R. S., and Parkes, C. M. (1974). *The First Year of Bereavement*. New York: Wiley.

Gold, J. H. (1996). The intolerance of aloneness [editorial]. *American Journal of Psychiatry* 153:749–750.

Goldberg, S. (1997). Attachment and childhood behavior problems in normal, at risk, and clinical samples. In *Attachment and Psychopathology*, ed. L. Atkinson and K. J. Zucker, pp. 171–195. New York: Guilford.

Golden, G. K. (1990). Attachment—not dependence. *Social Work* 35:101.

Goodman, L. A., Koss, M. P., Fitzgerald, L. F., et al. (1993). Male violence against women. *American Psychologist* 48:1054–1061.

Gorer, G. (1965). *Death, Grief and Mourning in Contemporary Britain*. London: Tavistock.

Green, B. L. (1993). Identifying survivors at risk: trauma and stressors across events. In *International Hand-*

book of Traumatic Stress Syndromes, ed. J. P. Wilson and B. Raphael, pp. 135–144. New York: Plenum.

Green, B. L., Wilson, J. P., and Lindy, J. D. (1985). Conceptualizing post-traumatic stress disorder: a psychosocial framework. In Trauma and Its Wake, ed. C. R. Figley, pp. 53–69. New York: Brunner/Mazel.

Greenberg, J. R., and Mitchell, S. A. (1983). Object Relations in Psychoanalytic Theory. Cambridge: Harvard University Press.

Greenberg, M. T., DeKlyen, M., Speltz, M. L., and Endriga, M. C. (1997). The role of attachment processes in externalizing psychopathology in young children. In Attachment and Psychopathology, ed. L. Atkinson and K. J. Zucker, pp. 223–274. New York: Guilford.

Griffin, D. W., and Bartholomew, K. (1994). The metaphysics of measurement: the case of adult attachment. In Advances in Personal Relationships, vol. 5, ed. K. Bartholomew, and D. Perlman, pp. 17–52. London: Jessica Kingsley.

Grosskurth, P. (1986). Melanie Klein: Her World and Her Work. New York: Knopf.

Grossman, K. E. (1995). The evolution and history of attachment research and theory. In Attachment Theory: Social, Developmental, and Clinical Perspectives, ed. S. Goldberg, R. Muir, and J. Kerr, pp. 85–121. Hillsdale, NJ: Analytic Press.

Grossman, K. E., Grossman, K., and Zimmerman, P. (1999). A wider view of attachment and exploration. In Handbook of Attachment, ed. J. Cassidy and P. R. Shaver, pp. 760–786. New York: Guilford.

Grotstein, J. S. (1990). The contribution of attachment theory and self-regulation theory to the therapeutic alliance. Modern Psychoanalysis 15:169–184.

Guidano, V. F., and Liotti, G. (1983). *Cognitive Process and Emotional Disorders*. New York: Guilford.

Gunderson, J. G. (1996). The borderline patient's intolerance of aloneness: insecure attachments and therapist availability. *American Journal of Psychiatry* 153:752–758.

Gut, E. (1989). *Productive and Unproductive Depression*. New York: Basic Books.

Hamilton, N. G. (1989). A critical review of object relations theory. *American Journal of Psychiatry* 146:1552–1560.

Hamilton, V. (1985). John Bowlby: an ethological basis for psychoanalysis. In *Beyond Freud: A Study of Modern Psychoanalytic Theorists*, ed. J. Reppen, pp. 1–28. Hillsdale, NJ: Analytic Press.

——. (1987). Some problems in the clinical application of attachment theory. *Psychoanalytic Psychotherapy* 3:67–83.

Hansburg, H. G. (1972). *Adolescent Separation Anxiety: A Method for the Study of Adolescent Separation Problems*. Springfield, IL: Charles C Thomas.

Harlow, H. (1958). The nature of love. *American Psychologist* 13:673–685.

Harris, T. O. (1997). Adult attachment processes and psychotherapy: a commentary on Bartholomew and Birtchnell. *British Journal of Medical Psychology* 70:281–290.

Harris, T., and Bifulco, A. (1991). Loss of parent in childhood, attachment style, and depression in adulthood. In *Attachment Across the Life Cycle*, ed. C. M. Parkes, J. Stevenson-Hinde, and P. Marris, pp. 234–267. New York: Tavistock/Routledge.

Hart, S. N., Brassard, M. R., and Karlson, H. C. (1996). Psychological maltreatment. In *The APSAC Handbook* on *Child Maltreatment*, ed. J. Briere, L. Berliner, J. A. Bulkley, et al. pp. 72–89. Thousand Oaks, CA: Sage.

Hazan, C., and Shaver, P. R. (1987). Romantic love conceptualized as an attachment process. *Journal of Personality and Social Psychology* 52:511–524.

———. (1990). Love and work: an attachment-theoretical perspective. *Journal of Personality and Social Psychology* 52:270–280.

———. (1994). Attachment as an organizational framework for research on close relationships. *Psychological Inquiry* 5:1–22.

Hazan, C., and Zeifman, D. (1999). Pair bonds as attachments. In *Handbook of Attachment*, ed. J. Cassidy and P. R. Shaver, pp. 336–354. New York: Guilford.

Heiman, M. (1965). Psychoanalytic observations on the relationship of pet and man. *Veterinary Medicine/Small Animal Clinician* 60:713–718.

Heinicke, C., and Westheimer, I. (1966). *Brief Separations*. New York: International Universities Press.

Hendrick, C., and Hendrick, S. S. (1994). Attachment theory and close relationships. *Psychological Inquiry* 5:38–41.

Herman, J. (1992). *Trauma and Recovery*. New York: Basic Books.

Herman, J., Perry, C., and Kolb, B. (1989). Childhood trauma in borderline personality disorder. *American Journal of Psychiatry* 146:490–495.

Herman, J. L., and van der Kolk, B. A. (1992). Traumatic antecedents of borderline personality disorder. In *Psychological Trauma*, ed. B. A. van der Kolk, pp. 111–126. Washington, DC: American Psychiatric Press.

Hinde, R. A., and Stevenson-Hinde, J. (1991). Perspectives on attachment. In *Attachment Across the Life Cycle*, ed. C. M. Parkes, J. Stevenson-Hinde, and P. Marris, pp. 52–65. New York: Tavistock/Routledge.

Hofer, M. A. (1984). Relationships as regulators: a psychobiologic perspective on bereavement. *Psychosomatic Medicine* 46:183–197.

———. (1995). Hidden regulators: implications for a new understanding of attachment, separation, and loss. In *Attachment Theory: Social, Developmental, and Clinical Perspectives*, ed. S. Goldberg, R. Muir, and J. Kerr, pp. 203–230. Hillsdale, NJ: Analytic Press.

Holmes, J. (1982). Phobia and counterphobia: family aspects of agoraphobia. *Journal of Family Therapy* 4:133–152.

———. (1993a). *John Bowlby and Attachment Theory*. New York: Routledge.

———. (1993b). Attachment theory: A biological basis for psychotherapy? *British Journal of Psychiatry* 163:430–438.

———. (1994). The clinical implications of attachment theory. *British Journal of Psychotherapy* 11:62–76.

———. (1995). "Something there is that doesn't love a wall.": John Bowlby, attachment theory, and psychoanalysis. In *Attachment Theory: Social, Developmental, and Clinical Perspectives*, ed. S. Goldberg, R. Muir, and J. Kerr, pp. 19–43. Hillsdale, NJ: Analytic Press.

———. (1996). *Attachment, Intimacy, Autonomy: Using Attachment Theory in Adult Psychotherapy*. Northvale, NJ: Jason Aronson.

———. (1997). Attachment, autonomy, intimacy: some clinical implications of attachment theory. *British Journal of Medical Psychology* 70:231–248.

———. (1999a). Defensive and creative uses of narrative in psychotherapy: an attachment perspective. In *Heal-*

ing Stories, ed. G. Roberts and J. Holmes, pp. 49–66. New York: Oxford University Press.

———. (1999b). Ghosts in the consulting room: an attachment perspective on intergenerational transmission. *Attachment and Human Development* 1:115–131.

Hooven, C., Gottman, J. M., and Katz, L. F. (1995). Parental meta-emotion structure predicts family and child outcomes. *Cognition and Emotion* 9:229–264.

Horowitz, M. J. (1988). *Introduction to Psychodynamics*. New York: Basic Books.

———. (1993). Stress-response syndromes: a review of posttraumatic stress and adjustment disorders. In *International Handbook of Traumatic Stress Syndromes*, ed. J. P. Wilson, and B. Raphael, pp. 49–60. New York: Plenum.

Hunter, V. (1991). John Bowlby: an interview. *Psychoanalytic Review* 78:159–175.

Insel, T. R. (1997). A neurobiological basis of social attachment. *American Journal of Psychiatry* 154:726–735.

Jacobs, S., and Douglas, L. (1979). Grief: a mediating process between a loss and illness. *Comprehensive Psychiatry* 20:165–176.

Jacobs, S., and Ostfeld, A. (1977). An epidemiological review of the mortality of bereavement. *Psychosomatic Medicine* 39:344–357.

Jacobson, A. (1989). Physical and sexual assault histories among psychiatric outpatients. *American Journal of Psychiatry* 146:755–758.

James, B. (1989). *Treating Traumatized Children*. New York: Lexington.

Janoff-Bulman, R. (1985). The aftermath of victimization: rebuilding shattered assumptions. In *Trauma and Its Wake*, ed. C. R. Figley, pp. 15–35. New York: Brunner/Mazel.

Johnson, H. C. (1991). Borderline clients: practice implications of recent research. *Social Work* 36:106–173.

Jones, B. A. (1983). Healing factors of psychiatry in light of attachment theory. *American Journal of Psychotherapy* 37:235–244.

Kahn, R. L., and Antonucci, T. C. (1980). Convoys over the life course: attachment, roles, and social support. In *Life-span Development and Behavior*, vol. 3, ed. P. B. Baltes and O. Brim, pp. 253–286. New York: Academic Press.

Kale, M. (1992). What you already know: Fluffy and Fido are good for you. *Interactions* 10:19–20. Renton, WA: The Delta Society.

Karen, R. (1990). Becoming attached. *The Atlantic*, February, pp. 35–70.

———. (1994). *Becoming Attached*. New York: Warner.

———. (1998). *Becoming Attached*. 2nd ed. New York: Warner.

Katcher, A. (1982). Are companion animals good for your health? A review of the evidence. *Aging*: September-October 2–8.

Keddie, K. M. G. (1977). Pathological mourning after the death of a domestic pet. *British Journal of Psychiatry* 131:21–25.

Kernberg, O. F. (1967). Borderline personality organization. *Journal of the American Psychoanalytic Association* 15:641–685.

———. (1975). *Borderline Conditions and Pathological Narcissism*. New York: Jason Aronson.

———. (1984). *Psychoanalytic Treatment of Personality Disorders*. New York: Academic Press.

Kincaid, S. B., and Caldwell, R. A. (1995). Marital separation: causes, coping and consequences. *Journal of Divorce and Remarriage* 22:109–128.

Klein, M. (1940). Mourning and its relation to manic-depressive states. *International Journal of Psycho-Analysis* 21:125–153.

———. (1946). Notes on some schizoid mechanisms. *International Journal of Psycho-Analysis* 27:99–110.

———. (1948). *Contributions to Psycho-Analysis*. London: Hogarth.

Knapp, C. (1998). *Pack of Two: The Intricate Bond Between People and Dogs*. New York: Dial.

Kobak, R. (1999). The emotional dynamics of disruptions in attachment relationships: implications for theory, research, and clinical intervention. In *Handbook of Attachment*, ed. J. Cassidy, and P. R. Shaver, pp. 21–43. New York: Guilford.

Kobak, R., and Hazan, C. (1991). Attachment in marriage: effects of security and accuracy of working models. *Journal of Personality and Social Psychology* 60:861–869.

Kobak, R. R. and Sceery, A. (1988). Attachment in late adolescence: working models, affect regulation and representations of self and others. *Child Development* 59:135–146.

Kobak, R. and Shaver, P. R. (1987). *Strategies for maintaining felt security: a theoretical analysis of continuity and change in styles of social adaptation*. Paper presented at the Conference in Honor of John Bowlby's 80th Birthday, Bayswater, London, June.

Kohut, H. (1977). *The Restoration of the Self*. New York: International Universities Press.

Kottler, T., and Omodei, M. (1988). Attachment and emotional health: a life span approach. *Human Relations* 41:619–640.

Kraemer, G. W. (1992). A psychobiological theory of attachment. *Behavioral and Brain Sciences* 15:493–541.

Krystal, J. H. (1978). Trauma and affects. *Psychoanalytic Study of Children* 33:81–116.

———. (1990). Animal models for posttraumatic stress disorder. In *Biological Assessment and Treatment for Posttraumatic Stress Disorder*, ed. E. L. Gillere, Jr., pp. 3–26. Washington, DC: American Psychiatric Press.

Kunce, L., and Shaver, P. R. (1994). An attachment-theoretical approach to caregiving in romantic relationships. In *Attachment Processes in Adulthood*, ed. K. Bartholomew and D. Perlman, pp. 205–237. London: Jessica Kingsley.

Leach, P. (1994). *Children First*. New York: Knopf.

Levinson, B. M. (1965). Pet psychotherapy: use of household pets in the treatment of behavior disorders in childhood. *Psychological Reports* 17:695–698.

Levinson, P. (1972). On sudden death. *Psychiatry* 35:160–173.

Levitt, M. J. (1991). Attachment and close relationships: a life span perspective. In *Intersections with Attachment*, ed. J. L. Gewirtz and W. F. Kurtines, pp. 183–206. Hillsdale, NJ: Lawrence Erlbaum.

Levitt, M. J., Coffman, S., Guacci-Franco, N., and Loveless, S. C. (1994). Attachment relationships and life transitions. In *Attachment in Adults: Clinical and Developmental Perspectives*, ed. M. B. Sperling and W. H. Berman, pp. 232–255. New York: Guilford.

Lewis, M. (1994). Does attachment imply a relationship or multiple relationships? *Psychological Inquiry* 5:47–51.

Lieberman, A. F. (1997). Toddlers' internalization of maternal attributions as a factor in quality of attachment. In *Attachment and Psychopathology*, ed. L. Atkinson and K. J. Zucker, pp. 277–291. New York: Guilford.

Lieberman, A. F., and Pawl, J. H. (1990). Disorders of attachment and secure base behavior in the second year of life. In *Attachment in the Preschool Years*, ed. M. T. Greenberg, D. Cicchetti, and E. M. Cummings, pp. 375–397. Chicago: University of Chicago Press.

Lieberman, A. F., and Zeanah, C. H. (1999). Contributions of attachment theory to infant–parent psychotherapy and other interventions with infants and young children. In *Handbook of Attachment*, ed. J. Cassidy and P. R. Shaver, pp. 555–574. New York: Guilford.

Lindemann, E. (1944). Symptomatology and management of acute grief. *American Journal of Psychiatry* 101:141–149.

Links, P. S., Offord, D. R., and Eppel, A. (1988). Characteristics of borderline personality disorder: a Canadian study. *Canadian Journal of Psychiatry* 33:336–340.

Liotti, G. (1991). Insecure attachment and agoraphobia. In *Attachment Across the Life Cycle*, ed. C. M. Parkes, J. Stevenson-Hinde, and P. Marris, pp. 216–233. New York: Tavistock/Routledge.

———. (1995). Disorganized/disoriented attachment in the psychotherapy of the dissociative disorders. In *Attachment Theory: Social, Developmental, and Clinical Perspectives*, ed. S. Goldberg, R. Muir, and J. Kerr, pp. 343–363. Hillsdale, NJ: Analytic Press.

Logan, D. E., and Graham-Bermann, S. A. (1999). Emotion expression in children exposed to family violence. *Journal of Emotional Abuse* 1:39–64.

Lohman, C. P. (1981). The social origins of femininity. *Smith College Studies in Social Work* 51:162–191.

Lorenz, K. (1952). *King Solomon's Ring*. London: Methuen.

Loring, M. T. (1994). *Emotional Abuse*. New York: Lexington.

Loring, M. T., and Myers, D. L. (1994). Differentiating emotional abuse. In *Emotional Abuse*, ed. M. T. Loring, pp. 15–24. New York: Lexington.

Lourie, M., and Stefano, L. (1978). On defining emotional abuse: child abuse and neglect: issues in innovation and implementation. *Proceedings of the Second Annual National Conference on Child Abuse and Neglect*. Washington, DC: U.S. Government Printing Office.

Lowenstein, S. F. (1985). Freud's metapsychology revisited. *Social Casework* 66:139–151.

Lundin, T. (1984). Long-term outcome of bereavement. *British Journal of Psychiatry* 145:424–428.

Lynch, J. J. (1977). *The Broken Heart*. New York: Basic Books.

Lyons, L. S., and Sperling, M. B. (1996). Clinical applications of attachment theory: empirical and theoretical perspectives. In *Psychoanalytic Perspectives on Developmental Psychology*, ed. J. Masling and R. Bornstein, pp. 221–256. Washington, DC: American Psychological Association Press.

Mackie, A. J. (1981). Attachment theory: its relevance to the therapeutic alliance. *British Journal of Medical Psychology* 54:203–212.

Maddison, D. C., and Viola, A. (1968). The health of widows in the year following bereavement. *Journal of Psychosomatic Research* 12:297–306.

Magai, C. (1999). Affect, imagery, and attachment. In *Handbook of Attachment*, ed. J. Cassidy, and P. R. Shaver, pp. 787–802. New York: Guilford.

Mahler, M. (1972). Rapprochement subphase of the separation-individuation process. In *Selected Papers of*

Margaret Mahler, vol. 2, pp. 131–148. New York: Jason Aronson.

Mahler, M., Pine, F., and Bergman, A. (1975). *The Psychological Birth of the Human Infant*. New York: Basic Books.

Main, M. (1981). Avoidance in the service of attachment: a working paper. In *Behavioral Development: The Bielefeld Interdisciplinary Project*, ed. K. Immelman, G. Barlow, M. Main, and L. Petrinovitch, pp. 651–693. New York: Cambridge University Press.

———. (1991). Metacognitive knowledge, metacognitive monitoring and singular (coherent) vs. multiple (incoherent) model of attachment: findings and directions for future research. In *Attachment Across the Life Cycle*, ed. C. M. Parkes, J. Stevenson-Hinde, and P. Marris, pp. 127–159. New York: Tavistock/Routledge.

———. (1995). Recent studies in attachment: overview, with selected implications for clinical work. In *Attachment Theory: Social, Developmental, and Clinical Perspectives*, ed. S. Goldberg, R. Muir, and J. Kerr, pp. 407–474. Hillsdale, NJ: Analytic Press.

———. (1999). Epilogue. Attachment theory: eighteen points with suggestions for future studies. In *Handbook of Attachment*, ed. J. Cassidy, and P. R. Shaver, pp. 845–887. New York: Guilford.

Main, M., and Goldwyn, R. (1984). Predicting rejection of her infants from mother's representation of her own experience: implications for the abused-abusing intergenerational cycle. *International Journal of Child Abuse and Neglect* 8:203–217.

Mallinckrodt, B., Gantt, D. L., and Coble, H. M. (1995). Attachment patterns in the psychotherapy relationship: development of the client attachment to therapist scale. *Journal of Counseling Psychology* 42:307–319.

Marks, I. M. (1970). Agoraphobic syndrome. *Archives of General Psychiatry* 23:538–553.

Marmor, J. (1974). *Psychiatry in Transition*. New York: Brunner/Mazel.

———. (1988). Psychiatry in a troubled world: the relation of clinical practice and social reality. *American Journal of Orthopsychiatry* 58:484–491.

Marris, P. (1958). *Widows and Their Families*. London: Routledge and Kegan Paul.

———. (1974). *Loss and Change*. London: Routledge and Kegan Paul.

———. (1982). Attachment and society. In *The Place of Attachment in Human Behavior*, ed. C. M. Parkes and J. Stevenson-Hinde, pp. 185–201. New York: Basic Books.

———. (1991). The social construction of uncertainty. In *Attachment Across the Life Cycle*, ed. C. M. Parkes, J. Stevenson-Hinde, and P. Marris, pp. 77–90. New York: Tavistock/Routledge.

Marrone, M. (1998). *Attachment and Interaction*. Philadelphia: Jessica Kingsley.

Masterson, J. F. (1981). *The Narcissistic and Borderline Disorders*. New York: Brunner/Mazel.

Mathews, A. M., Gelder, M. G., and Johnston, D. W. (1981). *Agoraphobia: Nature and Treatment*. New York: Guilford.

McCulloch, M. (1981). The pet as prothesis: defining criteria for the adjunctive use of companion animals in the treatment of the medically ill, depressed outpatients. In *Interrelations Between People and Pets*, ed. B. Fogel, pp. 104–123. Springfield, IL: Charles C Thomas.

McDougall, J. (1989). *Theaters of the Body*. New York: Norton.

Melges, F. T., and DeMaso, D. R. (1980). Grief resolution therapy: reliving, revising, and revisiting. *American Journal of Psychotherapy* 34:51–61.

Melges, F. T., and Swartz, M. S. (1989). Oscillations of attachment in borderline personality disorder. *American Journal of Psychiatry* 146:1115–1120.

Meloy, J. R. (1992). *Violent Attachments*. Northvale, NJ: Jason Aronson.

Melson, G. F. (1989). Studying children's attachment to their pets: a conceptual and methodological review. *Anthrozoos* 4:91–99.

Michelson, L. (1987). Cognitive-behavioral assessment and treatment of agoraphobia. In *Anxiety and Stress Disorders*, ed. L. Michelson, and L. M. Ascher, pp. 213–279. New York: Guilford.

Mikulincer, M., and Florian, V. (1998). The relationship between adult attachment styles and emotional and cognitive reactions to stressful events. In *Attachment Theory and Close Relationships*, ed. J. A. Simpson and W. S. Rholes, pp. 143–165. New York: Guilford.

Mikulincer, M., and Orbach, I. (1995). Attachment styles and repressive defensiveness: the accessibility and architecture of affective memories. *Journal of Personality and Social Psychology* 68:917–925.

Mills, L. (1996). Empowering battered women transnationally: the case for post-modern interventions. *Social Work* 41:261–268.

Minde, K., and Frayn, D. (1992). The contribution of infant studies to understanding borderline personality disorders. In *Handbook of Borderline Disorders*, ed. D. Silver and M. Rosenbluth, pp. 87–108. Madison, CT: International Universities Press.

Mireault, G. C., and Bond, L. A. (1992). Parental death in childhood: perceived vulnerability, adult depression and anxiety. *American Journal of Orthopsychiatry* 62:517–524.

Modell, A. H. (1986). Primitive object relationships and the predisposition to schizophrenia. In *Essential Papers on Object Relations*, ed. P. Buckley, pp. 329–349. New York: New York University Press.

Moeller, T. P., and Bachman, G. A. (1993). The combined effects of physical, sexual and emotional abuse during childhood: long term health consequences for women. *Child Abuse and Neglect* 17:623–640.

Monahan, D. J., Green, V. L., and Coleman, P. D. (1992). Caregiver support groups: factors affecting use of services. *Social Work* 37:254–260.

Muenzenmaier, K., Meyer, I., Struening, E., and Ferber, J. (1993). Childhood abuse and neglect among women outpatients with chronic mental illness. *Hospital and Community Psychiatry* 44:666–670.

Mugford, R., and McComisky, J. (1975). Some recent work on the psychotherapeutic value of cage birds with old people. In *Pet Animals and Society*, ed. R. S. Anderson, pp. 55–64. London: Bailliere Tindall.

Muir, R. C. (1995). Transpersonal processes: a bridge between object relations and attachment theory in normal and psychopathological development. *British Journal of Medical Psychology* 68:243–257.

Muschel, I. (1984). Pet therapy with terminal cancer patients. *Social Casework* 65:451–458.

Nelsen, J. (1995). Varieties of narcissistic vulnerable couples: dynamics and practice implications. *Clinical Social Work Journal* 23:59–70.

Nelson, K. (1999). Event representations, narrative development and internal working models. *Attachment and Human Development* 1:239–252.

Netting, F. E., Wilson, C. C., and New, J. C. (1987). The

human–animal bond: implications for practice. *Social Work* 32:60–64.

Noller, P., and Feeney, J. A. (1994). Whither attachment theory? Attachment to our caregivers or to our models. *Psychological Inquiry* 5:51–56.

O'Hare, T. M. (1991). Integrating research and practice: a framework for implementation. *Social Work* 36:220–223.

Ohman, A. (1993). Fear and anxiety as emotional phenomena: clinical phenomenological, evolutionary perspectives and information-processing mechanisms. In *Handbook of Emotions*, ed. M. Lewis, and J. M. Haviland, pp. 511–536. New York: Guilford.

Osofsky, J. D. (1988). Attachment theory and research and the psychoanalytic process. *Psychoanalytic Psychology* 5:159–177.

Osofsky, J. D., Hannk, D. M., and Peebles, C. (1993). Adolescent parenthood: risks and opportunities for mothers and infants. In *Handbook of Infant Mental Health*, ed. C. H. Zeanah, pp. 106–119. New York: Guilford.

Parad, J. (1988). Attachment theory and agoraphobia. In *Anxiety Disorders*, ed. B. Crocker, pp. 5–7. Los Angeles: University of Southern California Press.

Parad, H. J., Selby, L. G., and Quinlan, J. (1976). Crisis intervention with families and groups. In *Theories of Social Work with Groups*, ed. R. W. Roberts and H. Northen, pp. 304–330. New York: Columbia University Press.

Parker, G. (1979). Reported parental characteristics of agoraphobics and social phobics. *British Journal of Psychiatry* 135:555–560.

Parkes, C. M.(1965). Bereavement and mental illness. *British Journal of Medical Psychology* 38:1–26.

———. (1969). Separation anxiety: an aspect of the search

for a lost object. In *Studies of Anxiety*, ed. M. H. Lader, pp. 87–92. *British Journal of Psychiatry Special Publication No. 3*. Published by authority of the World Psychiatric Association and the Royal Medico-Psychological Association, London.

———. (1970). The first year of bereavement. *Psychiatry* 33:444–467.

———. (1972). *Bereavement: Studies of Grief in Adult Life*. New York: International Universities Press.

———. (1973). Factors determining the persistence of phantom pain in the amputee. *Journal of Psychosomatic Research* 17:97–108.

———. (1975). Unexpected and untimely bereavement: a statistical study of young Boston widows and widowers. In *Bereavement: Its Psychosocial Aspects*, ed. B. Schoenberg, I. Gerber, A. Wiener, et al., pp. 119–138. New York: Columbia University Press.

———. (1982). Attachment and the prevention of mental disorders. In *The Place of Attachment in Human Social Behavior*, ed. C. M. Parkes, and J. Stevenson-Hinde, pp. 295–309. New York: Basic Books.

———. (1991). Attachment, bonding, and psychiatric problems after bereavement in adult life. In *Attachment Across the Life Cycle*, ed. C. M. Parkes, J. Stevenson-Hinde, and P. Marris, pp. 268–292. New York: Tavistock/Routledge.

Parkes, C. M., Relf, M., and Couldrick, A. (1996). *Counseling in Terminal Care and Bereavement*. Leicester, UK: British Psychological Society.

Parkes, C. M., and Weiss, R. S. (1983). *Recovery from Bereavement*. New York: Basic Books.

Patrick, M., Hobson, R. P., Castle, D., et al. (1994). Personality disorder and the mental representation of early social experience. *Development and Psychopathology* 6:375–388.

Peterfreund, E. (1971). *Information, Systems and Psychoanalysis. Psychological Issues*, 7, Monograph 25/26. New York: International Universities Press.

Phillips, J. (1999). The psychodynamic narrative. In *Healing Stories*, ed. G. Roberts and J. Holmes, pp. 27–48. New York: Oxford University Press.

Pine, F. (1990). The interpretive moment. In *From Inner Sources: New Directions in Object Relations Psychotherapy*, ed. N. G. Hamilton, pp. 53–73. Northvale, NJ: Jason Aronson.

Podell, C. (1989). Adolescent mourning: the sudden death of a peer. *Clinical Social Work Journal* 17:64–78.

Pottharst, K. (1990). The search for methods and measures. In *Research Explorations in Adult Attachment*, ed. K. Pottharst, pp. 9–37. New York: Peter Lang.

Provence, S. A. (1991). Separation and deprivation. In *Child and Adolescent Psychiatry: A Comprehensive Textbook*, ed. M. Lewis, pp. 376–389. Baltimore: Williams & Wilkins.

Prudo, R., Brown, C. W., Harris, T., and Dowland, J. (1981). Psychiatric disorder in a rural and an urban population 2: Sensitivity to loss. *Psychological Medicine* 11:601–616.

Pynoos, R. S. (1994). *The traumatic moment revisited: toward a developmental psychoanalytic model of internal and external danger.* Lecture, Southern California Psychoanalytic Institute, Los Angeles, September.

Pynoos, R. S., and Nader, K. (1993). Issues in the treatment of posttraumatic stress in children. In *International Handbook of Traumatic Stress Syndromes*, ed.

J. P. Wilson and B. Raphael, pp. 535–549. New York: Plenum.

Raina, P., Waltner-Toews, D., Bonnett, B., et al. (1999). Influence of companion animals on the physical and psychological health of older people: an analysis of a one-year longitudinal study. *Journal of the American Geriatrics Society* 47:323–329.

Raphael, B. (1975). The presentation and management of bereavement. *Medical Journal of Australia* 2:909–911.

———. (1977). Preventive intervention with the recently bereaved. *Archives of General Psychiatry* 34:1450–1454.

Raphael, B., and Wilson, J. P. (1993). Theoretical and intervention considerations in working with victims of disaster. In *International Handbook of Traumatic Stress Syndromes*, ed. J. P. Wilson and B. Raphael, pp. 105–117. New York: Plenum.

Raphael, E. I. (1989). Grandparents: a study of their role in Hispanic families. In *Promoting Quality Long-Term Care for Older Persons*, ed. E. D. Taira, pp. 31–62. Binghamton, NY: Haworth.

Rees, W. D., and Lutkins, S. G. (1967). Mortality of bereavement. *British Medical Journal* 4:13.

Reite, M., and Boccia, M. L. (1994). Physiological aspects of adult attachment. In *Attachment in Adults: Clinical and Developmental Perspectives*, ed. M. B. Sperling and W. H. Berman, pp. 98–127. New York: Guilford.

Reite, M., and Capitanio, J. (1985). On the nature of social separation and social adjustment. In *The Psychobiology of Attachment and Separation*, ed. M. Reite and T. Field, pp. 223–255. Orlando, FL: Academic Press.

Richman, N. E., and Sokolove, R. L. (1992). The experience of aloneness, object representation and evocative memory in borderline and neurotic patients. *Psychoanalytic Psychology* 9:77–91.

Roberts, J. E., Gotlib, I. H., and Kassel, J. D. (1996). Adult attachment security and symptoms of depression: the mediating roles of dysfunctional attitudes and low self-esteem. *Journal of Personality and Social Psychology* 70:310–320.

Robertson, J., and Bowlby, J. (1952). Responses of young children to separation from their mothers. *Courier, Centre International de l'Enfance*, II :131–142. Paris.

Robertson, J., and Robertson, J. (1969). Young children in brief separation: Film No. 3: *John, 17 Months: For 9 Days in a Residential Nursery*. London: Tavistock Child Development Research Unit.

———. (1971). Young children in brief separation: a fresh look. *Psychoanalytic Study of the Child* 26:264–315. New Haven, CT: Yale University Press.

Robinson, G. E. (1992). Adult survivors of sexual abuse. *The Medical Clinics of North America* 4:4232–4233.

Rohner, R. P., and Rohner, E. C. (1980). Antecedents and consequences of parental rejection: a theory of emotional abuse. *Child Abuse and Neglect* 4:189–198.

Rosenblum, L. A., Coplan, J. D., Friedman, S., et al. (1994). Adverse early experiences affect noradrenergic and serotonergic functioning in adult primates. *Biological Psychiatry* 35:221–227.

Routh, D. K., and Bernholtz, J. E. (1991). Attachment, separation, and phobias. In *Intersections with Attachment*, ed. J. L. Gewirtz and W. M. Kurtines, pp. 295–309. Hillsdale, NJ: Lawrence Erlbaum.

Rubin, Z. (1980). *Children's Friendships*. Cambridge: Harvard University Press.

Ruderman, E. G. (1992). Countertransference: a vehicle for reciprocal growth and repair in women psychotherapists treating women patients. *Clinical Social Work Journal* 20:47–56.

Rynearson, E. K. (1978). Humans and pets and attachment. *British Journal of Psychiatry* 133:550–555.

Sable, P. (1979). Differentiating between attachment and dependency in theory and practice. *Social Casework* 60:138–144.

———. (1981). Attachment theory. In *Manual for Child Health Workers in Major Disasters*, ed. N. L. Farberow and N. S. Gordon, pp. 7–9. Rockville, MD: NASW.

———. (1983). Overcoming fears of attachment in an adult with a detached personality. *Psychotherapy: Research and Practice* 20:376–382.

———. (1989). Attachment, anxiety and loss of husband. *American Journal of Orthopsychiatry* 59:550–556.

———. (1991a). Attachment, loss of spouse, and grief in elderly adults. *Omega* 23:129–142.

———. (1991b). Attachment, anxiety, and agoraphobia. *Women and Therapy* 11:55–69.

———. (1991c). Pets, attachment, and well-being across the life cycle. *Social Work* 40:334–341.

———. (1992a). Attachment theory: application to clinical practice with adults. *Clinical Social Work Journal* 20:271–283.

———. (1992b). Attachment, loss of spouse, and disordered mourning. *Families in Society* 73:266–273.

———. (1994a). Separation anxiety, attachment and agoraphobia. *Clinical Social Work Journal* 22:369–383.

———. (1994b). Attachment, working models, and real experiences. *Journal of Social Work Practice* 8:25–34.

———. (1994c). Anxious attachment in adulthood: therapeutic implications. *Journal of Analytic Social Work* 2:5–24.

———. (1995). Attachment theory and post-traumatic stress disorder. *Journal of Analytic Social Work* 2:89–109.

———. (1997a). Attachment, detachment, and borderline personality disorder. *Psychotherapy* 34:171–181.

———. (1997b). Disorders of adult attachment. *Psychotherapy* 34:286–296.

———. (1998a). Almost all in the family: emotionally abusive attachments. *Journal of Emotional Abuse* 1:51–67.

———. (1998b) The science of cute. *World of Wonder, Discovery TV Channel*, January 22.

Sack, A., Sperling, M. B., Fagen, G., and Foelsch, P. (1996). Attachment style, history and behavioral contrasts for a borderline and normal sample. *Journal of Personality Disorders* 10:88–102.

Sanders, C. M. (1988). Risk factors in bereavement outcome. *Journal of Social Issues* 44:97–111.

Sanville, J. (1991). *The Playground of Psychoanalytic Therapy*. Hillsdale, NJ: Analytic Press.

———. (1994). Editorial. *Clinical Social Work Journal* 22:347–353.

Scharlach, A. E. (1991). Factors associated with filial grief following the death of an elderly parent. *American Journal of Orthopsychiatry* 61:307–313.

Schmale, A. H. (1971). Psychic trauma during bereavement. *International Journal of Clinical Psychology* 8:147–168.

Schneider, E. L. (1991). Attachment theory and research: a review of the literature. *Clinical Social Work Journal* 19:251–266.

Schore, A. N. (1994). *Affect Regulation and the Origin of the Self*. Hillsdale, NJ: Lawrence Erlbaum.

———. (1997). Interdisciplinary developmental research as a source of clinical models. In *The Neurological and Developmental Basis for Psychotherapeutic Intervention*, ed. M. Moskowitz, C. Monk, C. Kaye, and S. Ellman, pp. 1–71. Northvale, NJ: Jason Aronson.

———. (2000). Foreword. *Attachment and Loss, Volume I: Attachment*, by John Bowlby, 2nd ed., pp. xi–xxv. New York: Basic Books.

Scott, J. P. (1987). The emotional basis of attachment and separation. In *Attachment and the Therapeutic Process*, ed. J. L. Sacksteder, D. P. Schwartz, and Y. Akabane. Madison, CT: International Universities Press.

Selan, B. H. (1982). Phobias, death, and depression. In *Phobia*, ed. R. L. Dupont, pp. 133–139. New York: Brunner/Mazel.

Shaver, P. R., and Hazan, C. (1993). Adult romantic attachment: theory and evidence. In *Advances in Personal Relationships*, vol. 4, ed. D. Perlman and W. Jones, pp. 29–70. London: Jessica Kingsley.

Shuchter, S. R. (1986). *Dimensions of Grief*. San Francisco: Jossey-Bass.

Siegel, A. (1962). Reaching the severely withdrawn through pet therapy. *American Journal of Psychiatry* 118:1045–1046.

Siegel, D. J. (1995). Memory, trauma, and psychotherapy: a cognitive science view. *Journal of Psychotherapy Practice and Research* 4:93–122.

———. (1999). *The Developing Mind*. New York: Guilford.

Siegel, J. M. (1990). Stressful life events and use of physician services among the elderly: the moderating role of pet ownership. *Journal of Personality and Social Psychology* 58:1081–1086.

Siegel, J. P. (1999). Destructive conflict in non-violent couples: a treatment guide. *Journal of Emotional Abuse* 1:65–85.

Silverman, D. K. (1994). Attachment themes: theory, empirical research, psychoanalytic implications and future directions. *Bulletin of the Psychoanalytic (Section VI) of APA's Division of Psychoanalysis* 31:9–11.

Simos, B.G. (1979). *A Time to Grieve*. New York: Family Service Association of America.

Simpson, J. A. (1999). Attachment theory in modern evolutionary perspective. In *Handbook of Attachment*, ed. J. Cassidy, and P. R. Shaver, pp. 115–140. New York: Guilford.

Slade, A. (1999). Attachment theory and research. In *Handbook of Attachment*, ed. J. Cassidy, and P. R. Shaver, pp. 575–594. New York: Guilford.

Slade, A., and Aber, L. (1992). Attachments, drives, and development: conflicts and convergences in theory. In *Interface of Psychoanalysis and Psychology*, ed. J. Barron, M. Eagle, and D. Wolitzky, pp. 154–185. New York: APA Publications.

Solnit, A. J. (1990). The Bowlby legacy: continuity in theory building. *Readings* 5:4–7.

Solomon, J., and George, C. (1999). The measurement of attachment security in infancy and childhood. In *Handbook of Attachment*, ed. J. Cassidy, and P. R. Shaver, pp. 287–316. New York: Guilford.

Spencer-Booth, Y., and Hinde, R. A. (1967). The effects of separating rhesus monkey infants from their mothers for six days. *Journal of Child Psychological Psychiatry* 114:673–698.

Sperling, M. B. (1988). Phenomenology and developmental origins of desperate love. *Psychoanalysis and Contemporary Thought* 11:741–761.

Sperling, M. B., and Lyons, L. S. (1994). Representations of attachment and psychotherapeutic change. In *Attachment in Adults: Clinical and Developmental Perspectives*, ed. M. B. Sperling and W. H. Berman, pp. 331–347. New York: Guilford.

Sperling, M. B., Sharp, J. L., and Fishler, P. H. (1991). On the nature of attachment in a borderline population:

a preliminary investigation. *Psychological Reports* 68:543–546.

Spezzano, C. (1993). *Affect in Psychoanalysis*. Hillsdale, NJ: Analytic Press.

Sprang, M. V., McNeil, J. S., and Wright, R., Jr. (1989). Psychological changes after the murder of a significant other. *Social Casework* 70:159–164.

Sroufe, L. A. (1996). *Emotional Development*. New York: Cambridge University Press.

———. (1997). Psychopathology as an outcome of development. *Development and Psychopathology* 9:251–268.

Sroufe, L. A., and Waters, E. (1997). Attachment as an organizational construct. *Child Development* 48:1184–1199.

Stanford, C. (1998). The science of cute. *World of Wonder, Discovery TV Channel*, January 22.

Stein, H., Corter, J. E., and Hull, J. (1996). Impact of therapist vacations on inpatients with borderline personality disorder. *Psychoanalytic Psychology* 13:513–530.

Stein, M., and Susser, M. (1969). Widowhood and mental illness. *British Journal of Preventive Social Medicine* 23:106–110.

Stern, D. N. (1985). *The Interpersonal World of the Infant*. New York: Basic Books.

Stewart, M. (1983). Loss of a pet–loss of a person: a comparative study of bereavement. In *New Perspectives on Our Lives with Companion Animals*, ed. A. H. Katcher and A. M. Beck, pp. 390–404. Philadelphia: University of Pennsylvania Press.

Stone, M. H. (1992). The borderline patient: diagnostic concepts and differential diagnosis. In *Handbook of Borderline Disorders*, ed. D. Silver and M. Rosenbluth, pp. 3–27. Madison, CT: International Universities Press.

Sugarman, A. (1995). Psychoanalysis: Treatment of conflict or deficit? *Psychoanalytic Psychology* 12:55–70.

Summers, F. (1988). Psychoanalytic therapy of the borderline patient: treating the fusion–separation contradiction. *Psychoanalytic Psychology* 5:339–355.

————. (1994). *Object Relations Theories and Psychopathology*. Hillsdale, NJ: Analytic Press.

Suomi, S. J., Collins, M. L., and Harlow, H. F. (1973). Effects of permanent separation from mother on infant monkeys. *Developmental Psychology* 9:376–384.

Sussman, M. B. (1985). *Pets and the Family*. New York: Haworth.

Suttie, I. (1935). *The Origins of Love and Hate*. London: Kegan Paul.

Tearnan, B. H., Telch, M. J., and Keefe, P. (1984). Etiology and onset of agoraphobia: a critical review. *Comprehensive Psychiatry* 25:51–62.

Teitelbaum, S. (1998). Soothing and anxiety regulation: clinical applications. *Journal of Analytic Social Work* 5:57–73.

Tinbergen, N. (1951). *The Study of Instinct*. Oxford, England: Clarendon.

Tolman, R. M. (1992). Psychological abuse of women. In *Assessment of Family Violence*, ed. R. T. Ammerman and M. Hersen, pp. 159–172. New York: Wiley.

Tosone, C. (1997). Sandor Ferenczi: forerunner of modern short-term psychotherapy. *Journal of Analytic Social Work* 4:23–41.

Traupman, J., and Hatfield, E. (1981). Love: its effects on mental and physical health. In *Aging: Stability and Change in the Family*, ed. J. March, S. Kiesler,

R. Fogel, et al., pp. 253–274. New York: Academic Press.

Tronick, E. Z. (1989). Emotions and emotional communication in infants. *American Psychologist* 44:112–119.

Trowell, J., and Miles, G. (1991). The contribution of observation training to professional development in social work. *Journal of Social Work Practice* 5:51–60.

van der Kolk, B. A. (1987). *Psychological Trauma*. Washington, DC: American Psychiatric Press.

———. (1994). Biological considerations about emotions, trauma, memory, and the brain. In *Human Feelings*, ed. S. L. Ablon, D. Brown, E. J. Khantzian, and J. E. Mack, pp. 221–240. Hillsdale, NJ: Analytic Press.

———. (1996). The complexity of adaption to trauma: self-regulation, stimulus discrimination, and characterological development. In *Traumatic Stress*, ed. B. A. van der Kolk, A. C. McFarlane, and L. Weisaeth, pp. 182–213. New York: Guilford.

———. (1997). The psychobiology of posttraumatic stress disorder. *Journal of Clinical Psychiatry* 58:16–24.

van der Kolk, B. A., and McFarlane, A. C. (1996). The black hole of trauma. In *Traumatic Stress*, ed. B. A. van der Kolk, A. C. McFarlane, and L. Weisaeth, pp. 3–23. New York: Guilford.

van der Kolk, B. A., McFarlane, A. C., and van der Hart, O. (1996). A general approach to treatment of posttraumatic stress disorder. In *Traumatic Stress*, ed. B. A. van der Kolk, A. C. McFarlane, and L. Weisaeth, pp. 417–440. New York: Guilford.

van der Kolk, B.A., Weisaeth, L., and van der Hart, O. (1996). History of trauma in psychiatry. In *Traumatic Stress*, ed. B. A. van der Kolk, A. C. McFarlane, and L. Weisaeth, pp. 47–74. New York: Guilford.

van Dijken, S. (1998). *John Bowlby: His Early Life*. New York: Free Association Books.

Varkas, T. (1998). Childhood trauma and post-traumatic play: a literature review and case study. *Journal of Analytic Social Work* 5:29–50.

Volkan, V. D. (1970). Typical findings in pathological grief. *Psychiatric Quarterly* 44:231–250.

———. (1975). Re-grief therapy. In *Bereavement: Its Psychosocial Aspects*, ed. B. Schoenberg, I. Gerber, A. Weiner, et al., pp. 334–350. New York: Columbia University Press.

Waddington, C. H. (1957). *The Strategy of the Genes*. London: Allen and Unwin.

Walker, L. E. (1984). *The Battered Woman Syndrome*. New York: Springer.

Wallerstein, J. S. (1995). *The Good Marriage*. New York: Houghton Mifflin.

Waters, E. (1978). The reliability and stability of individual differences in infant–mother attachment. *Childhood Development* 49:483–494.

Weiner, H. (1978). The illusion of simplicity: the medical model revisited. *American Journal of Psychiatry* 135:27–33.

Weinfield, N. S., Sroufe, L. A., Egeland, B., and Carlson, E. A. (1999). The nature of individual differences in infant–caregiver attachment. In *Handbook of Attachment*, ed. J. Cassidy and P. R. Shaver, pp. 68–88. New York: Guilford.

Weisaeth, L., and Ettinger, L. (1993). Posttraumatic stress phenomena: common themes across wars, disasters, and traumatic events. In *International Handbook of Traumatic Stress Syndromes*, ed. J. P. Wilson and B. Raphael, pp. 69–77. New York: Plenum.

Weiss, E. (1964). *Agoraphobia in the Light of Ego Psychology*. New York: Grune & Stratton.

Weiss, J. (1993). *How Psychotherapy Works*. New York: Guilford.

Weiss, R. S. (1974). The provisions of social relationships. In *Doing Unto Others*, ed. Z. Rubin, pp. 17–26. Englewood Cliffs, NJ: Prentice Hall.

———. (1975). *Marital Separation*. New York: Basic Books.

———. (1978). After divorce. In *The Couple*, ed. M. Corbin, pp. 137–153. New York: Penguin.

———. (1982a). Attachment in adult life. In *The Place of Attachment in Human Behavior*, ed. C. M. Parkes and J. Stevenson-Hinde, pp. 171–184. New York: Basic Books.

———. (1982b). Relationship of social support and psychological well being. In *The Modern Practice of Community Mental Health*, ed. R. Schulking, pp. 148–162. San Francisco: Jossey-Bass.

———. (1988). Loss and recovery. *Journal of Social Issues* 44:37–52.

———. (1991). The attachment bond in childhood and adulthood. In *Attachment Across the Life Cycle*, ed. C. M. Parkes, J. Stevenson-Hinde, and P. Marris, pp. 66–76. New York: Tavistock/Routledge.

———. (1994a). Foreword. In *Attachment in Adults: Clinical and Developmental Perspectives*, ed. M. B. Sperling and W. H. Berman, pp. ix–xv. New York: Guilford.

———. (1994b). Foreword. In *Patterns of Relating: An Adult Attachment Perspective*, ed. M. L. West and A. E. Sheldon-Keller, pp. v–ix. New York: Guilford.

Welu, T. C. (1975). Pathological bereavement: a plan for

its prevention. In *Bereavement: Its Psychosocial Aspects*, ed. B. Schoenberg, I. Gerber, A. Wiener, et al., pp. 139–149. New York: Columbia University Press.

West, M. L., and Sheldon-Keller, A. E. (1994). *Patterns of Relating: An Adult Attachment Perspective*. New York: Guilford.

Westen, D. (1991). Social cognition and object relations. *Psychological Bulletin* 109:429–455.

Westen, D., Ludolph, P., Misle, B., et al. (1990). Physical and sexual abuse in adolescent girls with borderline personality disorder. *American Journal of Orthopsychiatry* 60:55–66.

Westphal, C. (1871). Die agoraphobie: eine neuropathische ersheinung. *Archives Für Psychiatre und Nervenkrankheiten* 3:384–412.

Winnicott, D.W. (1952). Anxiety associated with insecurity. In *Collected Papers: Through Paediatrics to Psycho-Analysis*. London: Tavistock.

———. (1965). *The Maturational Processes and the Facilitating Environment*. New York: International Universities Press.

Wolfe, B. E. (1984). Gender imperatives, separation anxiety and agoraphobia in women. *Integrative Psychiatry*: March-April 57–61.

Worden, J. W. (1982). *Grief Counseling and Grief Therapy*. New York: Springer.

Zasloff, R. L. (1996). Cats and their people: a (nearly) perfect relationship. *Journal of the American Veterinary Medical Association* 208:512–515.

Zimmerman, M., Coryell, W., Corenthal, C., and Wilson, S. (1986). A self-report scale to diagnose major depressive disorder. *Archives of General Psychiatry* 43:1076–1081.

Zisook, S. (1987). *Biopsychosocial Aspects of Bereavement*. Washington, DC: American Psychiatric Press.

Zisook, S., Devaul, R. A., and Click, M. A. (1982). Measuring symptoms of grief and bereavement. *American Journal of Psychiatry* 139:1590–1593.

Credits

The author gratefully acknowledges permission to reprint material from the following sources:

Lyrics to the song "On My Own," from the musicale *Les Misérables*, music by Claude-Michel Schonberg, lyrics by Alain Boulbil, Herbert Kretzmer, Jean-Marc Natel, Trevor Nunn, and John Caird.

Excerpts from "Differentiating between Attachment and Dependency in Theory and Practice," by Pat Sable, in *Social Casework* 60:138–144. Copyright © 1979 and used by permission of Manticore Publishers.

Excerpts from "Attachment, Loss of Spouse, and Disordered Mourning," by Pat Sable, in *Families in Society* 73:266–273. Copyright © 1992 and used by permission of Manticore Publishers.

Excerpts from "Pets, Attachment and Well-Being across the Life Cycle," by Pat Sable, in *Social Work* 40(3):334–341. Copyright © 1995 and used by permission of National Association of Social Workers Press.

Excerpts from "Overcoming Fears of Attachment in an Adult with a Detached Personality," by Pat Sable, in *Psychotherapy: Research and Practice* 20:376–382. Copyright © 1983 and used by permission of *Psychotherapy*.

Index

ABOUT THE AUTHOR

Pat Sable, Ph.D., is Adjunct Associate Professor at the University of Southern California, School of Social Work. She also maintains a private psychotherapy practice. Dr. Sable became interested in attachment theory in the early 1970s, at the time Bowlby published the second of his trilogy, *Attachment and Loss*, and has lectured and written extensively on application of attachment theory to clinical practice with adults. She has discussed attachment in appearances on radio and television.

Born in St. Joseph, Missouri, Dr. Sable earned her Bachelor of Arts from Northwestern University, and her M.S.W. and doctorate from the University of Southern California School of Social Work.